Child
Effects
on Adults

Child
Effects
on Adults

RICHARD Q. BELL
UNIVERSITY OF VIRGINIA

LAWRENCE V. HARPER
UNIVERSITY OF CALIFORNIA, DAVIS

 LAWRENCE ERLBAUM ASSOCIATES, PUBLISHERS
1977   Hillsdale, New Jersey

DISTRIBUTED BY THE HALSTED PRESS DIVISION OF

JOHN WILEY & SONS

New York   Toronto   London   Sydney

Lawrence Erlbaum Associates, Inc., Publishers
62 Maria Drive
Hillsdale, New Jersey 07642

Distributed solely by Halsted Press Division
John Wiley & Sons, Inc., New York

Library of Congress Cataloging in Publication Data

Bell, Richard Q.   1919-
    Child effects on adults.

    Bibliography: p.
    Includes indexes.
    1. Socialization—History. 2. Socialization—
Research. 3. Parent and child—History. 4. Parent and
child—Research. 5. Mammals—Behavior. 6. Parental
behavior in animals. I. Harper, Lawrence V., joint
author. II. Title.
HQ783.B37   301.15'7   77-24115
ISBN 0-470-99267-0

Printed in the United States of America

Contents

Preface

We expect parents to influence their children. People who live together usually affect each other, but what is often overlooked is the extent to which children influence their parents and other adults. This book is devoted to this other side of child-rearing or socialization: the way in which parents and other caregiving adults are themselves molded by the very children they are trying to rear. Although one book and several articles have appeared on this subject in the last decade, this orientation is still overshadowed by a massive literature devoted almost entirely to the effects of adults on children. The new perspective has excited much interest and stimulated some research, but the tide of more traditional, unidirectional thought has yet to be stemmed. Further effort against the strong current of the past is called for before a truly balanced view can gain widespread acceptance.

Because many of the articles relevant to the new approach have been published in different journals, even those who recognize the need to examine the other side of the equation have had difficulty tracking down the relevant materials. A mere compendium of this scattered literature would not only leave many questions unanswered but would overlook some that need to be asked. For example, it may well be important to consider why the effects of children on parents and other caregiving adults have been so long neglected. Further, we need to ask whether anything can be done so that studies of adults and children will yield more clear results. It has been shown that the direction of effects, adult to child or child to adult, is unclear in most of the findings from the past forty years of research. Until the present volume, no one has systematically examined research strategies that could isolate adult- from child-effects.

Even if we now had ready access to strategies that could clarify the flow of influences in this most basic human social system, it is unlikely that another viewpoint would receive much empirical attention, or become assimilated into theory, until it had been translated into a set of coherent alternatives to traditional thinking. As yet, with few notable exceptions, most advocates of the new perspective have focused upon the *logical* possibility that the parent-offspring/adult-child relationship could be reciprocal, without providing the substantive content needed to replace the possibilities with actualities. Finally, some of the most provocative models of reciprocity in the caregiving-offspring relationship, as well as the most thoroughly documented analyses of offspring effects on parents or other adults, have emerged from work on animals. Yet, few students of human socialization are even aware of these reports.

This book is an effort both to raise and answer a number of pertinent questions, to forge some links between theory and methods, to bring together research and theory emanating from work with other mammals and, from the latter, to sketch a broader comparative context within which the human caregiver-child relationship may be viewed.

Because we obtained our material from such a wide variety of sources, each chapter other than the first was written as a unit by the author or coauthor; only this preface and the concluding chapter are joint efforts. Our writing styles, the technical language of the various fields from which we have drawn our material, and our methods of organizing the data are noticeably different, but the underlying premise is the same. We hope that, in the transitions, the reader does not miss the underlying message—that it is high time to look at the "other side of the coin," and to work toward truly interactive models of parents and children, the young and adults.

It would be ideal, of course, if a single unifying conceptual structure could be developed for the work on both man and other mammals. This is clearly not possible at this stage in the development of the field, when the first-order task is to locate and draw together in one volume the available facts and ideas. We were tempted to use a common expositional framework developed from studies on mammals. Unfortunately, there is so much more data on the latter that there would be more blanks than entries if the classification system were applied at the human level. However, in the chapters on man, it was possible to use some elements from the classification system developed for other mammals. As readers move along from the chapters on history, through the research literature on humans, to the data from other mammals, they will hear some bars from a refrain that becomes sufficiently clear to be discriminated from the ambient noise level of facts. This is the expositional framework. They will read about behavioral matching of parent and offspring, the buffering of the system against adverse physiological or social circumstances, and its modifiability as both participants grow and adjust to each other. They will find descriptions of how the young initiate, maintain, differentiate, and terminate adult behavior. They will also encounter in the chapters on mammals, many efforts to integrate findings from man.

Children's influence on parents, even when acknowledged in the past, has usually been treated as if it were unimportant. The pursuit of the historical reasons for this view took us far beyond recent events in the social sciences. Thus, the first chapter of the book starts with an historical treatment that flows as beautifully as the Egyptian and Sumerian literature from which it draws many fascinating examples. We are delighted that Valerie French, an expert on ancient history, was able to contribute this chapter.

The second chapter, written by Bell, covers the period from medieval to modern times and turns up some interesting trends. For example, recognition of the child's importance has varied with not only our scientific, religious, and educational movements, but also with the social and political changes that fed the American and European revolutions.

Harper's history chapter then describes how an intellectual apartheid has kept behavioral scientists from seeing the continuity of interaction processes from other animals to man. Because of this dualism, students of human development have been late in getting the basic message of biology—namely, that we adults are intricately fitted to our young, just as they are to us. We become aware of this reciprocal relation of parental and filial behaviors when we try to rear the young of other species such as chimpanzees.

In Chapter 4, we try to show that the very best data from studies of human socialization can often be interpreted as showing the effects of children on parents, rather than the other way around. In the course of developing this interpretation, this chapter also presents a control systems model of parent-child interaction.

Because future research must find ways of unscrambling the problem of direction of effects, 17 research approaches are described in Chapter 5. These make it possible to separate the contribution of each participant more clearly than the traditional correlational study of parent and child characteristics. Many make it possible to generalize beyond the laboratory to parents and children in the natural setting.

Chapter 6 presents a theory of how an infant socializes its mother in the first year. We believe that this theory and the control systems model, used in conjunction with the research strategies that have been described, may give rise to new and productive lines of research.

Chapter 7 through 11 offer a comparative perspective on caregiver-young relationships. Field observations made by open-air zoologists help us achieve some notion of the boundaries of the problem. Data from well-controlled studies of animals clearly show how offspring affect parents and vice versa. The caveat is that we cannot expect the underlying processes to be the same at the human level. However, there are some interesting parallels, and we can develop a picture of what we might want to look for in our own species.

Chapter 11 presents an idea that may have rather far-reaching implications. Those of us over thirty have always known and resented the fact that most great advances in fields ranging from literature through science have been made by mere children in their twenties. Now, a review of the literature on other mammals suggests that in evolutionary history the young mammals were also the ones who led their elders into new territory, ate new foods, and accounted for the adaptive radiation of species into new environments. With that idea, we leave you to the book, and hope you enjoy it.

THE AUTHORS

Child
Effects
on Adults

Part I

HISTORY

1

History of the Child's Influence: Ancient Mediterranean Civilizations

Valerie French

INTRODUCTION

Children—how to care for them, how to rear them, how to make them into adults—have always been of concern to parents in particular and to society in general. Despite the oft-repeated observation that our children are our tomorrow, and the converse that we are the children of yesterday, historians have traditionally paid scant attention to the historical dimensions of childhood. Even the limited study that is available in historical literature has concentrated almost exclusively on what parents and society have done to and for their children. Historians, probably unconsciously, have conceptualized the infant as a Lockian *tabula rasa,* a passive recipient or object of the adult community's efforts to rear and educate. Yet a moment's reflection will tell any adult who has had more than casual contact with a small child that the child—even an infant—can exert definite and sometimes very strong influences on the adult's behavior. Childhood has not yet been investigated historically to ascertain how children in the past have affected their parents, caregivers, and society.

In addition to examining past societies' treatment of their young, historians of childhood must broaden their inquiry to include consideration of the stimulus effects of children on adults. The present study was undertaken to meet that objective. The data will be discussed according to five kinds of effects exerted by the young on the world of adults. The first of these has to do with the extent to which the infant or child itself is seen as very important or powerful—or is used to symbolize something important or powerful. Is the child merely recognized as an enjoyable object that is also necessary to complete a family, or do members of the society see in the child an inspiring influence, even a representation of the society's destiny?

The second kind of effect involves the extent to which the distinctive

3

characteristics of the young are recognized, such as their size, appearance, and behavior. Do the documents available to us indicate something more than a vague awareness of some inherent differences between children and adults, a recognition of some obvious and visible differences, or a sensitivity to basic differences in not only behavior but inferred needs and potentialities?

Third, although adults may have recognized the special characteristics of the young, it does not necessarily follow that the members of that society pay any particular attention to individual or age differences amongst the young. Infants may simply be seen as infants, children as children, and their general distinctiveness from adults may overshadow the wide range of variation in behavior at the same age level.

The fourth kind of effect has to do with the extent to which adults are aware that the young affect their parents or caregivers during specific interactions. The final effect to be considered concerns recognition on the part of adults of the special contribution made by the young to their larger social group, neighborhood, community, and even culture. The young contribute behaviors not ordinarily manifested by adults in the same society. The fourth and fifth effects have been recognized only rarely and have been given most attention in recent time.

An effort will be made to trace an awareness of these effects in documents from the ancient societies of the Near East, Greece, and Rome, largely using primary historical sources. There will be more reliance on secondary accounts in Chapter 2, which covers the period beyond Roman civilization and the present. The latter treatment will be more cursory, by necessity, in order to give the reader some grasp of the flow of concepts throughout the entire period.

Eliciting evidence from historical sources about these five effects is a difficult business at best. Childhood is such a commonplace—after all, nearly everyone has one—that few have taken the time to ponder it, much less seriously to reflect and write about it. Thus the historian of childhood must be prepared to draw on every conceivable piece of evidence from a particular period—not only written texts but also iconography, public art, folk arts, and material remains such as toys, baby and child equipment and furniture, floor plans of various kinds of houses, even lexicology. Often the historical "conclusions" are but inferences drawn from an offhand remark or from some battered artifact.

Some general problems in obtaining and handling historical evidence about childhood should be mentioned here. The first and greatest arises from the fact that in almost any society, the primary responsibility for the care of young children (from birth to about seven years of age) has been entrusted almost exclusively to women. Yet the bulk of our surviving evidence—literary and artistic works, legal codes, and other legislation, indeed even most of the household equipment—has been designed and produced by men. Thus, whenever possible, the historian must try to determine what, if any, contact each particular source actually had with young children. Unfortunately, the amount and nature of the association with children for a given source is often impossible to ascertain exactly, although in some cases a reasonable conjecture can be made, especially if the source is a literary figure of note.

A second obstacle in the evaluation of the historical sources is the determination of the extent to which they represent the thinking, habits, and attitudes of the society as a whole. Literary sources often reflect only the lifestyle of the elite of a society, and historians must take care not to extrapolate to the larger society. To ferret out the life-style of society in general—particularly in more differentiated societies that have lost their homogeneity—historians must turn to laws and physical remains and fasten on to those passages in the literary sources that refer specifically to distinctive groups. Though the ''aristocratic bias'' of much of the evidence can be troublesome, it can, nonetheless, be overcome.

One source merits a further remark—literary and dramatic productions intended for the community at large. Outstanding examples would be the Bible or the corpus of Greek plays of the fifth and fourth centuries B.C. To this category also belong such diverse items as the *Enuma Elish,* the great ancient Babylonian creation epic recited yearly at the New Year's festival, Roman triumphs and circuses, and today's movies and television programs. How children are portrayed in these productions can tell us something about prevailing social attitudes concerning their roles and special characteristics, although, again, the producers may not be representative of the larger society.

The use of pictorial representations of children as evidence for a society's concept of childhood must be accompanied by consideration of that society's conventions of pictorial representation taken as a whole. Recent examinations of children in art have made the point that in only a few periods have children been drawn or sculpted realistically (i.e., as in a photograph). Historians have too often drawn from this observation the inference that the artists and the consumers of the art did not pay attention to what children really looked like as distinct from adults, and that therefore the society had no concept of childhood. This is an unwarranted conclusion. In most periods of art, formal styles and conventions of representation dictate what the individual artist draws, paints, or sculpts. Are we to conclude that because ancient Egyptians almost invariably drew faces in profile with only one eye visible that ancient Egyptians had no concept of what a face really looked like? Or, that during all those centuries before artists learned perspective, society had no realistic concept of space or distance? Although it is true that most of the time in the past, artists have pictured children as miniature adults, we can not necessarily infer that they *thought* of children as miniature adults. When examining pictures, statues, and other pieces of art of a given society for concepts of childhood, historians will do well to see how the art of that society represents other groups of people, such as the old, the sick, and women. If a particular form or style dominates the representation of all kinds of people, then the historian must refrain from drawing inferences about children in particular. Pictures of children can be extraordinarily valuable, however, as evidence for the actual activities of children.

THE ANCIENT NEAR EAST

When attempting to survey a theme or development in Western Civilization, historians almost invariably begin with Greece. But the roots of our modern culture and its attitudes toward family and children extend far back beyond the Greeks both in time and geographical extent. Ancient Greek civilization did not arise in a vacuum; rather, it was built in part upon the vast and even more ancient base of Mesopotamian, Anatolian, Egyptian, and Hebrew cultures. Therefore, our Western heritage also commences in the "Cradle of Civilization," the Ancient Near East.

Any sort of inquiry into the history of these ancient peoples is fraught with difficulties—exotic languages, scanty evidence, to point out the more obvious. The investigation of the young child is particularly formidable because there are few references in the extant literature to children before they are school–age. In addition, because the thought processes of ancient Near Easterners were mythopoeic (Frankfort, 1946) rather than logical and analytic, we find in their writings nothing whatsoever like a treatise on the concept of childhood. Everything is stated in terms of empirical observation. Yet the historian can infer from these observations something about what a generalized picture of childhood might have been.

For Egypt, the abundance of paintings in which young children are portrayed provides additional and welcome evidence; but even when considering both the meager literary scraps and the paintings, the historian can draw only the sketchiest picture of early childhood.

Importance of the Young

Whatever the reason for the comparative silence of the literary sources—accidental survival or failure to discuss such a commonplace topic—children, the young ones as well as the adolescents, were active participants in the life of families at all levels of society. A delightful example of the real presence of children is contained in an Egyptian story from the Middle Kingdom (ca. 2000–1800 B.C.) about a courtier, Sinuhe, who returns to the pharaoh's court after a long absence. Sinuhe is welcomed back not only by the pharaoh and his queen but also by their children. In the story, the children shriek out their joy at Sinuhe's return and show him their necklaces, rattles, and other noisemaking toys (Erman, 1966). The children of Pharaoh Akhenaten and Nefertiti are prominently featured in the art produced during his reign (ca. 1378–1362 B.C.)

(Aldred, 1968). They are present at all official state ceremonies and are often shown caressing their parents or sitting on their laps. The king and queen display great affection for the royal brood, kissing and embracing them warmly.

Expressed fondness for children was by no means confined to the royalty and aristocracy of Egypt. Another story, also from the Middle Kingdom, tells of a sailor shipwrecked in the land of Punt and of his good fortune in being able to return to his home. The Prince of Punt sends him off, saying "Farewell, farewell . . . to your home! You will see your children . . ." (Simpson, 1972, p. 55). In fact, Egyptians seem to have thrived on large families and endeavored to rear each child that was born. The Egyptian bureaucracy kept records of all births (Montet, 1958).

Recognition of the child's place and importance in the family and society is also seen in Mesopotamian culture. Two Sumerian proverbs reflect the prominent position of the child in the family. "Marry a wife according to your choice; have a child as your heart desires!" and "Who has not supported a wife or child has not borne a leash!" (Kramer, 1963, p. 255). Judging from the number of provisions for the maintenance of children in Hammurabi's law code (ca. 1750 B.C.), the Babylonians also viewed the child as an important constituent of the community (Gordon, 1957). For example, the purpose of a dowry in Babylonia was to insure a proper upbringing for a woman's children, and the code of Hammurabi also foreshadows modern notions of community property law. "They shall return her dowry to that (divorced) woman and also give her half of the field, orchard and goods so that she may rear her children" (Gordon, 1957, p. 13).

Here is an implicit recognition of the need to sustain children, their physiological dependence, and the economic demands that they create. Motherless children are also protected. "If, after a man has acquired a wife and she has borne him children, and that woman has gone to her fate (died), her father may not lay claim to her dowry, for it belongs to her children" (Gordon, 1957, p. 15).

Carthaginian society (fl. 800–150 B.C.) attached particular importance to the small child—though the manifestation of this importance was gruesome, indeed horrendous. Punic religious beliefs demanded the sacrifice of the children of the nobility to the gods. Once, when threatened by a rival power in Sicily, the Carthaginians slew 500 noble children at one time. Filicide as an act of ritual sacrifice has been practiced by many primitive societies and must reflect somehow that society's use of the infant or small child as a symbol of extraordinarily powerful forces (DeMause, 1974). Howsoever contemporary psychologists now explain this act of sacrifice, the ancient Carthaginians believed that they were handing over to the gods their precious possessions. One has only to spend an hour or so in one of the two infant Necropolises excavated in Carthage and to consider the thousands of tiny grave stelae that mark the sacrifice of each child to sense the potency of the forces that drove the Carthaginians to kill their children, many of whom were as much as three years old when delivered up to the gods.

Hebrew tradition also accorded a place to the child, especially to the male child as the carrier and preserver of the family succession. The Old Testament has, however, comparatively few incidents that center on children. Where children are mentioned, the infant or babe often symbolizes the Hebrew hopes for the future, for it is in those passages of the Old Testament that describe the promised land that children stand out. In fact, the whole tenor of the relationship between Yahweh and his people resembles that between a father and his children, and in this sense, the Hebrews saw themselves as still being "in childhood," implying helplessness and dependence before God.

Recognition of Special Characteristics of Children

In most of the ancient Near-Eastern cultures, children were recognized as being important either in their own right—as seems to be the case for the Egyptians and Mesopotamians—or as symbols for powerful foes—as with the Carthaginians and perhaps the Hebrews. But attention to the importance or value of children does not necessarily imply that a society or community had a clear idea of those characteristics that pertain particularly to children. How far were parents and observers in these cultures able to recognize "childish" behaviors or needs? How well do these ancient Near-Eastern notions of "childish" behavior correlate with modern ones? With regard to this latter question, the contemporary historian must be particularly careful not to impose present concepts of childhood upon past civilizations.

In all ancient Near-Eastern cultures, the child was seen as a being who was helpless, not capable of directing his own affairs, who had to be legally represented in the community by an adult, usually the father. In most societies, the father had great authority over his children, sometimes even absolute authority. There seems to be some correlation between the level of militarism in a given society and the extent of paternal authority. In the gentler and more peaceful cultures of Sumer and Egypt, the father's authority seems to have been leavened by a general desire to promote the well-being of the individual child. Protection of the child against some abuses stands out clearly in Babylonian society in Hammurabi's Code. We have already mentioned how the code protects the children's rights to their mother's dowry. The code also protects the interests of adopted children by preventing their reclamation by their natural parents and also by preventing their disinheritance if the adoptive parents have other children. The more warlike Assyrians, Hittites, and early Hebrews allowed fathers to exercise almost unlimited control over their offspring. Children could be killed, deposited as security for debts, sold outright, or disinherited according to the decision of the father (Contenau, 1954; Gurney, 1954).

That children had physical needs separate from adults, all these societies saw. They created special equipment to care for small children. Feeding bottles have been found in Carthage (Charles–Picard & Charles–Picard, 1958). In most other cultures, breast feeding seems to have been the norm either by the mother or a wet nurse. The Egyptians provided for the comfort of the newborn by placing the infant on a cushion on bricks, a make-shift cradle (Simpson, 1972). Egyptian mothers carried their children around with them, probably until two or three years of age, in a kind of sling that kept the babe near the breast and left the arms free (Montet, 1958).

These ancient cultures also appeared to have recognized some emotional needs in their children. At least, many responded to their children with tenderness and affection. Even in militaristic Assyria, family members kissed one another as part of the morning greeting (Contenau, 1954). Egyptian paintings reveal warmth and attentiveness on the part of parents toward their children, affection that found expression in fondling and other physical contact. But it is in Sumerian literature that we find the most direct expression of the family's need for mutual love. A Sumerian proverb puts these needs succinctly: "A loving heart builds the home; a hating heart destroys the home" (Kramer, 1963, p. 226). Other passages (see Kramer, 1963) reflect the Sumerian ideal of loving home life; one passage described the terrible conditions that the gods might inflict on the city of Ur.

> The mother will not care for her son,
> The father will not cry out, O my wife
> The concubine will not rejoice in the lap,
> The children will not be fondled on their knees [p. 256].

Another depicts the cruelty of underworld demons who,

> Take away the wife from the man's lap,
> Take away the child from the nursemaid's breast [p. 257].

and who

> Sate not with pleasure the wife's lap,
> Kiss not the well-fed children,
> Take away the man's son from his knee [p. 257].

There is yet another piece of evidence that possibly testifies to the close and positive bond that united parents, particularly the mother, and children in Sumerian culture. In about 2500 B.C., for the first time in man's recorded history, a word that means "freedom" appears in the literature. The word used by the Sumerians for "freedom"—*amargi*—means literally "return to the mother" (Kramer, 1963, p. 79). The context of this word's appearance clearly indicates that "amargi" was valuable, something to be prized and worked for.

Thus its association with motherhood probably also reflects the society's positive view of the mother—she was someone to whom it was possible to go to be protected and safe without being imprisoned or constrained.

Most of the ancient Near-Eastern cultures also recognized the child's need and desire to play. Once again the Egyptian paintings provide some of the best evidence. In these, one sees children playing with balls and at jumping games—leapfrog and hopscotch—and running about and participating in other activities whose nature is not immediately obvious (White, 1963). In addition, the Egyptians provided for their girls many kinds of dolls, some of which even had wardrobes of clothes—there were "Barbie Dolls" at least three to four thousand years ago (White, 1963). Excavations in Carthage have produced a whole set of crockery—dishes, cups, oil lamps, jugs—all in miniature, apparently meant to accompany play with dolls (Charles–Picard & Charles–Picard, 1958).

Children's play among the upper classes in Assyria seems to reflect the warring ways of that culture. The boys were taught early, probably at about three years of age, to ride a horse and were given bows and arrows and targets as playthings. Boys spent their early years before going to school in play that simulated war, in shooting at targets or small game (Saggs, 1965).

Concerning those character or personality traits that adults associated with childhood, we have very little evidence indeed. In fact, the references are so few that we must be wary of drawing any conclusions about generally recognized childhood traits. However, some tentative inferences can be made. First, all of these societies stressed in their school systems the need for discipline, and often discipline of what seems to us a harsh and abusive nature. This emphasis on discipline—at least for children in the schools—probably implies that these societies saw children as lacking self-control, prone to disorder, unable or unwilling to pay attention or to sit still.

Second, Egyptian sources point out two other qualities associated with children in particular. One occurs in, of all places, one of the many beautiful love songs and poems that grace Egyptian literature.

If I were made the doorkeeper
I could make her mad at me;
Then at least I'd hear her voice when she is angry,
And I'd play the child afraid of her [Simpson, 1972, p. 301].

Certainly fear is not felt only by children. But what the hapless suitor here reflects is an awareness of a child-like way of expressing fear that differs from an adult expression of the same emotion.

The second passage, composed originally in the Old Kingdom (ca. 2400 B.C.), comes from the Instructions of the Vizier Ptahhotep to his son who will succeed him in that post. He remarks on the importance of a good education and good personal examples for the "children of the great." Ptahhotep explains this need by saying, "There is no child [i.e., not even those of the royal family] that of itself hath understanding'' (Erman, 1966, p. 56). Although this is hardly a ringing proclamation of a *tabula rasa* view of the child, it certainly portends that concept.

Other Aspects

Regarding the three effects not yet discussed (recognition of individual differences amongst the young, of the extent to which the young affect their parents during specific interactions, and of the special contribution made by the young), the limited sources allow no inferences or conclusions to be drawn. The apparent silence of our sources about these matters does not necessarily mean, however, that ancient Near-Eastern societies were totally oblivious to these effects. All pieces of extant evidence certainly ought to be carefully examined by specialists in each of these cultures.

ANCIENT GREECE

Ancient Greek society was every bit as concerned about its children as the older cultures of the Near East. Evidence of the importance attached to the young abounds. Nowhere is it more striking than in the attention Greek lawgivers and philosophers gave to the education of children, beginning from infancy. Greek drama also shows that children and their welfare were strong concerns of the Greek people.

Importance of the Young

As early as Homeric times (ca. 1000–750 B.C.), Greek society felt that a family without children was incomplete. The view that a complete family by definition included children still prevailed in the fourth century. In his treatise on politics, Aristotle insists that to be complete, a family or household has to have children.

Like the Hebrews, the Greeks saw themselves linked to the future through their children at both the familial and larger community levels. For Greek fathers it was of supreme importance to have either a natural or an adopted son to continue the family line. In Euripides' great tragedy, *Medea,* Aegeus the king of Athens is finally persuaded by Medea to promise to give her asylum in return for her pledge to supply him with drugs that will end his childlessness. Indeed, the awful revenge Medea wreaks on her husband Jason depends entirely on leaving him child*less*. Of all the ways in which she could conceive to hurt and torture him, leaving him absolutely bereft of children and without hope of begetting more was the most horribly painful. To kill only one of the two little boys would not suffice. Medea speaks, "The children are dead. I say this to make you suffer."

Continuance of the family name and line was not a matter only for kings and nobility. The law courts of Athens in the fourth century heard considerable litigation over adoption rights even among the lower classes of the citizenry.

At the larger community level, all Greek citizens, regardless of class, saw children as the future bearers of their culture and civilization. All the great lawgivers and philosophers devoted significant attention to the education and training of the young. It is important to note that for most of the Greek communities, the ideal goal of education was cultural rather than practical or vocational. The aim of education was to develop the child's moral character for his future participation in the life of the community (Beck, 1964). The Greeks even created in their households a special position for the *paidagogus* whose primary function was to protect and oversee the moral environment of the young male children (Beck, 1964).

Children were important to the Greeks as their link to the future, but they also seem to have been valued as family members just for themselves. Certainly their naming and acceptance into membership of the family was attended by elaborate ritual (Flacelière, 1965). Once a father, community, or tribal official had accepted the newborn into the family, the family was obliged to rear it.

This decision to accept or to reject the newborn raises, of course, the issue of infanticide. There can be no doubt whatsoever that infanticide was practiced in the ancient world to an extent that chills the blood of contemporary historians (Langer, 1973). What is of importance for this study is that the ancients were by no means sanguine about these actions. The act was not casual, the decision not lightly made. There are three major indications of some reluctance to resort to infanticide. First, the sources contain references to sickly or deformed children and to illegitimate sons, the very ones who could have been exposed and were not. Second, although we find few outright condemnations of infanticide as murder, we do find many passages that signify real unease about the act. A poignant description of the feelings of malaise and despair that attended infanticide is contained in the letters of a merchant to a friend which invoked such justifications for the abandonment of his infant as high taxes, support of actors, and other drains on his resources (Payne, 1916). Third, although the literature provides grisly pictures of scrapheaps of discarded babies, there are just as many stories of men and women from all walks of life rescuing discarded infants from their plight. Despite the legal and cultural approval for the practice of infanticide, many Greeks showed considerable compassion for the abandoned newborns. No doubt the helplessness of the infants aroused their emotions and prompted them to engage in rescue efforts. It is noteworthy that these adoptive parents were moved by the plight of individual infants, yet no one tried to do anything about the general practice of infanticide. It is thus a reasonable inference that adults were not moved by the idea of suffering infants so much as by seeing actual suffering and helpless infants.

Once accepted into the family, the infant's safety and position in the family were secure, and the child was usually seen as a source of pleasure, as something important and loved. Medea recognizes and capitalizes on the power of parental affection for children. Just as she took revenge on her husband by depriving him of children, just as she inveigled Aegeus of Athens into granting her asylum by promising him children, so also she finally persuaded Creon of Corinth (the king and father of the princess Jason abandoned her for) to grant her one more day in Corinth by appealing to his feelings about children. "Have pity on them! You have children of your own. It is natural for you to look kindly on them."

Perhaps Plutarch's letter to his wife to console her grief after the death of their two-year-old daughter shows better than any other piece of evidence remaining from the ancient world a parent's recognition of the special joys a child can bring.

> The delight it gives is quite pure and free from all anger or reproach . . . just as she was herself the most delightful thing in the world to embrace, to see, to hear, so too must the thought of her *live* with us and be our companion, bringing with it joy in greater measure, nay in many times greater measure, than it brings sorrow.

Children occupied, then, a position of importance in Greek civilization. They were seen as the carriers of both the individual family's and the larger community's line and culture. They were also viewed as suppliers of pleasure and comfort for their parents. It is surprising how few remarks one finds that characterize the rearing of children in a decidedly negative manner, and even these passages are relatively free from rancor or bitterness—feelings almost any parent experiences once in a while!

Recognition of Special Characteristics of Children

Characteristics and traits.   The Greeks also seem to have had a clear idea of qualities they believed to pertain especially to children. While artistic style and convention until well into the fourth century visually represented children—even infants—as miniature adults, literary descriptions of the young show clearly that the Greeks saw that there were physical differences between adults and children other than mere size. Medea comments on the sweet smile of her sons and the "bright look" of their eyes. Jason begs Medea to let him once more "touch my boy's delicate flesh." In an ode, Pindar calls the body of an infant "delicate," "dainty."

The Greeks noted the plasticity of the limbs of infants, and most believed that the limbs should be protected and molded. The most prevalent method of dealing with this plasticity was to swaddle infants.

The Greeks also recognized behavioral characteristics or traits that they believed were displayed more often or more appropriately by children than by adults. The range of these characteristics or traits is quite extensive but can be divided into the following groups: (1) *unformed or capable of being molded,* amoral, impressionable, ignorant, gullible, imaginative; (2) *helpless,* unable to speak, weak; (3) *fearful,* easily frightened, tending to cry or to beg and implore; (4) *cheerful and affectionate,* happy, loving, playful; (5) *unruly or difficult to control,* boorish, willful, wild; (6) *imitative;* and (7) *innocent.* While no Greek would maintain that these characteristics pertained exclusively to children, they seem to associate them especially with children's behavior.

Of the kinds of characteristics ascribed to children, Greeks seem to have been most attentive (as judged by the number of ancient references) to the "unformed" or "moldable" quality they perceived in their children. The parallel between the attention given to moldable character and plastic limbs is striking. Of course, the belief that a child can be trained equally well in mind and body underlies the whole system of Greek education. As the twig is bent, so grows the tree.

Some Greeks also believed that the young were ignorant, that their knowledge must be acquired. A passage from the philosopher Epictetus typifies this *tabula rasa* view of the child. "For what is a child? Ignorance. What is a child? Want of instruction. For where a child has knowledge, he is not worse than we are." This lack of knowledge made the child impressionable, sometimes gullible; and the Greeks laid great stress on telling young children only those stories and tales that would uplift them, avoiding those stories that might glorify immoral behavior.

As to the physical helplessness of children, we should not be surprised to find that Greek society saw this rather obvious trait. Plutarch remarks that nothing at all is so helpless as the newborn. One aspect of the infant's helplessness seems to have impressed the Greeks particularly—the inability to communicate with words. Orestes' nurse mentions this. Plato considers at some length how speechless infants can still manage to communicate some of their wants. Although the Greeks recognized that the young were relatively helpless and therefore needed care, their "helplessness" does not seem to be a dominant theme in descriptions of childish characteristics or traits.

The group of characteristics or traits that receive the most stress after those depicting the young as being "unformed" and "moldable" are those seeing the child as fearful, easily frightened, easily brought to tears, hiding in mother's skirts, begging to be picked up for comfort. Often Greeks took advantage of the ease with which children were frightened by conjuring up images of ghosts and other horrible creatures that would attack and punish children for misbehaving. While most passages in the literature indicate that ideas of horrible monsters were imposed on the child's mind by adults, some indicate an awareness that children can be frightened by specters contrived by their own unaided imaginations.

Furthermore, the literature shows an appreciation for childhood fears provoked by strangeness, bigness, or a change in the child's family situation. Homer portrays Hector's infant son reacting in tearful terror to the sight of his father's magnificant, large, shiny, plumed helmet. Euripides is sensitive also to the child's fear of being left alone.

The other characteristics attributed especially to children figure less prominently in the sources. Almost all writers who discuss children at all remark that they are cheerful, affectionate, and playful. Less often directly mentioned but surely tacitly assumed are their willful, boorish, and wild qualities, and their inability to sit still or to pay attention. The great concern with discipline and control indicates that Greeks believed the young had these latter characteristics. Interestingly enough, cruelty and viciousness do not seem to be traits ascribed to children. Finally, a few references are found in which children are described as innocent and as imitative.

Special needs.   In addition to a recognition of characteristics and traits belonging particularly to children, the Greeks also saw the many special needs of children. Just as they recognized the child's playfulness, they recognized the child's need for toys.

Greek society's appreciation of the child's need to play expressed itself in more than the mere supply of physical toys. The sources reveal an awareness of the kind of games children play and how important these games are for the child's development into an adult. Plutarch recognized the element of pretending in his little daughter's play and apparently encouraged both the child and her nurse to continue these games.

The most extensive and sensitive statement about children's play comes from Plato's *Laws:*

> To form the character of the child over three and up to six years old there will be need of games. . . . Children of this age have games which come by natural instinct; and they generally invent them of themselves whenever they meet together. As soon as they have reached the age of three, all the children from three to six must meet together at the village temples. . . . I assert that there exists in every State a complete ignorance about children's games—how that they are of decisive importance for legislation, as determining whether the laws enacted are to be permanent or not. For when the programme of games is prescribed and secures that the same children always play the same games and delight in the same toys in the same way and under the same conditions, it allows the real and serious laws also to remain undisturbed.
>
>   . . . Alterations in children's games are regarded by all lawgivers . . . as being mere matters of play and not as the causes of serious mischief; hence, instead of forbidding them, they give in to them and adopt them. They fail to reflect that those children who innovate in their games grow up into men different from their fathers.

Plato's observations about games and play reveal several interesting points. He and apparently most Greeks saw play and games as part of children's nature; they believed play to be such a vital need of children that civil legislation might have provisions for it. However, Plato differed from most Greeks in that he saw a connection between the way the child plays and the way that the child as an adult will think and act. Whereas most Greeks believed play was important but best left to the children themselves, Plato believed that the way children played should be regulated by the state.

The physical helplessness of infants and small children meant that they needed nursing and protection, and the Greeks clearly saw this. But they also seem to have felt that the young required something over and above rudimentary nursing and protection—love and physical affection. Greek literature is full of descriptions of or references to the fondling, kissing, embracing, hugging, stroking, and rocking of infants and small children. The Greeks are now and have always been physically demonstrative people. They touch one another freely and draw pleasure, comfort, and reassurance from physical contact. Hector's response to his infant son's frightened reaction to the shiny helmet is to remove the helmet, lay it aside, take the small boy into his arms, and kiss him and smile at him.

Plutarch advises mothers to nurse their infants themselves, because suckling makes mothers ''come to be more kindly disposed towards their children and more inclined to show them affection.'' Plutarch also advises fathers not to be too harsh or austere but rather to

in many cases concede some shortcomings to the younger person and remind themselves that they were once young . . . (and) bear misdeeds with good humor. . . . Our friend's shortcomings we bear with; why should it be surprising that we bear with our children's?

The most important need of children was seen by the Greeks to be discipline. The comparison between the Greek view of the child's nature and that of the Puritans is instructive. The Puritans beat and punished their young in an effort to drive from them the congenital sin of willfullness (Demos, 1970). This motivation for harsh discipline seems to be absent from Greek thinking. Indeed, when Greeks, except for the Spartans and outright Laconophiles, talked about the rigor and quality of discipline, they generally spoke of the need to temper it, to render it less harsh and abusive. Discipline of the young connoted to the Greeks less the idea of punishment for evildoing than close supervision to insure proper growth and development.

This study has so far indicated that

1. The Greeks viewed their children as important constituents of both family and community, as future bearers of Greek culture, and as valuable in their own right;

2. Greek parents and society recognized many characteristics, traits, and

needs that pertained especially to the young and to some extent based their treatment of children on that recognition (this finding anticipates the next kind of stimulus effect the study considers).

The Greeks then had a clear conception of "the world of the young" as distinct from "the world of adults." Did they see within the "world of the young" any differences either among various stages of development within the period of youth or among individual children at the same age level?

Recognition of Age and Individual Differences

Aristotle and Plato both describe stages of development and assign to each appropriate modes of parental care and education. For convenience, we shall tabulate these stages. (See Table 1 on p. 18.)

While the two schemes of developmental stages do not correspond exactly to one another or to contemporary theories of development (both miss the "toddler stage," for example), they do have enough in common with one another and with current descriptions of development to warrant the conclusion that the Greeks made an effort to discriminate stages through which the young pass from birth to adulthood, and they showed a striking cognizance of the physiological and psychological aspects of development, such as protection of the child's body and mind, the importance of infancy, and the sequence of physical and psychological training.

Despite the Greek's great stress on nurture in the development of children, they were not oblivious to differences in the nature of different children. It is not unusual for the sources to comment on differences between individual children or to remark that a certain child was brighter, quicker, or somehow different from his or her peers. Strepsiades, the father in Aristophanes's *Clouds,* recalls how bright his now rebellious son was as a small boy. Dio Chrysostum remarks that some children are naturally more timid than others. I have already made reference to the passage in Plato that argues for regulation of children's play. In his argument, Plato recognizes that some children are apt to innovate in their games.

It is in the biographies of Plutarch that we find the most frequent mention of differences in individual children. This attention to individual differences is, of course, to be expected in a biographer. Whether or not Plutarch's close observation of individuals as adults led him to an especially keen appreciation of children as individuals cannot be determined. But he remarked on these differences at both the concrete and conceptual levels. In a general discussion of education for children, Plutarch stresses that not all children—not even those of high birth—have the same natural gifts, but that even the child with a poor endowment can be trained to be better.

TABLE 1
Two Schemes of Development

Age level	Characteristics and/or proper care	Source
	Plato	*Laws*
Birth–2 years	Swaddled	789E
	Much rocking and crooning	790D
2–3 years	Carried by nurses	789E
	Nurses/mothers ascertain wants according to cries	792A
	Shield from pain, fear, grief, or corruption	792B
	"It is in infancy that the whole character is most effectually determined"	792E
3–6 years	Games played together with other children	793E
	Mild discipline	793E
6–puberty	Separate sexes	794C
	Boys go to school; gymnastics and music	794C, 795E
	Girls learn gymnastics also	694D
	Aristotle	*Politics*
Birth–weaning, 2 years	Bodily development most important	1336a
	"Training of the body (comes) before training of the mind"	1338b
	Plenty of milk; no wine	
	As free movement of limbs as possible	
	Accustom to endure cold	1336a
2–5 years	Bodily exercise	
	Play in preparation for adult activities	
	Allow to cry	
	Protect from base influences	1336a
5–7 years	Still at home	
	Protect from indecent talk, pictures, and statues	
	May not attend lampoons and comedy	1336b
7–Puberty	Begin school for boys	
	Avoid hard diet and severe exercise	1336b
Puberty–21	Rigorous training	1336b

Aristotle also noted that there were differences among children of the same age and background. And from this observation he drew the conclusion that just as it is better for the doctor to treat each patient as a particular case, so also it is better for the child to be given individual attention in education in order that he receive what he particularly needs.

Recognition of the Effects of the Young

Implicit in many of the passages so far discussed is an awareness that adults—parents, nurses, caregivers, teachers—perform certain acts and respond in certain ways to children. In considering the fourth kind of effect exerted by the young on adults—recognition of the extent to which the young affect their parents or caregivers during specific interactions—a distinction ought to be drawn between those responses that take cognizance of the child as a stimulus and those that do not. Is the adult aware that his response has been induced by the child? Or does the adult apprehend himself as acting upon or reacting to the child only in response to feelings or thoughts that originate within the adult?

Reactions or responses to children that are seen by the adult as originating within the adult probably reflect the adult's conception of the child (at least at the moment of interaction) as a *tabula rasa*. For example, Plutarch argues that parents love their offspring by nature. He thinks of the emotion as generated from within the adult and then proceeding out of the adult to the child. Philo Judaeus expresses much the same idea when he discusses the reasons that adults rescue abandoned infants. He says that a passerby is stirred up by compassion and humane feeling (already present within the adult) and then as a consequence picks up the castaway and gives it food and drink. Whereas modern psychologists would argue that Plutarch and Philo are describing behaviors that respond to a perceived helplessness in the newborn, Plutarch and Philo see the newborn as simply there, as the recipient of the adult feelings.

There are a surprisingly large number of instances in which the adult sees himself or herself acting in direct response to something the child has said or done, or sees feelings that children provoke in adults. I have already remarked that most of the telling points in the arguments in Euripides's *Medea* depend upon adult feelings about children: Medea knows full well how Creon will react to her plea to pity her two boys. Of a similar nature are all the references to orators and lawyers especially playing on the sympathies of Athenian jurymen by placing before them the children of their clients.

There is another group of passages that shows adults trying to ascertain what it is that the child wants and then to fill that want or need. The most charming description of this kind of response is the speech of Orestes' nurse Cilissa in Aeschylus's *Libation-Bearers:*

> A baby is like a beast, it does not think
> but you have to nurse it, do you not, the way it wants.
> For the child still in swaddling clothes can not tell us
> if he is hungry or thirsty, if he needs to make
> water. Children's young insides are a law to themselves.

The picture of an adult trying to do what the child wants or needs is found also in Homer's *Iliad,* in which the aged Phoenix recalls caring for the young Achilles:

> for you would not go with another out to any feast,
> nor taste of any food in your own halls until I had set
> you on my knees, and cut little pieces from the meat,
> and given you all you wished, and held the wine for you.

Stark recognition of the power that a child could exert over an adult is evidenced by a passage in Plutarch, in which the biographer records a saying attributed to the great hero of the Persian Wars, Themistocles:

> Of his son, who lorded it over his mother, and through her over himself, he said, jestingly, that the boy was the most powerful of all the Hellenes; for the Hellenes were commanded by the Athenians, the Athenians by himself, himself by the boy's mother, and the mother by her boy.

Although Themistocles was obviously joking, the crux of the jest nonetheless depends upon the recognition that children can often direct the actions of their parents.

The last of the five kinds of effects exerted by the young—recognition of their special contributions to the family and larger society—can be seen in Plato's *Laws,* already cited. There is an implication in these laws that most Greeks thought children's games were best left to the children themselves, but Plato saw in their spontaneity and ''mischief'' a threat to the continuity of the games that had molded their fathers. Thus, a latent capability of a childhood activity to change society at a later time was a concern of one of the great philosophers of ancient Greece. More often, however, an enjoyment of the carefreeness and playfulness that marks the young runs through the literature. They have fun and bring pleasure and amusement to their families and communities. Surely the most beautiful and moving description of the special joys that can be brought into a home by a young child is Plutarch's letter of consolation to his wife on the death of their daughter, Timoxena. Passages of this letter have already been cited, but these few lines are worth repeating here.

> Our affection for children so young has, furthermore, a poignancy all its own; the delight that it gives is quite pure and free from all anger or reproach.

Plutarch here expresses a kind of love and emotion that is unconstrained by fear or convention, a love he can feel only for a small child.

It will be helpful at this point to recapitulate the similarities and differences between the Greek and ancient Near-Eastern societies. In both the earlier and Greek societies, the child's endearing qualities as an object of affection were recognized, as well as the child's importance in completing the family. The child was also an important symbol of the society's hopes for the future.

It is not difficult to detect an awareness of the special characteristics of the young in the ancient societies prior to Greek civilization. They saw the child's need for love and provided toys to meet their needs for play as well as providing legal and other protection to offset their helplessness. All these special characteristics were also recognized by the Greeks, but they apparently began "education" at an earlier age. Again and again, Greek writers stress the need for training in early childhood in an attempt to mold and shape the child. The Greeks show a greater awareness of age and individual differences. Their leaders of thought differentiated many stages of development; moreover, they pointed out the extent of individual differences among children and tried to explain how these developed in various environments. With respect to recognition of immediate and larger social effects of the young, the writings of the Greeks again show an awareness of these effects not reflected in the ancient Near-Eastern literature.

ROME

The picture of childhood held by Roman society is in many ways very much like that of Greek society. Such a resemblance is no cause for surprise, because Greek culture—literature, philosophy, science, art—formed the base of much of Roman civilization. There were, however, two aspects in which the Romans differed considerably from their Hellenic predecessors: (1) the theoretically absolute, total control exercised by the father over his children and family, the *patria potestas*—paternal power; and (2) the continual struggle of the upper classes (and perhaps of the lower classes also) of Roman society to replenish themselves over nearly a millenium. These two facets of Roman culture seem to be as old as Rome itself.

Power the Roman father surely had. In almost all ancient societies, the father had the right of life or death over all newborn children. But in other societies, once the decision for life was made, the father's legal right to inflict death upon his child terminated. Not so with the Romans; until well into the Empire, Roman fathers retained the legal right to kill their children, even if those children had attained adulthood.

Gradually over the long course of Roman history, the power of the father to injure and abuse his children was circumscribed. In the second century A.D., Hadrian ruled that a father who killed his grown son should be banished. It was not, however, until 374 A.D. that the final step in limiting the father's power of life and death over his offspring was taken when an imperial edict was issued that anyone who even exposed his infant would be subject to punishment.

Such absolute power as the *patria potestas* appears to us repugnant and dangerous. The Romans also seem to have recognized the inherent danger of monstrous perversion. Almost as hoary as the institution itself is the first attempt to check its abuse. Roman tradition credits the city's founder,

Romulus, with a law limiting the father's power of life and death over his newborn children. He obliged families to rear to adulthood all sons and at least their firstborn daughters.

The long struggle to eventually limit the father's right to dispose of unwanted children is paralleled by the equally long struggle to maintain the numbers of the upper classes of Rome. The intent of Romulus's check on the *patria potestas* was clearly to provide more male children and future soldiers. Rome had always been a militaristic society, acutely aware that her survival and prosperity depended upon her sons' numbers and prowess on the field of battle. The law also implies, however, that Roman families needed encouragement to raise large numbers of children. Why this was so, we simply do not know. We do know that the disinclination to have sizable families persisted and remained a problem for the upper classes throughout Rome's long history.

I have pursued these two topics, the extraordinary authority of the father and the pervasive and persistent tendency of Romans to limit the number of children reared, because they reveal that the Romans must have had some difficulty in coming to terms with parenthood and in relinquishing their society (and hence themselves) to the coming generation. There must have been something that the Romans perceived in children—whether directly or symbolically—that deterred them from rearing enough of them to replenish their families.

Importance of the Young

In other respects, the Romans seem to have attached to their children and their upbringing much the same importance as the Greeks. Strong evidence that the Romans attached positive importance to their children is found in the number of oaths and appeals that refer to children. For example, Sallust reports that the Numidian prince Adherbal in a plea for asylum before the Roman Senate in 116 B.C., concluded his speech:

> Members of the Senate, I conjure you, as you respect yourselves, your children, your parents, and the majesty of the Roman people, aid me.

The birth and naming of a Roman child was attended by ceremony and ritual (Balsdon, 1969). In addition the Romans had a goddess, Rumilia, of "the rearing of young children."

Romans were every bit as concerned about their children's education as were the Greeks. In early times, fathers were their sons' principal teachers and gave their boys personal instruction in reading and writing as well as in physical skills such as swimming, riding, hurling the javelin, etc. By the middle of the second century B.C., however, fathers seem to have turned more and more to professional tutors or to schoolmasters and to have either hired private tutors or to have sent their sons out for instruction in reading and writing. Intimate parental involvement in children's education did not completely vanish, however. The emperor Augustus

> taught his grandsons reading, swimming, and the other elements of education, for the most part himself, taking special pains to train them to imitate his own handwriting.

Recognition of Special Characteristics of Children

Just like the Greeks, the Romans seem to have had a clear idea of characteristics and traits that especially marked children. The poet Catullus remarked on the particular smoothness of a child's earlobe. St. Jerome advises that the constitution of the young cannot endure too much severity, either physically or emotionally. St. Augustine mentions the singing voices peculiar to children and how it is impossible to distinguish between the voices of girls and boys.

The behaviors and characteristic traits associated particularly with children by the Romans is roughly comparable to that seen by the Greeks. As with the Greeks, the most remarked upon quality is the "unformed" nature of the child. The Romans saw the young as moldable, teachable, ignorant, unaware, even witless, and also, therefore, corruptible. The Romans seem to have been more inclined to see negative characteristics in their children than were the Greeks. Latin literature has many more references to the child as being unruly, quick to anger, prone to deceit, and naturally jealous than does Greek literature. Perhaps concomitantly, the Romans paid less attention to the qualities of weakness, helplessness, and fearfulness in their young. Both the Greeks and Romans recognized that their children were playful, cheerful, affectionate, and lovable. The Romans perhaps laid more stress upon the child's natural tendency to imitate than did the Greeks and more often remarked upon the natural innocence of the child. The latter trait is due no doubt to the influence of Stoicism and Christianity. Finally, three characteristics are connected with the child by the Romans that are not mentioned by the Greeks—competitiveness, curiosity, and natural facility of memory.

For the Romans as well as the Greeks, the notion of the child as unformed or moldable—a *tabula rasa*—provided the basis of their educational practices and theories. They believed that good examples were essential to the formation of good character, and, like the Greeks, they attempted to shield their young from potentially corrupting influences.

The single most comprehensive Roman treatise on education is that of Quintilian, the *Institutio Oratoria,* written at the end of the first century A.D. This great teacher of the art of rhetoric took a very positive view of the child and of his innate ability to learn.

> I would, therefore, have a father conceive the highest hopes of his son from the moment of his birth . . . you will find that most (children) are quick to reason and ready to learn. . . . Those who are dull and unteachable are as abnormal as prodigious births and monstrosities,

and are but few in number. . . . Let us not therefore waste the earliest years: there is all the less excuse for this, since the elements of literary training are solely a question of memory, which not only exists even in small children, but is specially retentive at that age. . . . He will remember such aphorisms even when he is an old man, and the impression made upon his unformed mind will contribute to the formation of his character.

Some recognition of the notion that children often live up to expectations is obviously present in Quintilian's views.

Quintilian and other Romans also believed that children were naturally competitive and tried to apply that observation to their educational practices. Both Cicero and St. Augustine emphasize the competitiveness of young boys. Quintilian urged that the child's natural instinct for competition be used to further his learning, but he urged teachers to make use of the positive aspects of competition rather than its destructive qualities.

With respect to the needs of children, the Romans here too conform to the picture already established for the Greeks. Their recognition that the child needs a balance of love, affection (both physical and emotional), and discipline is apparent in the literature, perhaps nowhere more so than in the writings of Quintilian. However, a broad cross section of Roman literary figures—St. Augustine, Aulus Gellius, St. Jerome, Lucretius, Plutarch, Pliny, Senaca, and Suetonius—comment on the child's need to be loved and fondled.

Likewise most writers also mention the child's need for guidance and discipline and indicate an appreciation that harsh, abusive treatment of children can be undesirable. Roman children, like their Greek counterparts, received spankings, beatings, and whippings. Quintilian deplores such practices, but his comment makes it clear that flogging students was an all too common habit of most schoolmasters. Other Romans also expressed an aversion to harsh, corporal punishment. The otherwise stern Cato the Elder, a paragon of discipline and austerity, "used to say that the man who struck his wife or child laid violent hands on the holiest of holy things." There existed then in Roman society alongside the all too obvious use of harsh, bodily punishment a countertrend that recognized the physical and psychic damage that such severity could produce.

Recognition of Age and Individual Differences

The Romans apparently observed the stages of development and growth in their young and of individual differences in children of the same age as keenly as the Greeks. The Roman biographies of Plutarch and the lives of Suetonius abound with examples of differences among children.

The teacher Quintilian, as might well be expected, was keenly aware of differences among the native abilities of his students and advised tailoring a boy's program to his own abilities and needs.

The skillful teacher will make it his first care, as soon as a boy is entrusted to him, to ascertain his ability and character . . . the teacher must next consider what treatment is to be applied to the mind of his pupil. There are some boys who are slack, unless pressed on; others again are impatient of control; some are amenable to fear, while others are paralysed by it; in some cases the mind requires continued application to form it, in others this result is best obtained by rapid concentration.

The Romans also had a fairly developed and consistent picture of stages of development within childhood. Three writers—Quintilian, St. Augustine, and Macrobius—present a reasonably detailed account of stages of growth in children, and many other passages exist that allude to or assume such developmental processes.

Table 2
Three Schemes of Development

Age Level	Characteristics and/or proper care	Source
	Quintilian	*Instituto Oratoria*
Birth–3 years	In charge of nurses and then paidagogus	
	Highly impressionable; therefore nurses and paidagogus must speak properly and set fine moral examples	
	Has learned to speak	1.1.5–11
3–7 years	Still at home but education and training should commence	1.1.15–19
	Memory is acute and retentive	1.1.36
	Not capable of originality	1.1.36
	Needs studies to be amusing	1.1.20
	Needs stimulation of praise and sometimes of competition	1.1.20
	Suit tasks to child's limited ability	1.1.22
	Do not push too hard	1.1.32–33
7–adolescence	Boys should be sent out to school	1.2.1–13
	Instruction should be tailored to individual pupil	1.3.6
	Needs rest and relaxation	1.3.8
	Play is good for boys	1.3.11
	Character formation crucial before boys learn deceit	1.3.12
	Avoid flogging and abusive punishment	1.3.13–17
	St. Augustine	*Confessions*
Infancy–3(?) years	At first could only suck and cry	
	Began to smile and laugh	1.6
	Frustrated at being unable to communicate and thus cried more	
	Easily angered; often sullen	1.7
	Jealous of other infants	

(continued)

Table 2 (Continued)

Age level	Characteristics and/or proper care	Source
3(?)–7(?) years	Remained at home	1.8
	Learned to speak	
	Learned one word at a time	
	Made lots of grunting noises	
	Learned without an adult really teaching	
	Aware of "body language," of non-verbal forms of communication	
	At beck and call of elders	
	Disobedient	1.9
7(?)–adolescence	Went to school	1.9
	Unruly and still disobedient	1.9–10
	Did not like to study	1.9, 1.12
	Loved to play	1.9–10
	Prayed to be spared the rod at school	1.9
	Irrational likes and dislikes	1.13
	Concluded that curiosity led to learning and that frightful punishment hampered learning	1.14
	Macrobius *(early fifth century A.D.)*	*Commentary on the Dream of Scipio*
7th hour	Critical hour after birth: those who survive to this hour are likely to live	67
7th day	Umbilical cord cast off	68
14th day	Eyes respond to light	
7th week	Eyes follow moving object	
7th month	Teeth begin to appear	69
14th month	Sits up without fear of falling	
21st month	Begins to talk	
28th month	Can stand firmly and walk	
35th month	Begins to be weaned	
7th year	Permanent teeth begin to appear Speaks plainly	70
14th year	Onset of puberty in both male and female	71

For convenience, Table 2 recapitulates the stages of development found in these three writers. These schemes of development are quite obviously independent of one another, yet all show a similar pattern of empirical observations about the development of children. Quintilian's is written from the point of view of the teacher of rhetoric, the trainer of orators. Of the three, his is most like those of Plato and Aristotle and treats both the physiological and psychological aspects of the child. St. Augustine shows a much more personal, emotional approach to describing the various stages of development. His description of how he learned to speak is truly marvelous. St. Augustine is one of those rare individuals who possess an exceptional recollection of their own childhoods. There is little in his adult life that would have allowed him opportunity for close observation of children, and indeed he expressly disavows any fondness for children. The most impressive aspect of Augustine's description of his own childhood is the intense sympathy, even empathy, he displays as an adult for the conditions and difficulties of being a young child. Macrobius' commentary shows an evident attempt to schematize the maturation process on the number seven and its multiples and plainly focuses on the physiological aspects of the child.

These three schemes all see roughly three stages of development: infancy, young childhood, and adolescence. Although modern theories postulate more stages, recognize other areas of development (psychosexual), and elaborate some much more fully (motor, cognitive, moral), the general outline presented in each of these schemes corresponds roughly to contemporary models. Indeed, St. Augustine's recollections describe behaviors—sullenness, disobedience, angriness—that suggest what Gesell called the "terrible two's." Augustine also shows an implicit awareness of nonverbal communication.

Recognition of the Effects of the Young

There was not among the Romans much inclination or ability to see themselves as acting in response to their children. There are very few passages in the extant Roman literature that reveal any awareness that adults react in response to children. The Roman culture, unlike the Greek, was not given to such subtle observations of human behavior. Perhaps this inability to see themselves as acting in response to children has some connection with the idea of *patria potestas*—power and hence the agency of action resides in the father. The few examples of adult reaction usually assume that the adult is in charge of his actions. All the oaths and appeals issued in the name of children attest to a perception on the part of the adult community that the child could somehow invigorate the noblest instincts or actions already in men.

St. Augustine remarks that parents bear childishnesses because they know that the child will outgrow them. Cato the Elder declared "that his son's presence put him on his guard against indecencies of speech as much as that of the so-called Vestal Virgins." Suetonius reports that the soldiers in the German camp in which the young (two- or three-year-old) emperor, Caligula, was raised were so devoted to the little fellow that "when they threatened mutiny after the death of Augustus and were ready for any act of madness, the mere sight of Gaius (Caligula) unquestionably calmed them." Thus, about the only strongly perceived motivating force exerted by children was the one that uplifted or called forth strength and nobility.

There is an interesting connection perhaps between this one acknowledged motivating force and what some Romans saw as the child's particular contributions to society. Cicero twice remarks that man can see nature's plan best in children: "my own school, more than others, go to the nursery, because they believe that Nature reveals her plan to them most clearly in childhood."

Of course, this view of the child as bearing some special relationship to nature (and hence to the divine for Cicero) becomes a common theme in Christian writing. St. Augustine often expressed this idea: "For these things hast thou hid from the wise and prudent, and hast revealed them unto babes [*Confessions* 7.21]."

Here then is the child as something sacred and powerful. If this concept of the child existed before Cicero, indeed, if it too had its origins in the very beginnings of Roman civilization, perhaps a fear of this power accounts for the creation of the countervailing power of the *patria potestas* and the very curiously ambivalent attitude of the Romans toward their children.

SUMMARY

This discussion of the effects of the young leads us back to the topic of their importance and to a summary of the differences between the Greeks and the Romans. Although the power of the child was dwarfed by the power of the Roman father, the Roman child was at least as important as in Greek society, possibly even more so if there is any merit in the suggestion of a relation between the ambivalent attitude of Roman parents toward children and their perception of children as embodying sacred secrets of nature.

The Romans, building upon Greek culture, saw most of the same special characteristics in their young and added some new ones—competitiveness, curiosity, imitation, and memory facility. Again, reflecting their ambivalent attitude, they saw many more negative characteristics. Also, as would be expected in a society that had the psychological task of justifying arbitrary and sometimes monstrous parental power, they paid less attention to the helplessness and weakness of the young.

We might expect that the Romans would have amplified the perceptions of age and individual differences that were a part of their cultural acquisition from the Greeks. They did not. Furthermore, the Romans seem to have been considerably less aware of the influences exerted on them by their young. Although children were seen as capable of calling forth higher standards of behavior and speech from adults, the Romans did not show sensitivity to many other effects that had been detected by the Greeks. Perhaps the Romans' disinclination to consciously perceive the influences of their children may also be attributed to their ambivalent attitude toward their children.

I have reviewed data from the ancient societies of the Near East, Greece, and Rome to determine the extent to which these civilizations recognized and paid attention to the influences exerted on adults by the young. The evidence reveals both similarities and differences among the civilizations. All three saw the child as an important link to the future, but none romanticized the child. The Romans placed more emphasis on the power and importance of the father and never succeeded in producing as many children as their leaders wanted for practical, militaristic purposes. Both ancient Near Easterners and Greeks noted the distinctive qualities of helplessness and the need for love and play, but the Greeks showed the greatest recognition of the child's need for gentle shaping and guidance, along with strict (sometimes harsh) discipline to counter the child's apparent lack of self-control. Only the Greeks seem to have been much aware of the effects of the young on adults, families, community, and larger society. Finally, both Greeks and Romans saw definite patterns of child development and recognized differences among individual children.

2
History of the Child's Influence: Medieval to Modern Times

Richard Q. Bell

INTRODUCTION

It has been exciting to find a clear, unmistakable imprint of the child's power and uniqueness in the beautiful passages of literature from the ancient societies of the Mediterranean. Because classical literature has become relatively unfamiliar territory, we have included in Chapter 1 entire passages in which the message of the child's effects are embedded. However, we must quicken the pace and hence change the style. To move on toward our objective of developing an historical perspective, the review will now be more cursory and will rely more heavily on secondary sources. Fortunately, there now exists a substantial and respectable corpus of historical study on childhood from medieval times to our own (Sommerville, 1972). This will make it possible for us to merely summarize some of the more important findings of this work as it bears on our theme.

MEDIEVAL PERIOD THROUGH 17TH CENTURY

The history of the influence of the child in medieval Europe varies enormously according to geographic and temporal locations, but a few generalizations can be hazarded concerning historical developments that help establish a bridge to the philosophers, educators, and scientists from the 18th century whose work has most direct bearing on the current scientific climate with which we are concerned. Against the background of centuries of unremitting invasions, internal warfare, and famines, the standard measure of success in the medieval period was survival. Under such circumstances, all members of society were rendered equal in their face (Aries, 1962; McLaughlin, 1974). Thus it should be no cause for surprise if little conscious attention was paid to special characteristics and needs of children as opposed to other groups. However, as feudalism developed and gradually brought order out of chaos, ecclesiastical institutions established themselves in the fabric of medieval life and drew attention to children. These institutions perpetuated the Roman's incongruous attitudes toward children, though the terms of description were altered to conform with Christian culture. On the one hand, the child represented sweetness, purity, charm, and innocence in the popular image of religious devotion—the cult of the Virgin and Infant Jesus (Clark, 1969). On the other hand, Christian theologians associated the child with the doctrine of original sin. As this doctrine gained ascendency, the age of baptism became progressively lower, and the child came to represent evil, selfishness, willfullness, and vice.

Beginning in the 12th century and continuing through the 17th century, a renewed awareness of the unique qualities of childhood appeared in art, literature, and religion. Further development of various portrayals from earlier periods can be seen; and to the images of innocence and depravity, the Protestant Reformation and the Catholic Counter-Reformation added the notion that the child was possessed of a small soul that required careful nurture. Society was responsible for the proper development of the child. Its inherent evil had to be suppressed; its fragile soul had to be nourished. Increasingly, children were segregated from society into religious teaching institutions so that their presumed special needs could be met.

While the foregoing brief summary does violence to great regional and temporal differences from the medieval times through the 17th century, a full account of child–effects in the rich history of this period is clearly beyond the scope of this book. It will be sufficient to note the broad trends that will continue to be emphasized in the periods to follow. For our limited purposes, suffice it to say that as European societies emerged from centuries of pain, suffering, and death, adult and child were distinguished more clearly, and the child became symbolically important to religious movements as a representation of such varying characteristics as frailty, purity, and inherent depravity. Yet there was no indication that the teachings of the moralists had made adults any more consciously aware of (1) differences between children; (2) child–effects on adults during specific interactions; or (3) child–effects on the society. If anything, the intensity of emotional commitment to abstract concepts may have prevented parents and educators from reacting discriminatively toward children.

The preceding discussion suggests the need at this point for a terminological simplification that will be helpful in the remainder of the book—the use of "parent–effect" or "child–effect" rather than the full phrases parent effect on child or child effect on adult (or parent).

THE 18TH CENTURY

A reaction to the Reformation image of the inherently depraved child set in during the mid-18th century. A group of philosophers and educators set themselves against previous educational trends. John Locke, for example, argued vigorously against the existence of innate ideas. One can see the long shadow of Aristotle in Locke's counter-arguments for the concept of the infant as a *tabula rasa*. He also advised parents to observe their infants carefully in order to detect congenital characteristics. Locke, then, questioned the existence of *innate ideas* but not individual differences or innate characteristics. Thus, Locke advanced a view on the importance of detecting early individual differences, similar to the views expressed in classic antiquity by Aristotle, Epictetus, Plutarch, Quintilian, and others.

Although Locke inveighed against the notion of inherent evil, in one sense his basic orientation toward children complemented that of the religious leaders. He saw children as imperfect adults. Parents ought to observe them carefully in order to detect their basic characteristics; then with this information in mind, they should be shaped toward an adult–ideal.

It will be recalled that Plato emphasized *innate ideas* and the emergence of instincts under favorable circumstances—the "games which come by natural instinct." Jean Jacques Rousseau continued Plato's line of thinking, in contrast with that of Aristotle, in that he believed that the directions for growth were already in the child. However, Rousseau was far more confident than Plato that everything would work out satisfactorily if the child were simply left to its own resources. Rousseau placed primary trust in nature and in a belief that man is born basically good. Actually, Rousseau's contention that man is most likely to achieve happiness, if only allowed to follow his own instincts, is a stance just as extreme as the one it was intended to counteract. However, it did promote an acceptance of diversity in children, and it postulated the need of every child for individualized experiences that would permit the child's own proper growth. Rousseau's *Emile* was considered a charter of childhood, a declaration of the rights of children. The child was accorded a level of importance equal to that in Reformation doctrine, but in this case the emphasis was on the good in the child rather than the evil.

There were two other important implications of Rousseau's teachings. The child was seen as active and searching and thus could be expected to affect the physical and interpersonal environment in which he was developing. Rousseau also drew attention to age differences. The child's maturity, as well as his basic proclivities, should determine the means of education.

Pestalozzi and Froebel followed Rousseau with an insistence on the desirability of educating a child through the child's own activity. Child development had to be studied in order to provide an empirical basis for pedagogical techniques. The demonstration of new types of school environments set the stage for further developments in the 19th century that have been highly influential at all levels of public and private education.

There were broad political as well as philosophical movements in the west that affected the theoretical image of the child. The latter part of the 18th century witnessed many revolutionary or proto-revolutionary movements involving not only the United States but also Europe, from Poland to Ireland, from the Scandinavian countries to Italy. These revolutions, including the American, were part of a general though not necessarily interconnected series of reactions against constituted bodies such as parliaments, councils, assemblies, and magistries (Palmer, 1964). The composition of these bodies tended to be influenced by hereditary position. Thus, our own political and social philosophy developed in a period in which there was a strong reaction against hereditary determination of position in society. This reaction provided a favorable general context for the Lockean viewpoint that the child becomes what society provides in the way of training.

While the recognition of the unique status of the child was enhanced in many ways by the foregoing developments, it became easier to lose sight of the child's own potential for determining growth. Since political and social movements gain their strength at the outset with strong and necessarily simple declarations, it is not too surprising that a political and social philosophy that emphasized the rights of man and the child led to an emphasis on the results that could be achieved by training. An overly zealous advocacy of such a position made it difficult to encompass the possibility that the child makes its own contribution to the developmental process.

While significant developments in societal attitudes about the nature of children occurred at the theoretical level during the 18th century, at the practical level there was no corresponding change. Recent studies of 18th-century childhood show that parents generally adopted one of two postures toward their young: (1) a stance of indifference that separated parent and child both physically and emotionally; and (2) a determinedly intrusive vigilance over the child that made the parent a part of the child's every action (Lorence, 1974). The former dominated the aristocracy, especially in England and France; the latter was most prevalent among the middle classes and was clearly derived from the Reformation view of the child as inherently evil. For the child of the 18th century, the voices of Locke and Rousseau, of Pestalozzi and Froebel, represented the minority view, but they broke the intellectual ground for the practical developments of the 19th century.

EARLY 19TH CENTURY

Early 19th-century America saw the development of three basic points of view about children—views not entirely consistent with each other. These perspectives penetrated levels of society well beyond those of the aristocracy and intelligentsia (Sunley, 1955). The first was a continuation of Reformation doctrine, which is now augmented by the addition of more specific dicta aimed at helping parents guard their children against the effects of their own impulses. Absolute obedience was demanded. The child's will was to be broken by ignoring crying rather than responding to needs that the cry may have indicated. There was great concern over masturbation, and it was considered especially important to protect the child against the sexual effects of kissing and hugging by parents, nurses, and other caregivers.

The second line of thinking was an outgrowth of the writings of Locke and Rousseau, emphasizing the tempering effect on the child of exposure to experiences that challenged and developed mettle. There was great emphasis on motor development and independence of movement. Many writings that found wide readership in the general population opposed swaddling and encouraged parents to let their infants sit up and feed themselves, often too early by present standards. Children were generally encouraged to be independent.

The third point of view was an outgrowth of the teaching and educational demonstrations of Pestalozzi and Froebel. Children were to learn by their own activity or by encouraging expressions of impulses and feelings. Impulses were regarded as good rather than as indications of inherent depravity. The popularization of these educational viewpoints portrayed the child as a flower that would blossom according to a schedule. It would emerge showing the full beauty of its nature if the parent primarily served the function of a gardener by providing basic physical and experiential nourishment.

There were a variety of factors contributing to changes in the view of the child in America (Sunley, 1955). First, parents increasingly began to see children as an extension of their ambition and status needs. Second, the need to mold the child grew directly out of a value system that emphasized the ability of man to control and direct his future, rather than his being at the mercy of a fate preordained by God or heredity. There was also a need to find new directions for living and child-rearing in order to replace the very simple and rigid patterns of family life that were being disrupted by industrialization and urbanization.

LATE 19TH CENTURY AND EARLY 20TH CENTURY

This is the era during which revolutions in scientific thinking affected the behavioral and social sciences—an era during which American psychologists and sociologists developed a strong interest in the study of the child.

American sociology was still in its infancy at the end of the 19th century and, perhaps surprisingly, began by postulating that progress in civilization was related to superior genetic endowment, that instincts explained social behavior, and that inherited mental abilities and traits produced racial and ethnic differences (Clausen, 1967). These hypotheses emphasized the child as a repository of instincts that would be released at certain points in his development. Individual differences were slighted as merely minor variations in instinctual patterns. Instinct theory also dominated thinking in psychology in these, its early years.

The revolutions in thought were, of course, Darwin's theory of evolution, and the stage theories of development, principally Freud's and Piaget's. All tapped new empirical data and reorganized ways of thinking about existing phenomena.

This is also an era during which one of the most important records of child development was made—Preyer's (1882) diary of his child up to age three. Preyer's record has been recognized for its thoroughness of observation and painstaking care in recording. It is an impressive document that no doubt prompted many to become interested in children and helped those who were attempting to develop an educational theory based on actual knowledge of children. Preyer also recognized the influence on development carried within the child.

While Preyer's diary was primarily of interest to scientists who had an interest in child development, G. Stanley Hall had an influence on educational thought that eventually reached into practically all school systems in the United States. Essentially a synthetic rather than an original thinker, Hall was strongly influenced by evolutionary theory, particularly the notion that ontogeny recapitulates phylogeny (McCullers, 1969). Hall saw in the pre-adolescent years the opportunity for a recounting of the story of man's development across the span of unrecorded history. From this standpoint, children became important because they contained within them a growth process that could assist us in understanding the evolution of civilization.

Hall also contributed to an appreciation of individual differences by recording the range of information children possessed concerning the social and inanimate objects of their ordinary lives. Hall's early effort along these lines may be seen as an approximation to the more systematic empirical effect that Binet used later to develop a test of intelligence (Dennis, 1949). Following Darwin's lead, Hall moved the study of development beyond the philosophical approach of Locke, Rousseau, and Pestalozzi, to the level of actual scientific study. Child psychology developed in America largely as the result of Hall's empirical work as well as his other efforts, again inspired by Darwin, to link the fields of child and animal psychology (Kessen, 1965).

Hall's empirical work stimulated educators to find out what children actually know during given periods of development. He also developed themes originally launched by Rousseau, Pestalozzi, and Froebel, to make other contributions to educational thinking. The notion of a child-oriented versus curriculum-oriented educational program was the forerunner of progressive education. The latter movement, championed by John Dewey, continued to be highly influential up until the dissolution of its formal organization in 1955. The movement's credo of "learning by doing" appears quite similar to the emphasis on "learning by discovery" that has developed out of recent research on cognitive development (McCullers, 1969).

By far the most significant development in this period for our contemporary understanding of the child was Freud's theory. It had attracted many Europeans of diverse disciplines by the late 1800s. After the visit of the Austrian psychoanalyst to Clark University in 1910, his theories spread quickly and widely in the United States. The impact of psychoanalysis was profound, especially when related to the concept of the child. The picture that emerged from his early formulations was that of a frail, impressionable child, helpless in the face of trauma and vulnerable to a lifetime of neurotic conflict. As some doubt developed about the actual nature of the early sexual traumas reported by patients, the power of the child's fantasy to modify reality rather than submit passively was recognized. The concept of the child's place in the world was revised, and the child was seen as a much more hearty and viable representative of the instinctual forces. In fact, in *Civilization and Its Discontents* (Freud, 1953), the child takes on somewhat heroic proportions as a fundamental antagonist of civilization; the socialization process is pitted against the child's savage instincts, and society must force the child to give up the pleasure principle for the reality principle.

Whether as an easily traumatized victim of adult mistreatment or as an antagonist of civilization, the importance of childhood was recognized in psychoanalysis in a new light. Attention to individual differences was also stimulated by pointing both to the possibility of congenital variations in the ego apparatus and to the many different ways by which the child could resolve conflicts with society. The problems of psychological development were seen as stemming largely from the renunciation of instincts and from the internal conflict carried forth into adult life from this renunciation. Childhood was important because it shaped the entire course of adult life.

Although psychoanalytic theory did not speak directly to the fourth child–effect, the child's stimulus demand on parents was clearly evident in Freud's use of the term "King Baby."[1] Some of his followers such as Ferenczi pointed out that the child's power over the parent was in some sense tantamount to a tyranny. On the fifth category of child–effects—the contribution of children and youth to the society—the theory said much. According to Freud, the traumas of childhood in large part predetermined the attitudes and behaviors of the adult society.

As psychoanalysis was still gaining adherents and showing increased impact

---

[1] The authors are indebted to Donald Burnham of the Washington, D.C. Psychoanalytic Society for bringing this to our attention and for several other valuable contributions.

on the general public, particularly in America, sociologists were abandoning instinct theory and the search for innate differences between social classes and national groups. The liberal sociologists came to believe much more in educability and turned their attention toward the society's values, institutions, and child-rearing techniques. Psychologists also reacted against their previous commitment to biological factors and the theory of evolution. All that was left of biology in the new American behaviorism of the period around 1930 was a set of discrete, individual reflexes that became linked together and organized into habit hierarchies as a result of experience.

Both in sociology and in psychology, the contribution of children to their own development was equated with genetic and congenital factors, and dismissed with them. The child's contribution to interaction in the course of socialization was overlooked because of this change in perspective in the two academic disciplines. Infancy and childhood were still important, but their importance consisted in the fact that they provided a formative period in which parents and other agents of socialization produced their imprint. In the 1930s, John B. Watson's extreme behaviorism drew attention away from the capabilities of the child and from the special characteristics of immaturity. Individual differences were unimportant. However, as psychology and sociology began to turn away from biological thinking, Arnold Gesell brought attention back to it in a new way. Instead of seeking explanations at the abstract level of instincts, Gesell paid close attention to the detailed nature and sequence of sensory, motor, and psychological development.

It is some measure of the diversity of American science during this period that there were in existence such divergent views as those of Watson and Gesell, each with their adherents, and each developing a vigorous empirical approach. While many developmental psychologists resisted Gesell's conclusions because of his informal sampling techniques and inattention to problems of experimental design, pediatricians and other medical personnel were quick to respond to the concept of the child's biological nature expressing itself in an ever-unfolding pattern of maturation. He reported on the autonomy of motor developmental sequences that occurred despite different training or experience patterns. His motor and mental scales came into wide usage. The concept of stages of development, with intervening periods of reorganization and even regression, seemed to match what physicians saw in their private practice with infants and young children.

Gesell's nationally syndicated columns in newspapers conveyed the word to all parents that they could expect certain characteristics of children to appear as part of an orderly sequence, that they might find the young difficult to manage at some periods, easier at others. Physicians and child-care workers in contact with the public popularized Gesell's view of the importance of the child and of the latent power of the child's ever-unfolding and changing nature. He alerted parents to the fact that they could expect things to happen other than for reasons of their own ministrations and that they would be affected by these changes in the child.

Although there was great emphasis on the "child in general" and on the stages of development in the normal child (Gesell, Halverson, Thompson, Ilg, Castner, Ames, and Amatruda, 1940), Gesell and Ames (1937) drew attention to individual differences as well. Careful and detailed studies of films on five infants from the first to fifth years were used to develop and test predictions concerning the continuity of individual differences in energy output, motor demeanor, self-dependence, and expressive behavior.

LATE 20TH-CENTURY INFLUENCES

Only 10 years after Watson had enunciated the tenets of his radical behaviorism, students of social learning, such as Dollard, Miller, Whiting, Mowrer, and Sears, began the task of constructing a theory of socialization by bringing together Hullian learning principles and psychoanalytic hypotheses concerning sex, aggression, identification and dependency (Nowlis, 1952). The conceptualization of socialization reached a new level of sophistication and breadth. It was clearly seen that the child develops in a social context and that the basic unit of behavior must be at least dyadic (Sears, 1951). Children could also affect parents. However, at mid-20th-century, the child's contribution to the parent–child interaction was seen as deriving essentially from biological factors. Since it was difficult to identify the operation of biological factors, let alone experimentally manipulate their contribution, it is quite understandable that empirically oriented students of socialization would not wait for further research to make it possible to identify such factors. They moved on with conceptualization and measurement in an area in which research was feasible. Parents' reports on their child-rearing techniques were readily accessible to interviewers, so the efforts of these students of socialization centered around the parent as an independent variable and the child as a dependent variable.

By the 1960s, it was apparent that the approach had only generated low-order relationships between parent characteristics and child behavior and that findings from different studies were often contradictory. The conclusions of several reviewers to this effect are summarized in Chapter 4. The relative lack of productivity of the approach could well have been due to such methodological problems as the use of indirect questionnaire and interview measures from parents on both the independent and dependent variables. However, it was important to re-examine the question of whether the omission of the child's effects on the parent had also been damaging.

Piaget's theory of child development came into prominence initially in the 1930s and then experienced a revival of interest from the mid-1950s to the present. Developed from the field of epistemology in philosophy and from evolutionary theory in biology, the theory has excited great interest in the unique characteristics of infants and children. Out of the tremendous volume of research that Piaget's experiments stimulated, it has become apparent in a new and striking way that the young are not merely little or uninformed adults. They see things quite differently, violating all sorts of common-sense views. To a very young infant that has not yet reached the point of putting together different stimulation from the same object, the sight of the mother may be one thing, the sound of her voice another. At times the infant appears to be following the philosophy of Bishop Berkeley, refusing to concede that something appearing in two places is the same thing. A parent may get a glimpse into the other world of the child on seeing the delight of a boy at getting what he feels to be a much larger glass of a delicious drink than his sister, merely because the same amount is poured into a taller glass.

Although *aliment* from the environment is necessary to nourish schemata, the child's own active organization of this experience gives the primary thrust to growth, according to Piaget's formulation. The child acts on the environment—not merely receiving and storing information—and operates from some built-in principles about how the things with which it comes into contact should be put together.

The importance of the child's own internal structures and its capability of determining its own relation to the environment, also gained support during the same period from a revision of the classical formulations of psychoanalysis. Ego Psychologists Hartman, Kris, Loewenstein, and Rapaport found it necessary to postulate the existence of an autonomous conflict-free ego structure present from early infancy, in order to reconcile psychoanalytic formulations with the empirical findings of general psychology. It was evident that the infant is capable of many perceptual and cognitive responses long before an ego that should subserve these responses could have emerged out of the battle of the Id and the external world. Piaget's infant could gradually work toward a reasonably accurate construction of the world using anything handy, such as matchboxes or watch chains, and an adult or sibling to keep them near and occasionally make them move. So could the infant of the Ego Psychologists find sufficient support in the average interpersonal and inanimate environment present in most cultures throughout the world. The hypothetical infant with an autonomous ego and a conflict-free sphere of functioning is a more powerful infant than is pictured in classical psychoanalytic theory. The latter infant is one whose fiber and strength is only gradually forged out of, and precariously maintained in, the seething caldron of conflict between instinctual and environmental forces.

If the image of the competent infant and young child loomed larger than ever in the new formulations of the Ego Psychologists and Piaget, data from strong empirical thrusts in the 1930s and again in the 1960s filled out the form with substance. Watson had led American behaviorists to hospital nurseries to look for early reflexes, emotional responses, and evidence of conditionability. Once they had learned how to study their tiny subjects, the range of interests expanded to such topics as sensory discrimination, activity, and diurnal variation (Pratt, 1954). The psychoanalysts looked for evidence of ego functioning and for emotional responses that would help them understand the early development of what they called *object relations,* the functioning of the infant with its parents or caregivers. American governmental support of research fed a renewal of these interests in the '60s—an effort that produced an impressive picture of neonatal capabilities ranging from early learning and the ability to inhibit response, to visual form perception and response to human voice qualities (Kessen, Haith, & Salapatek, 1970). Also, by this time, longitudinal studies had uncovered evidence that congenital characteristics affected later development (see Bell, Weller, & Waldrop for a review, 1971, pp. 106–128).

By the late 1950s and early 1960s, the combined effect of theories and findings led many investigators to point to the increased evidence of infant capabilities (see Chapter 4) and the likelihood of infant effects on their family environments. There was the beginning of a corrective to the early behaviorists' image of the infant as a passive recipient of stimulation.

Unlike the early behaviorists, who discarded the possibility of child effects on the parent and other caregivers along with biological contributors, the modern behaviorists such as B. F. Skinner (1964) accept the fact of the child's contribution but do not attribute these effects solely to biological factors. Experimenters using operant conditioning principles adapt and change their procedure to fit the individual infant or child, and thus, in a very basic way, adjust to the fact of individual differences, even though they do not accord these differences any theoretical importance in their own right. Skinner (1971) details the many ways in which characteristics of the learner shape and modify those who are trying to bring about change in behavior. This latter position is a relatively recent pronouncement of Skinner's and thus has not yet had sufficient opportunity to affect scientific thinking. However, it is clear that the theory is flexible and can admit child–effects on a caregiver as well as the effects of the caregiver on the child.

SUMMARY

Due in large part to the chaotic conditions of the early medieval period, children were treated much as adults. In the later middle ages, however, society again became aware and appreciative of their unique qualities although religious teachings primarily drew attention to such contradictory symbolic aspects as sweetness or purity versus inherent depravity or original sin. From the 12th century to the 17th century, the leaders of the religious reformation were moved to protect what they saw as the frail and corruptible souls of the young. These leaders elevated the status of the young to a higher level of importance in the public mind, while, at the same time, bringing about changes in the family and in education that insulated children from the rest of society. These changes suppressed the recognition of many distinctive characteristics of childhood.

In the 18th century, the writings of philosophers and educators picked up themes from Plato and Aristotle, placing children and early development at a very high level of importance but for very different reasons than those of the Reformationists. According to some of these new views, whatever ideas the child possessed simply reflected the imprint of society. According to others, the child was inherently good and, left to its instincts, would develop optimally. Individual differences were clearly recognized by some philosophers, and it was pointed out that these should determine the means of education.

By the early 19th century, European influences had crystallized into three broad viewpoints on child-rearing that were being presented vigorously to the American public by professionals in the child-care field. These were the "break the will" school, the "hardening" school developed from Rousseau's doctrines, and the "gentle treatment" school based on the work of the educators.

In the late 19th and early 20th centuries, the impact of evolutionary theory, and of the biological viewpoint in general, led to a different kind of importance being attached to childhood. Sociologists and psychologists saw the child as a repository of a wide range of instincts. Presumably, children carried the imprint of phylogeny in the form of prenatal influences (the diarist Preyer) and could show in their development the story of how man himself emerged (G. Stanley Hall). The child also took on heroic proportions in psychoanalytic theory. Although initially depicted by Freud as vulnerable and helpless in the face of trauma, the later representation of the child in psychoanalytic theory was that of an antagonist of civilization.

A revolt by sociology and psychology against biological thinking began to develop in the early part of the 20th century. As a result of this revolt, children were viewed in a different way. In John B. Watson's radical behaviorism and in the extreme environmentalism that ensued, the child's contribution to the developmental process was equated with instinctual forces and rejected along with the entire biological approach. Individual differences became much less important than training procedures. However, it is indicative of the diversity of viewpoints existing during this period that the biological viewpoint had a vigorous champion in the person of Arnold Gesell. His empirical work supported a picture of considerable latent power residing in the child, as well as the importance of individual differences. The maturational-stage view of sensory, motor, and mental development gained wide acceptance amongst professionals and even had considerable impact on the general public after Gesell's views reached the mass media.

The Hullian-psychoanalytic students of socialization, starting their work in the late 1940s, recognized at the outset that children could affect parents, as well as parents affect children. Yet, at the level of actual empirical investigation, they primarily studied the child as a target on which parent child-rearing practices were registered. By the '60s it became apparent that this unidirectional approach had not been productive.

As Gesell's stage approach to development was gaining adherents, Piaget's biological–epistemological approach made its appearance, but it was nearly 20 years before social scientists in any great numbers became captivated with the cognitive achievements of the Piagetian infant—the infant that was represented as so active in organizing its experiences. During this latent period, Ego Psychology was revising classical psychoanalytic theory by postulating the early existence of relatively autonomous ego structures. For their emergence and maintenance, these structures needed only an average expectable environment. Thus, when Piagetian theory did set off a groundswell of interest in the 1950s, social scientists had been exposed to two successive theoretical approaches in which considerable capability and organizing power was attributed to infants. Then, extensive research attention to infancy in the 1960s filled in the theories with facts on early perceptual and cognitive capabilities, and it became apparent that an approach to socialization that ignored these capabilities had been relatively barren of results. It had become increasingly apparent that infants as well as young children have certain built-in or relatively autonomous emergent structures with which they react to and affect the things and people around them.

A still more recent scientific development has further set the stage for recognition of the effects of the young (but did not necessarily set the actors in motion, so to speak). Modern behaviorism, most vigorously championed by Skinner, has rejected the extreme stance taken by early behaviorism and has enunciated a theory that is sufficiently flexible to admit the possibilities of caregiver behavior being modified by child behavior, as well as the opposite. However, as with other learning theories in the behaviorist tradition, the theory has not yet directly generated research on the nature of immaturity or on the effects of children.

3
Trends Leading to Recognition of the Effects of Animal Young

Lawrence V. Harper

INTRODUCTION

In the preceding chapters, we saw that scientific recognition of the importance of the human offspring's contribution to their own upbringing has occurred only recently and represents a break with previous theories of parent–child relationships. In contrast, in the study of animal behavior, recognition of the effects of the young was favored by traditional concepts.

DUALISM

A history of Western scientific thought concerning the role of the young must begin with conceptions of the differences between animal and human behavior. According to Beach (1955), the dualist view, separating the behavior of man from that of other animals, can be traced to at least the fourth century B.C. when Heraclitus asserted that men (and gods) differed from all other animals in that men were created in possession of rational souls. This view was continued by the Stoic philosophers of the first century A.D. who felt that, unlike men, beasts acted without reflection. Although Aristotle placed man on the same scale as other animals, religious doctrine required separation of mankind, possessed of free will, and beasts, who responded blindly. Hence, Albertus Magnus and St. Thomas Aquinas both reaffirmed the view that man was created with the powers of reason and foresight, and animals were endowed with automatically adaptive behavior that was not subject to rational control or deliberate modification.

Until Darwin's publication of *The Origin of Species* (1859) and, more specifically, *The Expression of Emotions in Man and Animal* (1872), the behavior of other forms was largely regarded as distinct from human behavior in that it was thought to be automatic, the product of a different kind of divine creation, in which each species was endowed with uniform, infallible "instincts" appropriate to its place in nature. The theory of evolution, however, suggested a "continuity of mind" between man and animals and denied the doctrine of separate creation. Proponents of Darwin's theory set about to demonstrate the existence in animals of intellectual capacities comparable to those possessed by man. These efforts, based largely on anecdotal reports, were subject to and roundly criticized for anthropomorphism. Subsequent attempts to investigate the animal "mind" became embroiled in questions concerning the criteria for demonstrating consciousness in lower animals and, ultimately, in debates concerning the usefulness of attributing consciousness to any form (Boring, 1957). As indicated in Chapter 2, naive attempts to attribute instinctive "causes" for human traits and institutions similarly fell into disrepute. Thus, by the turn of the century, many American comparative psychologists who were concerned with evaluating behavioral similarities among humans and other animals sought experimental alternatives in such observable, manipulable phenomena as learning, imitation, and delayed response, processes which were felt to have demonstrable generality across species (Boring, 1957).

INSTINCT THEORY

Although the concept of continuity of mental processes from animals to humans represented a radical break with the past, evolutionary theory required only the acceptance of a different account of the origins of instincts (and their possible existence in humans). Instead of regarding instinctive behavior as the product of divine creation, the adaptive repertoires of animals were explained as the outcomes of the selective process. Animal behaviorists concerned with the unique adaptations of individual forms were encouraged to continue viewing the behavioral peculiarities of each species as important in their own right. Mechanistic conceptions of the nature of instinctive behavior required little modification; such responses continued to be seen as essentially automatic and unconscious. For example, William James (1890) presented the "common definition" of instinct as follows (italics his):

> the faculty of acting in such a way as to produce certain ends, without foresight of the ends and without previous education in the performance. [Instincts] . . . are the functional correlates of structure. With the presence of a certain organ goes, one might say, almost always a native aptitude for its use [p. 383].

In his subsequent discussion of the origins of instincts, James sided with

Darwinian, as opposed to Lamarkian, interpretations of the evolution of adaptive patterns. In the following discussion of the conditions leading to the display of such adaptive behavior, James sounds remarkably modern (italics his):

> A very common way of talking about these admirably definite tendencies to act is by naming abstractly the purpose they subserve, such as self-preservation, or defense, or care for eggs and young. . . . But this represents the animal as obeying abstractions which not once in a million cases is it possible it can have framed. The strict physiological way of interpreting the facts leads to clearer results. The *actions* we call instinctive all conform to the general reflex type; they are called forth by determinate sensory stimuli in contact with the animal's body, or at a distance in his environment. Although the naturalist may, for his own convenience, class these reactions under general heads, he must not forget that in the animal it is a particular sensation or perception or image that calls them forth [p. 383].

James' remarks on the adaptive nature of the relationship between instinctive reactions and the species' environment indicates that the foundations for the "modern" concept of instinct (cf. Tinbergen, 1951) had been laid before the end of the century—although it would be some time before the details were worked out sufficiently to allow a more extensive treatment of the topic (e.g., Lorenz, 1935/1957). Concerning the stimuli eliciting instinctive behavior, James (1890) wrote (italics his):

> At first this view astounds us by the enormous number of special adjustments it supposes animals to possess ready-made in anticipation of the outer things among which they are to dwell. *Can* mutual dependence be so intricate and go so far? Is each thing born fitted to particular other things and to them exclusively, as locks fitted to their keys? Undoubtedly this must be believed to be so. Each nook and cranny of creation, down to our very skin and entrails, has its living inhabitants with organs suited to the place, to devour and digest the food it harbors and to meet the dangers it conceals; and the minuteness of adaptation thus shown in the way of *structure* knows no bounds. Even so are there no bounds to the minuteness of adaptation in the way of *conduct* which the several inhabitants display [pp. 383–384].

Thus Darwinian theory focused attention upon the functional significance of different constellations of characteristics, including behavior, as both the products and determinants of a species' evolution. While the majority of American comparative psychologists concentrated upon general processes, largely abstracted from conceptions of the nature of "intellect," European ethologists and a few American naturalists continued in the Darwinian tradition of attempting to unravel the ways in which animals were "fitted to particular other things"—including their species mates (see Klopfer & Hailman, 1967, for an overview). The fact that birds, rather than forms more closely related to man, were among the principle objects of interest of early field observers probably made it easier for these investigators to eschew mentalistic explanations in favor of physiological or inductively derived concepts to account for the regulation of social interaction (Lehrman, 1962).

MUTUALITY IN ANIMAL SOCIAL RELATIONS

As Tinbergen (1951) has pointed out, it had become obvious that, although humans may regard their behavior as controlled by "foreknowledge," such speculation regarding animals was futile and frequently misleading. Thus, in order to achieve mechanistic explanations for finely regulated, "instinctive" exchanges among lower forms, zoologists quickly came to an appreciation of the mutuality of stimulation in animal social relations.

By the early 1930s, there existed substantial evidence from a number of infrahuman species that a reciprocal interchange of signals was essential for the regulation and maintenance of social interactions; James' "other things" to which species were "fitted" yielded to experimental analysis. The field of comparative ethology was then given new impetus as a result of a series of theoretical papers and experimental investigations by Lorenz and his collaborators. In one of his best known articles, Lorenz (1935/1957) wrote (italics his):

> The animal . . . and the lower animal in particular, is essentially fitted to his world by innate behavior. . . . A material or objective comprehension of his world is not a biological necessity. It is enough if an instinctive reaction which must respond to a specific object in order to maintain the species is set off by *one* of the stimuli which that object sends out [p. 85].

In line with the evolutionary view that species-typical features function to adapt the individual to his total environment, Lorenz proposed that:

> Consistent treatment of another member of the species . . . is often achieved by the purely extraneous circumstances that the releaser, the fellow member of the species, emits all the stimuli correlated to the various releasing mechanisms collectively. The functional design of innate behavior patterns localizes the biologically necessary element of unity in the stimulus-emitting object, rather than in the acting subject [p. 87].

Landmark that this paper was, the emphasis on mutual social stimulation nonetheless represented the refinement and extension of existing conceptions of instinctive behavior, rather than a radical break with the past. We have seen that James' review 45 years earlier emphasized how "conduct" was adapted to the stimulus qualities of the environment. In fact, to illustrate his thesis, James was already able to cite studies by German and American naturalists of the 1870s and 1880s who had demonstrated how parental and filial responses in birds were determined by exteroceptive stimuli provided by nest, eggs, and parental movements. Two years before Lorenz' theoretical paper appeared, Wiesner and Sheard (1933) had experimentally demonstrated several ways in which stimuli emanating from the young served to orient and control features of maternal caregiving in the laboratory rat.

In 1951, Beach was able to conclude a review of studies of parent–offspring relations in animals with the statement that: "The parental responses of animals that feed and protect their offspring depend heavily upon the behavior of the young themselves [p. 413]." Thus, both theoretically and empirically, off-spring determination of parental behavior had become an established principle among animal behaviorists. Indeed, by the mid-1950s this body of research was sufficient for Lehrman (1956) to use the evidence for reciprocal stimulation between parent and offspring as one basis for a critique of what he regarded as unduly simple models of instinctive behavior. (In contrast, scientific recognition of the effects of human young was minimal before the 1960s, cf. Ch. 2.) Further progress in this area, especially as it related to the role of the young in mammalian caregiving behavior, resulted from a resurgence of interest in a truly comparative approach to the study of animal behavior. By 1963, there was enough activity in the field to warrant publication of a collection of papers entitled *Maternal Behavior in Mammals* (Rheingold, 1963). The evidence presented in that volume made it clear that Beach's (1951) summary statement was entirely applicable to mammals.

CONDITIONS FAVORING THE RECOGNITION OF OFFSPRING-EFFECTS IN ANIMALS

In addition to the theoretical and empirical traditions characteristic of the study of animal behavior, several other factors probably help to explain why comparative psychologists and ethologists analyzed the effects of the young on parental behavior earlier than did students of human socialization. Certainly, it would have been both logically and scientifically absurd to ascribe purpose or foreknowledge to a naive, primiparous rat—let alone a hand-reared bird. Thus, investigators were forced to assume that the moment-to-moment adjustments between mother and young represented a reciprocal exchange of signals rather than parental anticipation of the effects of caregiving. In addition to the necessity of accounting for short-term adjustments between parent and young, there were other empirical phenomena that may have helped to focus attention on the peculiar contribution of offspring stimuli. For example, the simple fact that parents of many species discriminate their own from other offspring (cf. Beach, 1951) must have alerted investigators to the necessity of evaluating the stimulus qualities of the young. Although it is likely that the foregoing considerations combined to hasten the investigation of offspring–effects in animals, one of the most significant contributors to the rapid advance in the analysis of the parent–offspring relationship by comparative psychology—as contrasted to the study of human behavior—must have been the greater degree to which it was possible for investigators to manipulate the behavior of nonhuman subjects.

CONDITIONS DELAYING RECOGNITION OF
OFFSPRING-EFFECTS IN MAN

The fact that there was such a delay between the experimental demonstration and analysis of offspring effects in nonhuman mammals and a recognition of the effects of the human child is another matter. Many students of human behavior have ignored the results of studies of animal behavior. One frequently encounters statements to the effect that man—at least the adult—is not governed by biological impulses, that human actions are influenced primarily by expectations and cultural sanctions (if not by reason). Indeed, it would seem that, in one sense, the dualist views of Heraclitus and the medieval scholastics are only now bowing to evolutionary thought. This latter delay probably stems from reactions against attempts by late 19th-century psychologists and sociologists to adopt oversimplified models of the "survival of the fittest," and reactions against subsequent theories that turned descriptions of behavior into catalogs of instincts (cf. Boring, 1957). One gets the impression that many personality and social psychologists overreacted by rejecting not only simplistic neo-Darwinian models of survival, but also the essential theoretical constructs and empirical findings of biology—as evidenced also by the reluctance of developmentalists to consider the possibility that endogenous characteristics of the young could affect parental behavior in man (cf. Ch. 2).

Freud's theory of the traumatic origin of mental illness may have been a second factor delaying recognition of offspring effects in man. As Baldwin (1967) has pointed out, psychoanalytic theory influenced the thinking of most students of personality development and socialization. Although psychologists often criticized Freud's ideas about the biological bases of behavior, they accepted his emphasis on parent–effects and the ways in which the behavior of the young is shaped by the environment. In all fairness to Freud, we must remember that he advanced his theory at a time when enlightened opinion was just beginning to accept mental disorders as natural phenomena, and most people held that human behavior was guided by conscious choice. It would be asking too much to expect that he also would have illuminated the mutuality of the parent–offspring relationship. Indeed, this would have been particularly unlikely since Freud grew up and developed his theory in a culture in which the parent's authority—especially the father's—was unquestioned (cf. Lynn, 1974). In short, although it represented a revolutionary advance in man's understanding of himself, insofar as it focused attention on the role of the parent, psychoanalytic theory probably contributed to the relatively late recognition of the ways in which human young influence the behavior of their caregivers.

SUMMARY

Whatever the reason for the lag between the various branches of behavioral science, as a result of over 40 years of careful, controlled experimentation, the comparative literature now contains many thoroughly documented studies of the ways in which the young influence caregiver behavior and several provocative, descriptive models for conceptualizing the dynamics of the parent–offspring interaction in mammals (see Rheingold, 1963). Furthermore, at this writing, biological theory is moving toward quantitative models of animal social dynamics, one of which endeavors to predict the timing of weaning by evaluating the active role played by the young, as well as that of the mother, in the parent–offspring relationship (Trivers, 1974).

In later chapters of this volume, we will review in detail evidence for the effects of mammalian young on their caregivers. In order to underscore the heuristic value of the well-controlled animal studies, we will also discuss experimental, observational, or clinical studies of human caregiver–offspring relations that appear to document analogous phenomena. However, it should be emphasized from the outset that while we feel there are many parallels between human and animal behavior at the descriptive level, we are not suggesting that in each case comparable physiological or psychological mechanisms account for these similarities.

Part II

THEORIES AND RESEARCH
APPROACHES—MAN

4

Socialization Findings Reexamined

Richard Q. Bell

INTRODUCTION

H. L. Mencken once commented that there is an easy answer to every human problem—simple, plausible, and wrong. Four decades of socialization research have pursued a simple and plausible answer to the problems of human development—that most of the child's characteristics are brought about by the behavior of the parents. It has been plausible to conceptualize the human parent as the initial agent of culture and the infant or child as the object of acculturation, because the human infant seems so motorically helpless in comparison with the young of other species. To an observer who is not paying attention to its effects on the parent in the early years, the human infant seems initially in need of protection and support and then later in need of shaping and modification by the parent.

From the preceding chapters on history, it is apparent that it is no simple matter to escape traditional oversimplifications. To address the full complexity of the human socialization process, it is necessary to free ourselves from ideological fetters whose origins reach back for centuries. We must fully appreciate that it is no longer necessary to take stands so extreme on the malleability and educability of children that we find ourselves unable to recognize the ways that children can educate adults. There is some truth in Peter DeVries' (1954) quip: "The value of marriage is not that adults produce children, but that children produce adults [p. 98]." We can accept the possibility of children making their own contribution to the stream of development and to the changing parent–child social system without indicating approval of that period in the history of sociology and psychology in which instincts were sought in every human behavior pattern and in which biological determinants were hypothesized for national, ethnic, and individual differences.

To recapitulate some further historical trends still exerting an effect on current theories of socialization, the shift from overgeneralized models of biology to the radical behaviorism of the 1930s led to a greater emphasis on the nature of the environment in determining changes in behavior. The infant's own characteristics, other than health, were unimportant to Watson, who felt each could be molded into any desired pattern. What he overlooked is that the young are a part of the environment of adults and parents and thus must be accepted as a source of stimuli. We should be prepared to expect substantial control of parental behavior by the young on this ground alone. The most recent surge of interest in socialization was launched by investigators who were themselves troubled by indications of childrens' impact on parents (Nowlis, 1952, p. 294) and who emphasized the importance of dyadic models in treating social interactions (Sears, 1951). They focused on unidirectional effects from parent to child in order to see what might emerge from such research (not having at their disposal any very obvious methods of isolating child effects) rather than from any theoretical neglect of the child's stimulus value. Thus, the control of parent behavior by the young should take its place as a part of the general expectation by the modern psychologist that most behavior will be found to be under partial control of some stimuli that are external to the organism.

To complete our brief historical survey, it is necessary to turn to some developments of the last decade. Some observations seem self-evident once our attention is drawn to them, yet they have been anything but self-evident as judged from their neglect in past accounts of parent–infant interaction. First, even the youngest of infants, the newborn who has no behavioral repertoire traceable to social interactions, is in many respects much more powerful than the young parent.[1] Young parents are at the mercy of a cry, and further, can't escape the compelling quality of the infant's facial expression and the helpless, thrashing movements once the cry has brought them within visual range. Parents with a firstborn seem not only overwhelmed with their new responsibilities but also somewhat helpless and confused. In many respects, they appear to be much less powerful than the infant, whose behaviors are remarkably well organized to produce a given result. Rheingold (1966) was one of the first observers to state this fact succinctly: "So aversive, especially to humans, is the crying of the infant, that there is almost no effort we will not expend, no device we will not employ, to change a crying baby into a smiling one—or just a quiet one [pp. 12–13]." In the same context, she also pointed out the positive value of the stimuli provided by the infant in social situations. "The amount of attention and the number of responses directed to the infant are enormous—out of all proportion to his age, size, and accomplishments."

Second, one of the many productive outcomes of applying Skinnerian learning theory to problems of child development is the fact that interest has shifted from the product of socialization to its process. Burton, in Yarrow, Campbell, and Burton (1968, p. 123) has pointed out that the usual study of parent and child

---

[1] The author is indebted to Gene C. Sackett for this observation.

behavior, typically oriented toward the product of training at a single time, could not recapture the essence of the developmental process. Even if the investigator employs a retrospective interview to assess the historical aspects of child-rearing techniques, it seems unlikely that the parents will be able to relate the important temporal links in a long series of parent–child interactions. In discussing moral development, later in this chapter, an example of an extended developmental sequence given by Burton will be furnished that illustrates this point.

A third point is logically compelling once it is brought to our attention. If we view parents as capable of changing children, the very changes brought about during one period of interaction would by necessity expose parents to altered child behavior in the subsequent period. In other words, if parents are effective, they must be affected by the products of their tutelage. For present analytical purposes, we can ignore the possibility of maturational contributors, granting in any event that it is difficult to index them or bring them under experimental control. We can even close our minds for the moment to the fact that children are active organizers of the experiences provided by parents, adopting components selectively and forming new syntheses of their own. Given these considerations, it is still logically compelling that child behaviors are also consequences of parent training, and these emergents are a fact of life in the week-to-week and month-to-month experience of the parent.

Because the phrases "parent–effect" and child–effect" are used frequently in the remainder of the book the reader is reminded of the terminological simplification adopted in Chapter 2 that made it unnecessary to use a full phrase such as "parent effect on the child." It will be assumed the reader understands that an attribution of an effect only implies that the behavior of one of the participants plays some role in determining behavior of the other. Most behaviors are complex emergents of a variety of determinants.

Some discrepancies between theories and facts.   Progress in science very often comes from careful study of phenomena that do not fit existing conceptions. A theoretical orientation toward parent–effects could find confirmation in the fact that the mother of identical quadruplets who are schizophrenic was uniformly extreme in restrictiveness with her daughters. On the other hand, they might find it awkward trying to account for the fact that she was not uniform in affection (Schaefer, 1963), unless they paid some attention to the possibility that there were nongenetic congenital differences between the infants that could have affected the mother. Similarly, the unidirectional approach has a difficult time accommodating differences in foster mother care for two infants of the same sex and age assigned at the same time (Yarrow, 1963, pp. 109–110). Investigators hoping to see an immediate onset of the socialization process in the hospital nursery, and looking for evidence of the mother's impact on the earliest behavior, must be disappointed in the fact that the prior state of the infant before being brought to the mother from the nursery for a feeding accounted for subsequent maternal feeding behavior better than prior observation of other maternal behavior or estimates of "maternal attitudes" obtained from interviews (Bell, 1968, p. 83). In a similar vein, advocates of the unidirectional approach would find it disconcerting that the amount an infant consumed in a breast feeding during the newborn period was highly related to the subsequent duration of time the mother continued breast feeding throughout infancy, whereas a number of personality characteristics of the mother were not related (Hillenbrand, 1965).

Many of the discrepant findings have been in the literature for some time. Others continue to emerge. Owen, Adams, Forrest, Stoltz, and Fisher (1971) commented as follows on findings from their study of familial patterns in a sample of school children with learning disorders:

> In this research population the families of the . . . [children with learning disorders] . . . were rated as more disorganized and as less stable emotionally than the control families. Why, we may ask, if the families are so disorganized and emotionally unstable, should there be such a strong effect on the learning–disability child, and apparently less effect on his siblings? If these factors were primary antecedents to learning disability, one would expect that such difficulties would be rampant in these families, rather than restricted, in extreme form at least, to the one member. Our analysis suggested that children with learning difficulties experience the family life differently from the control children, and to a lesser extent, different from that of their same-sex siblings [p. 65].

This restriction of presumed family impact to one child is indeed puzzling to adherents of a unidirectional model.

There is no phenomenon in which the use of parental power is more evident than in "battering." Just as historians themselves have overlooked the disturbing evidence of infanticide and brutal child-beating in old documents, the average citizen today has found it difficult to accept fully the disturbing fact of flagrant child abuse. From studies of incidents (Gill, 1970) it appears that the abused child often was born at a time in the history of the family when there was unusual stress originating in problems such as subsistence or housing. It seems unlikely that the stimulus characteristics of children would by themselves constitute sufficient stress to result in mistreatment. However, it is necessary to recognize that demands or specific acts of the child were a part of the chain of events that led to the abuse. In the case of infants, the caregiving burden, the nagging and persistent crying, often set the stage. In young children, the abuse was quite often the outcome of a sequence in which ordinary disciplinary action was initially taken by the parents or caregivers in response to a specific behavior of the child. With the failure of these actions to produce the desired change, uncontrolled anger and violence was inflicted on the child.

Some inkling of bidirectional effects emerged from clinical studies in which parents reported their perception of the child as a cause of the problem. Many of the parents felt that they had been abused by the child, not that they had abused the child. By itself these reports would simply appear strange and difficult to explain on psychodynamic grounds. However, again, as in many other studies of differential effects within a family, it is quite typical to find that only one child in a family is abused. When it appears to social agencies that the conditions leading to the abuse cannot be corrected, the child who has been battered is often transferred to a foster home. In some instances, it has been reported (Gill, 1970, pp. 29–30) that battered children have been abused in a foster home, transferred, and abused in another foster home. It is unlikely that these foster homes had shown previous evidence of child abuse, otherwise the agency would not retain the family for foster care purposes.

Gill (1970, pp. 130–131) has also reported a compelling fact emerging from factor analysis. Deviance in the child was at least as substantial a factor in explaining the incidents as deviance in the parents. Constant fussing, a strange and highly irritating cry, or other exasperating behaviors were frequently reported for the one child in the family singled out for battering. According to a study by Morse, Sahler, and Friedman (1970), 15 of 25 battered children studied were considered "difficult" by their parents. While 10% of a normal cross section of births show low birth weights by a pediatric criterion, among battered children the rate runs as high as 40% (Klein & Stern, 1971). Many battered children whose birthweights are within normal limits have other significant medical illnesses, which may have overtaxed the limited resources of certain parents and thus led to an emotional crisis (Klaus & Kennell, 1970).

In families under stress, it could be expected that caregiving for the children would be less than optimal, and thus the deviance of the children may have originally been due to familial sources. Whatever the origins, the characteristics of the child played an important part in the situation that led to the battering.

Nutritional marasmus is another example of a clinical condition in which the young appear, at first glance, to be simply victims of extremely adverse circumstances but, on closer analysis, their behaviors are seen as contributing to a complex causal situation. Pollitt (1973) has countered the usual view that protein calorie malnutrition is a simple effect of a life in poverty on a helpless infant. Previous investigators had overlooked the fact that children with nutritional marasmus are usually weaned early and are commonly late in the birth order in large families. Pollitt has drawn together evidence that poverty and frequent closely spaced pregnancies, by disturbing nutrition of the fetus, retard intrauterine growth, leading to the likelihood of prematurity and low birth weight. According to his hypothesis, the latter conditions are associated with poor sucking and swallowing, to which the over-stressed mother in poverty responds with early weaning. Since her capability for maternal care is overtaxed, she is unable to prime and stimulate the infant's feeding. Again, as in the case of child battering, the characteristics of the young victim must be considered as one phase of the developing phenomenon, even though these characteristics do not arise *de nouveau* to produce their effects.

Child–effects demonstrated in research.   In addition to the discrepancies in child and family phenomena that the traditional unidirectional approach of socialization research always found it difficult to accommodate, impetus for a more complex view of socialization continues from research that directly shows child effects. This research will be described in detail in later chapters in the book, but for present purposes three findings should be noted. A sequence analysis of adult–child interactions in a nursery school setting (Yarrow, Waxler, & Scott, 1971) uncovered the fact that adults returned more quickly to initiate positive contacts with children who, in previous interactions, showed interest or compliance. When children's behavior was manipulated by role playing (Osofsky, 1971) or by designing special tasks (Osofsky & O'Connell, 1972), effects on adult or parent behavior could be detected. When children who differ in speech characteristics were placed in interaction situations with adults, the speech of the adults was affected (Siegel, 1963).

Most theories simply ignore data that are difficult to explain, unless crucial. Differences in normal or pathological development between children in the same family, and differences in parental response, would not destroy a theory of parent–effects but might force it into cumbersome elaborations. In contrast, such findings are precisely what we would expect if looking for the effects on parents of differences between children.

INTERPRETATION OF SOCIALIZATION FINDINGS

Not only has an exclusive commitment to the traditional unidirectional approach become increasingly difficult to justify on the foregoing grounds, but there are abundant indications that it has not been productive empirically. Seven out of eight reviews of human socialization studies have noted that research in this area has produced a relatively small number of consistent and well agreed upon findings (Becker & Krug, 1965; Caldwell, 1964; Fontana, 1966; Frank, 1965; Orlansky, 1949; Sewell, 1963; Yarrow, Campbell, & Burton, 1968). One reviewer who has claimed to find consistencies (Hoffman, 1970) has been able to cite very few studies that could not be reinterpreted equally well as showing child effects. Various possibilities have been suggested for the paucity of results: (1) excessive reliance on interviews or questionnaires from parents, in place of direct observation; (2) failure to obtain information directly from the child; and (3) over-reliance on field versus experimental studies. However, the observational, conceptual, and experimental developments of the last decade that we have just reviewed point to an additional and more basic problem—that we must return to the original doubts of Nowlis (1952) and Sears (1951). They were concerned that neglecting the child's effects might have a damaging effect on the productivity of socialization research. The failure to identify separately child– and parent–effects may, indeed, have made it difficult to uncover any substantial number of clear relationships between child and parent characteristics.

Source of the data to be explained.   In this section, a systematic effort will be made to develop explanations in terms of child–effects for the few consistent findings of socialization research. Since a previous effort at explanation (Bell, 1968), interest in comparative developmental studies has quickened, and the number of experimental studies with children has increased greatly, so that theoretical treatments are now no longer based predominantly on data from field studies of parents and children. However, the new formulations based on a wider range of evidence must still find corroboration in field studies in order to be convincing. Hoffman (1970) found little coherence between findings from field and experimental studies in an important area of socialization research— moral development. Furthermore, most experimental studies using human subjects have typically involved interactions between children and experimenters who are strangers to them. Bronfenbrenner (1974) has pointed out the logical difficulties of generalizing from such studies to child-rearing amongst familiar family members. In chapters to follow, we will review four studies that provide empirical support for Bronfenbrenner's cautions.

Although there has been a praiseworthy increase in the breadth of the evidence from which our theories are drawn, there are serious problems in fitting together findings from different kinds of studies. Only a few investigators such as Patterson, Cobb, and Ray (1973) are carrying out research to bridge the gap between experimental and field studies. Until a sufficient volume of research has developed in which the ideas from animal research and human experimental studies are tested by observation of actual behavior sequences shown by parents and children, we are largely dependent for our theories upon field studies that have characterized parents and children in relatively global terms and that have, in the main, simply correlated these parent and child characteristics as they appeared at a single time. This latter kind of study is still by far the most frequently summarized in theoretical treatments (Baumrind, 1966; Berkowitz, 1973; chapters by Feshbach, Hoffman, Mischel, and Maccoby & Masters in Mussen, 1970). These reviewers acknowledge the weakness of this kind of study as a basis for detecting parent–effects. Most go further and offer occasional substantive explanations for some of the findings in terms of child–effects—a distinct change since the present author's earlier review (Bell, 1968).

Though reviewers have been sensitized to child–effects, few of the reports of individual field studies sufficiently warn the reader that a correlation between parent and child characteristics obtained at the same time does not indicate direction of effects. They seldom admit that interpretations in terms of parent–effects are no more parsimonious than those in terms of child–effects.

To maintain vigilance concerning the equivocal nature of correlations, to caution those who still assume too readily that parent–effects are somehow more "reasonable" or parsimonious, and to consolidate fragmentary hypotheses about child–effects that have been enunciated in the last few years, the remainder of this chapter will consist of an effort to provide a coherent, systematic explanation for correlational findings in terms of child–effects. A set of propositions will be advanced that is not overly complicated or difficult to defend. The data to be explained are the few findings from correlational studies that reviewers consider relatively firm. A conscious emphasis on child–effects is acknowledged. There is little likelihood that the hypotheses to be offered will themselves lead to another one-sided approach, since over forty years of research on parent–effects would have to be offset.

Clarification of terms to be used.   Before proceeding to the explanatory system, some clarification of terms and a discussion of certain technical points are in order. To facilitate exposition, the terms *parent* and *child* will be used throughout this chapter, though in many cases the term parent could be expanded to cover nonparental caregivers, and the term child could be applied to infants as well as children. Furthermore, most of the findings to be explained involve mothers, not fathers. However, since we will be discussing some very general findings that seem to emerge from a wide variety of field studies primarily involving young children, the terms parent and child will be sufficiently precise.

It is not logically possible to offer exclusive interpretations in terms of either genetic or experiential determinants for sequences of parent and child interactions in the naturalistic setting. However, when certain samples are contrasted that have known genetic characteristics, when the behavior of parent or child is altered experimentally, or two samples of parent–child pairs receive different treatment, it is quite defensible to interpret the differences obtained in terms of genetic or experiential contributors. For this reason, the terms *genetically, congenitally,* or *experientially determined* are considered as abstractions derived from research operations—the analytic process in science. The same considerations apply to the terms *parent–effects* and *child–effects.* These effects may be teased apart by scientific analysis, but must be put together to understand behavior *in situ.* In material to follow, a child–effect will sometimes be ascribed to a prior interaction sequence with the parent, whereas in other cases a child–effect will be attributed, in part, to congenital contributors. The term *congenital* will cover both genetic and congenital determinants for further purposes of simplification. In no case is a fixed or predestined developmental outcome implied. A congenital contributor imparts a direction or line of flow to development, not a rigid, unalterable destiny. In an average expectable environment, this source of determination could lead to a detectable path of growth, but a number of environmental events could divert or block the flow of events for which a congenital contributor is assumed.

In many instances, there will be a reference to parent– or child–effects without an effort to trace these effects to their ultimate origins. It should be kept in mind that we can legitimately refer to the contribution of a parent or child to an interaction without implying any necessary experiential or congenital contributor to either. As we have already mentioned, studies of parent– and child–effects can take as their starting point any behavior available at the time of study in the repertoire of parent or child.

The fact that a child can modify a parent behavior at a single time carries no implication that the origin of that behavior is explained by such a demonstration. This is a fundamental point that needs to be emphasized, not only in the present context, but in efforts to derive explanations from a wide variety of experimental work in child development. Epstein (1964) made the basic point in another context when he pointed out, relative to studies of learning, that demonstrations of the modifiability of a response had no necessary implications for its origins.

GENERAL MODEL FOR EXPLANATION IN TERMS OF CHILD–EFFECTS

The explanatory model is presented first, and then we examine its utility and application to findings widely cited in the socialization literature. The model is most applicable to data from field studies of socialization by parents in ongoing interactions with young children, and the treatment is oriented toward the effects of the young. The present system of explanation also provides a very general set of concepts that may be useful in explaining the phenomena of ongoing social systems involving participants who differ widely in acquisition and performance of the behaviors common to the subculture and society.

An explanation for the origin and early development of the parent–child interaction system, a more specialized, though possibly more basic effort, will be offered in Chapter 6.

Causal Factors and the Nature of Control

Congenital contributors to competence, assertiveness, and social response. The demonstration of a child–effect does not require that we trace the effect to its ultimate origin. Yet there is sufficient evidence of congenital contributors to child behavior that it is useful to organize this evidence and begin looking for probable effects. Congenital influences are just one of many kinds of determinants, but they are especially important in that they clearly emanate from the child. Since the author's earlier paper on the same subject (Bell, 1968), some additional evidence from studies of human subjects has accumulated that provides relatively clear evidence of congenital contributions to variation in competence, assertiveness, and social response. By competence we mean the ability of the child to carry out tasks ordinarily considered as appropriate to its age level. Assertiveness involves the vigor and speed with which the child's goals are pursued. Social response or person orientation includes both positive and negative behaviors directed toward peers and adults as well as ability to induce such behaviors. More elaborate definitions could be provided, but these are sufficient to indicate to the reader the general class of behaviors intended under each rubric.

Rosenblith and Anderson (1968) have reported associations between responses of the neonate and impairments in later motor development. These impairments seem quite likely to adversely affect the parents' judgments of the child's competence. In several studies, minor physical anomalies, such as a single transverse palmar crease, have been used to index congenital contributors to behavior, because these anomalies are produced in early fetal development by chromosomal breakdowns or teratogenic agents such as viruses that mimic these breakdowns. It has been shown that the more of these anomalies a child has, the greater is the likelihood of (1) clinical hyperactivity, or fast-moving, object-oriented play in nonclinical samples (Waldrop & Halverson, 1971); (2) aggressiveness in early-school-age males (Halverson & Victor, 1976); and (3) shy, inhibited behavior in school-age females (Waldrop, Bell, & Goering, 1976). Additional evidence of a congenital contributor to variation in assertiveness has also appeared in the form of an association between insensitivity to tactile stimuli in the newborn period and assertive behavior in experimental barrier situations at the pre-school period (Bell, Weller, & Waldrop, 1971). There are differences between these clinical and nonclinical behavior patterns, but they share a common feature of variation in the imperative nature and force of goal-directed behavior that would be experienced as assertiveness by others in the child's interpersonal contacts.

In addition to the evidence from twin studies of a congenital contributor to social behavior or person orientation, (Freedman, 1965; Scarr, 1965), further findings have appeared of a congenital contributor (again, as indexed by minor physical anomalies) to defects in peer relations of early school-age children (Halverson & Victor, 1976). These problems of peer relations may indicate the existence of irritating behavior as well as a low orientation toward persons. Several leads have also emerged concerning the precursors of person orientation in earliest infancy. Four studies have shown relations between various aspects of the newborn's response to interruption of sucking and later behavior (Bell, 1975): (1) a positive relation between the latency of the newborn's response and positive emotional expression of the infant at the third month; (2) a negative relation between the activity level of newborns and rated happiness at eight months; and (3) a relationship between the newborn's crying (and its latency) and positive emotional expression in later infancy, as well as responsiveness to teachers in the preschool period.

Positive emotional response in infancy is very relevant to the social interaction out of which an orientation toward persons should develop. Accordingly, the foregoing findings fit in with a report (Clarke–Stewart, 1973) that the characteristics of the infant rather than those of the mother (both assessed toward the end of the first year) showed a significant relationship to the closeness of the mother–infant system at a year and one-half in a cross-lagged correlational analysis.

In the present context of providing an explanation for relations between global trait descriptors applied to children and parents at a single cross section in time, congenital factors are assumed to create individual differences in the probability of response to certain classes of situations. However, congenital contributors may only be a part of the total causal picture. For example, a congenital contributor to assertiveness may be expressed in the form of high-intensity behavior in the sense used by Walters (1964), but intensity is only one of several properties of behavior that lead to pain, distress, or discomfort, and thus become labeled in certain cultural contexts as aggression. High intensity may exist without leading to production of pain in others if the child has learned to modulate it in a certain kind of situation. As Berkowitz (1973) has pointed out:

> "Whether a person becomes openly aggressive after being thwarted depends upon such things as his characteristic degree of optimism and trust, the extent to which he has learned to respond constructively to the problems confronting him, his judgment as to how safe it is to attack available targets, or how proper it is to show any aggression in a given situation, his attitude toward the potential target, the motives he attributes to the frustrator, the degree to which the people around him are also suffering from the frustration inflicted upon him, and his interpretation of his own emotional reaction to the frustration [p. 102]."

Thus, a congenital contributor to human assertiveness involving speed and magnitude of goal-directed behavior takes its place in a complex of causal influences.

Control and power relations.   Perhaps one might argue that the model of an agent of socialization acting upon a malleable and unformed child is somewhat of an oversimplification—that the parent is much more mature than the child, has more power, and has a behavior pattern more closely approximating the adult patterns of the culture. We agree that it would be a mistake to simplify the parent–child interaction system by saying that the young child socializes the parents. Obviously, some perspective on the nature of controls exerted by each participant in the system is needed at this point before we proceed further.

As Skinner (1971) has pointed out, there is even a reciprocal relation between the physicist and the subatomic particles whose behavior the experiment is designed to control. Just as the experimenter's behavior is shaped and controlled by the nature of the particles, the nature of the child's behavior must require an adjustment of some sort by the parent, and, at this very basic level, there is a reciprocal relation despite the inequality of maturity. Some indications of the pervasiveness of the child's effects can be gained from the fact that the adjustment of operant conditioning procedures to an individual child has become almost a key element in the "art" by which successful experimenters finally establish operant control over specific child behaviors. This art receives scant mention, if at all, in journal articles reporting these experiments. Demonstration of control presupposes that the investigator found out what could and could not be shaped. A common joke is that if the child could speak he might say, just as the rat, "Have I got that experimenter under my control!"

Children start approximately 50% of interactions (Wright, 1967), indicating again that the greater maturity of the parent is no basis for assuming that the parent initiates most of the interactions that lead to socialization. The empirical evidence is that there is a balance relative to starting interactions; neither parent nor child dominates the situation. Research on attachment behavior has also pointed to a type of control that children exert over parents. The signal and executive aspects of a child's attachment repertoire affect parents in such a way as to bring about and maintain proximity. It is not necessary that the child "plan" to bring a parent, or have the intention of keeping the parent, nearby. It is only necessary that the child's behavior be effective, and there is little doubt that young children are very competent in affecting the proximity of their parents. Further, children get their way by their inherently appealing nature. Thus, it is necessary to keep in mind that competence, defined in terms of controlling the behavior of another person so as to produce a certain result, is not to be equated with maturity, which refers to the stage that any given individual has reached in attaining adult forms.

In one respect, there is a clear inequality and asymmetry in the relationship of parent and child, namely that involving intentional behavior. The younger the child, the less likely it is that the child is consciously controlling parental behavior in order to achieve certain consequences. A simple kind of intentional behavior can be identified in the last part of the first year of life (Wolff, 1960, p. 109). The quality and extent of intentional behavior will gradually develop in the second year so that this element increasingly comes to bear on parent behavior. Nonetheless, it is clear that throughout the early years of child-rearing, intention is much more characteristic of parent than child behavior. Parents' goals for child-rearing cover a much longer span of time and involve more general objectives. Parents frequently let things happen that are discordant with their values and expectations for their children. They make the judgment that nothing effective can be done at the time but that an opportunity to redirect the behavior may occur later. The parent can afford to lose a few interaction skirmishes to the child, even a battle, while still hoping to win the campaign, so to speak.

Parents have power as well as long-range objectives on their side. They have the physical size and control of resources to determine the outcome of an interaction more often than children. The dominance is not completely one-sided, and it is not without cost. In the Midwest study (Wright, 1967, pp. 234–236), children dominated a substantial number of interactions, and they met dominance with resistance. The steady and persistent resistance of children to some parental objectives may lead to the eventual abandonment of an objective, despite the fact that the parent dominates more specific interaction bouts. Children can also exercise control through a means that is sometimes overlooked as a source of power—appeal. In the same Midwest data, this was the category in which they exceeded all parents and other adults with whom they interacted.

To summarize, parent–child interaction occurs in a reciprocal social system in which much of the progress toward cultural norms involves mutual adjustment and accommodation. Parental control through power and long-range intentional behavior is offset to a certain extent by childrens' sheer activity in starting interactions, their resistance to domination, and their inherently appealing nature.

Basic Propositions of the Explanatory Model

Control theory.   With some findings concerning the child's congenital contribution in mind and with a general perspective on how children and parents control each other, we can introduce more specific propositions concerning control that are needed in the explanatory system. It is assumed that each participant in a parent–child interaction has upper and lower limits relative to the intensity, frequency, or situational appropriateness of behavior shown by the other. When the upper limit for one participant is reached, the reaction of the other is to redirect or reduce the excessive, inappropriate behavior (upper-limit control reaction). When the lower limit is reached, the reaction is to stimulate, prime, or in a variety of other ways to increase the insufficient or nonexistent behavior of the other (lower-limit control reaction). From the standpoint of the parent, upper-limit control behavior reduces and redirects child behavior that exceeds parental standards. Lower-limit control behavior primes and stimulates child behavior that is below parental standards. In other words, one very general principle about the activating power of children is that they contribute too much or too little or that they show some behaviors too early or too late in terms of parents' expectations. In a sense, then, the function of parent control behavior is to maintain child behavior within an optimal range.

Up to this point, the term *control* has been used in an absolute sense to simplify the argument, without indicating that there are degrees of control. Further, the term control is not used in terms of any specific conceptual model such as "reinforcement" in learning studies.

Parental repertoires.   A variety of behavioral reactions may be elicited from parents in response to a particular child behavior. Once the investigator of socialization descends from the level of global trait descriptions such as warmth, permissiveness, and restrictiveness, to concentrate on the sequences out of which child behavior emerges, it is likely to be readily apparent that parents do not have fixed techniques for socializing children. It may be that in certain areas of interaction, both child and parent behavior become rigid, each holding its own position and stimulating the other in a way that maintains a circular and unproductive pattern of interaction. However, even in such a case, it must not be assumed that the current behavior of the two participants can be taken as indicating the history by which they reached this stage, or that they are not capable of other responses if something disturbs the equilibrium.

Most investigators of parent–child interaction have adopted a minimum level of descriptive complexity that is appropriate to a social system, the discrete actions of each participant being at least of sufficient complexity to be recognized by the other and perceived as relevant. As Wright (1967) has pointed out in connection with the Midwest studies of behavior ecology, crying might be recorded, but not expiration and setting the vocal cords. Usually, investigators also attempt conceptual organization above the level of discrete, molar acts. In the present approach, it is assumed that actions or responses may occur in subsets, called *repertoires.* An example of such a subset is fussing, crying, grimacing, and thrashing shown by very young infants and comprising, in effect, an "alerting and proximity-maintaining" repertoire. Through the research that has been carried out on attachment behavior, we have come to appreciate the inherent organization of infant behavior, seeing the crying, smiling, babbling, and calling out as serving signal functions, while later, approach and following serve executive functions. Surely then, it should be possible for us to differentiate similar components of parental behavior. Indeed, the several acts a mother uses in soothing constitute such a repertoire.

Hierarchical and sequential organization.   Parents do not emit behaviors at random. In teaching a child a prohibition, for example, they may use explanation and reasoning in the initial stages and injunctions and physical force only in later stages or when an infraction is extreme. Items in the parental repertoire are interdependent in the sense that given one response to a stimulus, others in the same set are more likely to occur than those in another set. Further organization within the set also exists. The probability of occurrence of responses in a set may vary according to order and levels of stimulation. Parents respond differently to a compliant act followed by one that is defiant than to the opposite. They also respond differentially to independence, assertiveness, and aggression. That is, the sets are hierarchically organized. Also, the several responses in a subset may be released in a certain order, that is, a sequentially ordered repertoire may exist. Under a condition of constant stimulation such as fussing, a mother may first try talking, then jiggling the crib, turning the infant to another position, then picking it up, and holding it to her shoulder. Presumably, selective activation of elements in the repertoire is partially a function of parents' past experience in a given sphere of interaction.

Although repertoires may be labeled in terms of their likely effect on the other participant, they should be demonstrable from interaction data without reference to their stimulating effects. All that is required is that there be a temporal association of certain elements within one participant's total set of responses occurring during the interaction.

It is expected that differences in repertoires will be found. For example, the young should have fewer, more sparse, and less well-organized and differentiated repertoires than their caretakers.

Integration and Application of Explanatory Propositions

Concepts concerning congenital contributions to child behaviors, control, and the selective activation of items from parental repertoires may now be put together. In general, we would expect that parents would show an increase in upper-limit control behavior in response to children who, because of congenital contributors, are impulsive, hyperactive, or overly assertive. Although we lack research that would separately identify many different effects on parent repertoires of different congenital contributors, we can make some reasonable guesses. It seems likely that parents of hyperactive, erratic, and overly assertive children would be more likely to respond, in rough order, with distraction, quick tangible reinforcement or nonreinforcement, holding, prohibiting verbalizations, and physical punishment, having had past experiences that did not positively reinforce the use of reasoning, threat of withdrawal of love, and appeals to personal and social motives.

On the other hand, where congenital contributors exert a direction toward low activity, inhibited behavior, low assertiveness, slow development and general lack of competence, parent lower-limit control behavior would be released. In rough order, behaviors such as drawing attention to stimuli, positively reinforcing increases in activity, urging, prompting, and demanding increased performance would be more likely to emerge from the parent repertoire. In the context of this and the preceding explanatory example, phenotypically different child behaviors are considered to be similar only with respect to their effects on the appropriate parent–control pattern.

In an earlier theoretical treatment (Bell, 1968), speculations were offered concerning the probable impact on parents of young children in whom congenital factors favor responsiveness to persons. It was assumed that children high in person orientation would be attentive to their parents and responsive to their social behavior. Now we might add that they could induce upper-limit controls from their parents if they showed extreme attention-, approval-, or help-seeking. In contrast, children low in person orientation would induce lower-limit controls from parents. During infancy, their parents might be very responsive to the child's few social overtures such as smiles and vocalizations, hoping to prime and increase this kind of response. When they found that their efforts were relatively unsuccessful, as time went on, they might show less attention to social behaviors. When they found that the infant's behavior was controlled less well by variations in their social response; they might turn to providing physical activity or play with inanimate objects. Presumably, by early childhood the parents would be less likely to find love-oriented control techniques useful and would fall back on the use of material reinforcers. In extreme situations, they would be more likely to use power–assertion.

Thus, the concept of upper- and lower-limit controls is related to the notion of sequentially and hierarchically organized response repertoires; it provides a way of looking at interaction sequences in order to understand why certain elements in a repertoire are activated at a given time by certain child behaviors. By itself, this perspective is an important gain in clarifying the complexities of socialization, as can be seen from the examples already given and from others that will follow in which various authors have invoked the combination of control theory and organized response repertoires in order to explain their data, even though they may not have recognized or labeled the formal features of the model they were using.

To move beyond a level of *ad hoc* explanations for specific parent–child pairs, it is necessary to flesh out the skeletal model with information on the behavioral characteristics of the child, the family, subcultural, and larger societal demands on the parent, and the parents' own individual assimilation of all of these forces into a set of expectations for the child. Against this background, the child's behavior at a given time invokes lower- or upper-limit controls and "keys in" certain behaviors from a response repertoire of the parent.

The wider setting in which parent and child exist limits the ways in which parents react with respect to the foregoing model. The over-stressed mother of a large poverty-stricken family may respond to the lethargic infant's inadequate sucking and feeding-demand mechanisms by showing withdrawal and neglect rather than by lower-limit control behavior that would ordinarily occur in a family system that is not under stress (Pollitt, 1973). Under the circumstances, the mother has no lower limits as far as caregiving demands are concerned. Self-sufficiency has to reach certain levels before she can respond with nurturance.

Applications of the general model. In discussing the relationship of child aggression and punishment by the parent, Feshbach (1970) postulates differences between children in basic characteristics favoring the development of aggression. He assumes a hierarchical organization of parental responses in explaining how some parents may resort to physical punishment when an earlier, less drastic method of control failed with such children. In this case, the children presumably only elicited two responses from the parental repertoires, but, carrying Feshbach's thinking further, other children may very well escalate the action of their parents so that at one time or another, or even in a very demanding sequence, they release almost the entire set of responses. Then the child may reinforce or fail to reinforce specific parental behaviors, further exerting a selective effect on the repertoire and, conceivably, on its organization. From this standpoint, learning to be a parent consists very largely of expanding and sequentially organizing one's responses within repertoires to make possible appropriate responses to a variety of child behaviors, and to give primacy to those responses in the hierarchy that produce the desired results or other feedback with acceptable levels of effort.

In an observational study of 7-month-old adopted infants, Beckwith (1971) uncovered a correlation of .49 between verbal discouragement by the mother and the infant's Gesell score. The hypothesis offered to explain this finding was that verbal discouragement (an upper-limit control technique) was the response of a mother living in a property-conscious home to an infant that showed greater than average locomotion and reaching out for objects (thus scoring high on the Gesell).

In a two-year longitudinal study in the preschool period, Emmerich (1964) uncovered a curious developmental transformation indicating that children who were interpersonally negative at the beginning of the period changed in the direction of becoming more poised, while their counterparts, who were initially positive in interpersonal relations, began to show signs of feeling insecure toward the end of the period. Maccoby and Masters' (1970) hypothesis to account for these data was as follows: "Perhaps in anticipation·of the child's entry into the more formal kindergarten setting, socializing agents at this time were putting pressure on the outgoing child to modulate his aggressiveness, while a simultaneous attempt was being made to influence a self-contained child to become more outgoing [p. 99]."

INTERPRETATIONS OF FINDINGS

In this section, explanations in terms of child—effects will be offered for the small number of associations between parent and child characteristics that recent reviews of socialization research have considered deserving of explanation on the basis of consistency of findings. Studies of sex-role development, aggression, dependency, and moral development will be considered. Because failures to replicate have been so characteristic of this field of research (Yarrow, Campbell, & Burton, 1968), there should be little loss, in the long run, from not attempting explanations for findings from individual studies.

Figure 1 is an adaptation of Baumrind and Black's (1967) synthesis of results from three studies concerned with the interrelations of social and emotional behavior in young children. To simplify the diagram and to make it possible to represent a third dimension that has emerged more recently from the work of Schaefer (1971), most trait descriptors have been moved to the perimeter of the circle, and in some cases moved between adjacent sectors. The added dimension, Task-Oriented Behavior, involves continuous variation along a dimension marked by perseverance, conscientiousness, attentiveness, and achievement–orientation, at one pole, in contrast with distractability, hyperactivity, and other "inappropriate" behavior at the opposite pole. Schaefer has reported evidence

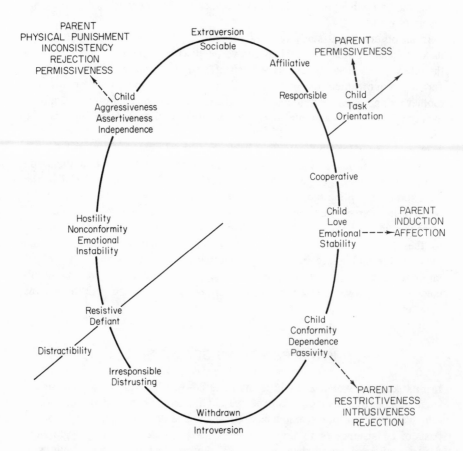

FIGURE 1   Projection of parent reactions onto a three-dimensional model of child behavior. (Adapted from Baumrind & Black, 1967 [© 1967 by the Society for Research in Child Development, Inc.], and Schaefer, 1971 [© 1971, University of Minnesota Press].)

obtained from large samples of children and a variety of methods, that this third dimension, along with the previously located Love–Hostility and Extraversion–Introversion dimensions, provides a relatively complete space within which most trait descriptors can be located.

Schaefer's three-dimensional model for parents involves dimensions of Autonomy–Control, Lax– versus Firm–Control, and Love–Hostility, as in the child model. An alignment of these two models is, of course, a major objective of socialization research, but Schaefer has indicated that this has not yet been accomplished. From our perspective, it may even be difficult to achieve in the future. The number of points at which alignment can be made are very few, owing to the sparcity of replicated associations between parent and child characteristics. In addition, the models do not provide differentiation of trait descriptors on the basis of intensity, a key factor in trying to align child characteristics with parental reactions. Figure 1 offers an improvement in this respect. The first concept listed in a group is considered most intense, the last, least intense. With this improvement, the dimensional child and parent schemes at least offer a useful synthesis of terms involved in socialization research and make it possible to discuss findings in the context of a general descriptive model.

Development of Sex Differences

At first glance, this is one area of development in which there is every reason to expect an impact of parents, on the basis of well-recognized sex-role stereotypes for males and females. However, it is now becoming increasingly evident that sex-role learning is influenced substantially by other children and that, whatever the origin of the child's status, this status itself affects the parents (Rosenberg & Sutton–Smith, 1968). Mischel's (1970) summary of research in this area is instructive. "Modeling is thus not a one-way process; children may serve as models for the sex-role of their parents as well as emulating them and their own peers and siblings. . . . [These findings] . . . undermine the traditional assumption that sex roles are learned chiefly or exclusively through the child's identification with the like-sexed parent [p. 32]."

Mischel notes that while observed relationships between parental practices and children's sex-typed characteristics are often highly suggestive, the statistical association is usually modest in magnitude, and there is neither a clear and definitive pattern of replication across sexes or clear sex-specific parental practices. Nonetheless, it was felt that one tentative conclusion could be drawn: "Permissiveness (as opposed to restrictiveness) by parents tends to be related to such masculine attributes as aggression, assertiveness, achievement, and independence in children. . . . In contrast, parents who are restrictive may tend to have children who are somewhat more dependent, compliant, conforming, fearful and polite [p. 50]." Maccoby and Masters (1970, pp. 143, 144) reviewed the same area with an interest in attachment rather than sex-role development and also concluded that there was an association between independence and autonomy in children and permissiveness in parents, and between high dependency in children and restrictiveness in parents. Interpreting the same kind of finding in their own study, Baumrind and Black (1967) reached the conclusion that the association of permissiveness with independence or autonomy reflects the parents' granting of sufficient social and spatial freedom to the child, but not to the extent of neglect. Guidance and demands for growth were considered to be necessary conditions also.

In terms of child–effects, a reasonable interpretation for the correlates of permissiveness would be that they involve to a considerable extent parental reaction to goal-oriented, competent, and independent behavior. If a child is capable and appropriately self-sufficient, one would expect less of a need for correction and direction on the part of the parent. Neither upper- or lower-limit controls are needed. In other words, the assumed reaction to appropriate capability and independence in children is for parents to give them relatively free rein. The arrow and dotted lines projected from the task-orientation pole of this dimension in Figure 1 represents one of these assumed child–effects. The same effect is also represented as a projection of child independence and assertiveness in the sector that orders these concepts according to intensity, with aggressiveness as most intense. For this explanation in terms of child–effects to be appropriate, it would be assumed that independence and assertiveness do not exceed parental standards for appropriate sex roles.

In keeping with the notion that different effects occur at various levels of intensity in child behavior, permissiveness is not considered a parental reaction to child aggression. The ordering of child and parent behaviors in this sector is intended to represent a changing pattern of parental behaviors in response to different child behaviors. It is much more likely that aggressiveness will trigger upper-limit controls in parents rather than responses in the neutral range of permissiveness. Thus, even if the variance that independence, assertiveness, and aggressiveness share is sufficient to result in their being located in adjacent points of a three-dimensional correlational plot of child characteristics, this does not preclude differential parental response on the basis of nonshared variance.

Thus, to other problems of interpretation issuing from findings of the studies reviewed in this section, we must add the fact that possible reactive factors in parents have not been isolated from those that may have been involved in the development of sexually dimorphic child behavior. In other words, the correlational studies do not tell us whether permissiveness was involved in the process by which independence emerged in the child or whether the parental behaviors were a response to independence displayed by the child for any number of other reasons.

Dependence

Before interpreting the relation between child dependence and parental restriction that has emerged from the studies of sex differences, some discussion of the meaning of the umbrella term *dependence* is needed. From Figure 1 it would appear that independence and dependence are polar opposites, but they are not. Negative correlations are not usually found between measures of the two—one reason being that dependence itself is not a unitary construct. Some aspects that are subsumed might be bipolar opposites, and other aspects might not be. Asking for help from others, or instrumental dependence, msut be distinguished from emotional dependence. Attachment should be distinguished from the latter, because it refers to a normal species-wide behavior rather than a fearful, overly intense relation to an adult. Unfortunately, these and many other facets of the term dependence have not been distinguished in most of the studies from which reviewers of socialization research have drawn their conclusions. In the present treatment, the position will be taken that the studies using global trait descriptors were primarily interested in emotional dependence but that instrumental dependence also affected the ratings.

Dependence and restriction.   The nature of Maccoby and Masters' explanation for the association of child dependence with adult restriction indicates that they also assumed that instrumental dependence was involved in most measurements of dependence. The explanation is that restrictiveness should prevent a child from exposure to physical and social situations in which skills needed for adequate coping can be developed. Although this is certainly a reasonable explanation for inadequate peer relations and for dependency on adults continuing beyond the expected age, there is also an alternative explanation that is equally reasonable and for which support is available from field and experimental research. This alternative explanation assumes that both the child's lack of competence and inability to *use* skills (because of fear or an overly intense relation to an adult) contribute to an adult's perception of a child as dependent. The child's lack of competence and failure to apply himself to a task leads to lower-limit parental control behavior involving urging, prompting, and directing, as well as more protective behavior. Such a reaction is not restricted to young children. Grown-ups appear "bossy" and "overprotective" when managing their elderly and infirm parents.

Any condition in children that impairs ability to cope should result in parents "taking over" child functions, as well as controlling and directing their activities. If this line of reasoning is sound, then the author's finding (Bell, 1964a) of a consistent attitude pattern in parents whose children had physical handicaps (cerebral palsy, congenital heart defects, mongolism, and congenital blindness) is relevant to the association of child dependence and parent restrictiveness.

Parents of children who had limitations in coping ability because of these handicaps were consistently high on a self-report questionnaire scale labeled "Intrusiveness." An experimental study (Osofsky & O'Connell, 1972) produced a result that matches with actual parental behavior the subjective aspect of restriction measured in the attitude questionnaire. (Such a correspondence is worth noting, because results from field and experimental studies are most often difficult to reconcile). Instrumental dependency behavior produced by instructions to the child and exposure to a difficult task, elicited controlling behavior on the part of parents. With these findings in mind, a more complete statement of the child–effect explanation may be made—dependent children evoke intrusive attitudes and controlling behavior from parents, and the latter features lead to ratings of restriction. The explanation for the effect of dependence on restriction is shown in Figure 1 as a projection along the line of increasing intensity running from conformity through dependence to extreme passivity.

There are other possible sources of variance in ratings of restriction, but it is not possible to identify separately such components as control, direction, suppression of impulses, and restriction of social or spatial opportunities for the development of skills. As in the case of child dependence, general trait descriptors of parent behaviors were used in many of the studies reviewed by Maccoby and Masters, and Mischel.

Dependence and rejection. Whereas no consistent association has been found between dependence and parental warmth, 6 of 8 studies reviewed by Maccoby and Masters (1970, pp. 139–141) have found an association between dependence and parental rejection. These reviewers offer an interpretation that recognizes the distinction that has been stressed in this chapter between the process of development and the product. They also recognize the possibility that a child–effect on parents might be involved. Their interpretation is that the association does not indicate the acquisition of dependency by the child in response to parental behavior but, rather, the elicitation or enhancement of previously established dependency–behavior. The elicitation could be a function of withdrawal and lack of availability of the rejecting parent for interaction. Presumably, the lack of parental availability acts as social deprivation, or any anxiety-arousing situation, to enhance the manifestation of dependency, regardless of the conditions under which it may have developed. Maccoby and Masters also add: "We must also not overlook the possibility that dependent children tend to have rejecting parents because they are dependent—their dependent behavior, beyond a tolerable level of intensity and frequency, that is graded according to age, alienates parents. In correlational studies, it is not possible to determine how important a factor this is [p. 141]." This interpretation is shown in Figure 1 as an increasingly likely parental response of rejection as child behavior increases in intensity from conformity through dependency toward passivity.

Aggression

In recent reviews of parent–child correlations in this area (Berkowitz, 1973; Feshbach, 1970), considerable space is devoted to finding consistencies in conflicting data. Part of the problem lies in reliance on correlational studies. It is also evident that the development and control of aggression is an extremely complex matter. Nonetheless, certain basic findings emerge in one form or another with sufficient frequency to warrant theoretical attention. These consist of the association of aggression in boys with inconsistent and physical punishment by parents (Berkowitz, 1973, pp. 114, 117) and with hostility or low warmth and nurturance (Feshbach, 1970, p. 217).

Aggression and punishment. Berkowitz offers a curious interpretation of the association between physical punishment and aggression. He sees it as indicating that punishment is ineffective. Nonetheless, there are indications of a general change in the way of thinking about such data, since the present author's (Bell, 1968) review of findings from a study by Lefkowitz, Walder, and Eron (1963), who had concluded that an association between peer ratings of aggression and parent reports of the use of physical punishment supported the hypothesis that punishment produces frustration and conflict, or affords a model of aggression that, in turn, produces aggressive behavior in the child. The alternative explanation offered by the present author was that congenital assertiveness in children that were aggressive with peers activated upper-limit controls in parents so that their responses escalated toward the extreme of physical punishment. It could be added now, that this parental response would be expected regardless of the origins of the child's aggressiveness, whether from congenital bases or from interactions with parent behaviors other than physical punishment. The fact that the most consistent findings involve the association of child aggression with severe physical punishment (Feshbach, 1970, p. 227) fits in with the picture of a provoked parent, although all of the other factors that have been mentioned in connection with child abuse, such as stress on the entire family system, must also be assumed. Feshbach concludes a review of the association of aggression and punishment as follows:

> In analyzing the effects of any of these factors, it is assumed that the behavior of the child is a constant. Parents, however, are not immune to their children's behavior, and their response to a particular act may be influenced by the history of their interaction with the child. The parent who uses severe punishment may have begun with soft words, which failed to achieve their objective of aggressive control. Children differ in their predisposition to aggression and in their docility. These variations in aggressiveness may evoke from the parent some portion of those very punitive behaviors which may be assumed to be their antecedents. Although one can exaggerate the influence of the child's aggression upon the parents' disciplinary practices, the possible contribution of the child's behavior to the parent–child interaction has been largely ignored and some attention to this dimension is required [p. 228].

Aggression and inconsistency.   Since laboratory and field research are in apparent agreement relative to the contribution of inconsistent punishment to aggressive behavior, this association deserves special attention. The agreement from the two lines of research is based on the assumption that the laboratory effects of intermittent reinforcement on aggressive behavior are the basis for the associations found in field studies. One possibility warranting consideration is that inconsistent discipline is, just as physical punishment, one indication of a parent who is at an extreme point relative to upper-limit controls. At times the parent may punish, and at other times he may fail to punish, for a number of reasons. Advice from experts in the mass media may produce guilt about the use of "last-resort" tactics and a desire to use more approved techniques. The child may initially respond to physical punishment by a reduction in aggression but may "slip back" after not receiving punishment for a subsequent offense. With a cycling of responses occurring in both participants to the interaction, an unstable control situation exists. The parent could quite understandably reach the conclusion that training techniques were ineffective if he were confronted with occasional high-magnitude behavior that threatened or produced injury to another and if the behavior persisted, despite a variety of responses including physical punishment. Frustration with such a situation could lead to outbursts of repeated severe physical punishment. In short, both severe physical punishment and inconsistency can be seen as extreme upper-limit parental control behavior in response to highly assertive or aggressive child behavior.

Aggression and rejection.   Feshbach (1970, pp. 217, 218) has detailed the many ways in which it is thought that a hostile, rejecting parent could produce aggressive behavior in a child. In comparison with an accepting parent, the rejecting parent presumably: Feels little warmth for and has minimal interest in the child and, therefore, may delay longer before relieving discomfort; provides less stimulation and assistance in developing the child's own concept of effectance; less often responds with reinforcement for nonaggressive behavior; shows fewer responses, such as affection, that are incompatible with aggression; and offers an unattractive model for development of ego controls through identification. The latter would ordinarily assist the child in modulating the expression of socially unacceptable behaviors. However, Feshbach is also very willing to concede the possibility of a child–effect. "This association [between the absence of warmth and aggressiveness in the child] is not necessarily unidirectional. The child's aggressiveness may elicit rejecting responses from the parent, which in turn fosters further aggression, thereby establishing an unhappy cycle of rejection–aggression [p. 217]." The important point is that the child's aggression, regardless of its origins, must be considered as having the capability of affecting the parent. At the present time, field studies of these findings do not make it possible to unravel the events leading to associations between rejection and aggression. With suitable research designs, to be discussed in Chapter 5, it should be possible to determine the life history of such cycles in individual parent–child pairs.

The postulated parental reactions of rejection, inconsistency, and physical punishment are shown in Figure 1. The ordering of the child and parent behaviors is intended to convey a change from permissiveness to rejection as child behavior moves beyond acceptable levels of independence and assertiveness to aggressiveness.

Moral Development

From Hoffman's review (1970) it appears that guilt and an internal moral orientation in children are negatively associated with power assertion on the part of the parents. The latter involves control of the child by capitalizing on physical power or by control over material resources. Physical punishment, deprivation of material objects or privileges, the direct application of force, or a threat of any of the preceding are included under this heading. This finding is consistent across the sexes and at several age levels. One other finding is not as consistent across the age levels but emerges with sufficient frequency that it cannot be dismissed. This is the positive association of guilt and internal moral orientation with inductive discipline and affection. Explanations or reasons for requiring the child to change behavior are the basis for the category of induction. Hoffman points out that one particular kind of induction is especially important, other-oriented induction, a technique in which the parent makes reference to the implication of the child's behavior for another person.

Hoffman expressed concern that the foregoing associations between child and parent characteristics had been derived almost entirely from studies that could not clearly point out the direction of causality—naturalistic or field studies. It is also disconcerting that the findings from laboratory studies have not followed the same pattern as that of the naturalistic research (Hoffman, 1970, pp. 300, 302–303). Experimentally controlled variations in the behavior of adults do not typically produce the same effects on children that are thought to be operating in naturalistic studies. This discrepancy between the two lines of research obviously suggests a need for caution before drawing conclusions about the direction of effects. The door is not only open to questioning the methodological differences between laboratory and field studies (such as use of an experimenter who is a stranger to a child subject) but also to a more basic issue. If the associations found in the naturalistic studies cannot be produced by experiments in which adults are deliberately attempting to have an effect on children, one of the substantive possibilities to be considered is that those associations were due to the effects of children on parents, and thus the laboratory studies could only reproduce them if they manipulated child behavior in order to detect the effects on adults.

One other basis for concern about the presumed parent–effect relations in moral behavior is that neither the correlational or experimental studies capture the developmental character of the process out of which such behavior emerges. Burton, in Yarrow, Campbell, and Burton (1968) has illustrated the necessity of considering the complete train of events rather than the end-point at which a moral behavior emerges:

> Jennifer, at 18 months, likes to climb up into her mother's new velvet chairs and bounce on the cushions. Her parents may try to "explain" to her at this age that their chairs will be "hurt," that her shoes will make the pretty velvet "ugly." But Jennifer's language development does not allow her to understand these reasons for not bouncing on the chair. Even if she might "understand" that her parents are not pleased when she bounces, it is such great fun that she does not care much about paying attention to what they are saying. . . . Sometimes in the month to follow, the parent may take Jennifer quite roughly from the velvet chair and place her in (another) chair. Another time she may shake her, another time she may raise her voice, and another occasion may elicit a spanking from the parent. . . . One day the parent may observe Jennifer saying to herself, "No, no, Jennifer. Naughty!" when Jennifer has one knee on the velvet seat and is about to climb into the chair. The mother may then say, 'Good girl, Jennifer," and watch her turn to something else. . . .
>
> As the months go by, Jennifer's linguistic ability increases so that she does comprehend many parental attempts to explain or reason with her about not breaking a rule. The parents also find that the verbal reprimands, which have accompanied the direct techniques, and which were originally ineffective because Jennifer ignored them, are eventually sufficient to terminate or to prevent her undesired behavior. Even certain facial expressions from the parent can now seem effective as punishment. Increasingly, the parents rely on these less direct forms of control, since they can be applied at a distance and with greater immediacy than the direct physical types of control [pp. 120–121].

Burton notes that if Jennifer's parents are interviewed at the end of the process we have described, they will report that she sometimes punishes herself, resists temptations, and confesses. As a result, she will be rated high on conscience development. If the techniques of Jennifer's parents described in this episode are a reflection of their general disciplinary practices (a necessary assumption in most of these studies), they will report that they currently use reasoning and explanations or some love withdrawal and little or no physical punishment. The developmental character of the sequence in Jennifer's history is lost. The early use of direct punishment techniques by the parents has dropped out.

Guilt and power assertion.   Considerable credence exists for an interpretation of the effects of power-assertive discipline that places emphasis on the duration of punishment (Hoffman, 1970, p. 283). According to this explanation, the application of force dissipates the parent's anger and relieves the child's anxiety or guilt quickly, thus reducing the child's motivation to alter behavior. We have already reviewed evidence of a congenital contributor to clinical hyperactivity, as well as to a pattern of fast-moving, impulsive, object-oriented play in nonclinical samples. It would seem reasonable that the latter pattern would lead to frequent and unexpected infractions of rules and to less continuity between current child behavior and past parent–child interactions. Thus, more upper-limit control behavior would be expected from the parents, and there should be many situations in which a quick build-up and release of anxiety or guilt in both parties would occur.

On the basis of congenital contributors to fast-moving, impulsive play, it is possible to devise a two-pronged hypothesis concerning child effects in this context. Children in whom the congenital contribution is strong, as indexed by their minor physical anomalies, would not only induce more power-assertion in their parents (which itself could, in turn, favor low guilt) but would also be more difficult to affect by non-power-assertive techniques, because their pattern of situationally controlled behavior does not favor internalization. The negative effects of parental power assertion on moral development may also be operative, but only as one link in the chain of events leading from a congenital contributor to low guilt.

Guilt, affection, and induction. Hoffman (1970) concluded that greater affection in the parent–child relationship makes it less necessary to resort to power-assertion or love-withdrawal and makes the child more amenable to induction. From this, it would seem to follow that any characteristics of the child that involved greater receptivity to social stimulation and greater responsiveness to adults would affect the frequency and quality of these same parental behaviors. Other-oriented induction would be particularly affected by these characteristics of the child, because it would be difficult to appeal to children on the basis of their effects on other adults or children unless they were involved with and concerned about others. Accordingly, from our standpoint, it is hypothesized that children who are high in person-orientation induce both more affection and more other-oriented inductive techniques from their parents, as well as show more receptivity to these techniques when applied by their parents.

Since congenital contributors to person-orientation have been demonstrated in substantial numbers of children in nonclinical samples, their presence in samples of school children and other groups used for studies of moral development should be sufficient to account for many of the associations that have appeared in past research.

Arguments for parent–impact on moral development. In concluding his review, Hoffman (1970, p. 325) concedes that definitive conclusions concerning causal direction cannot be drawn from the data of field studies and that clarification awaits the application of longitudinal or experimental studies. Unfortunately, experimental studies that have been carried out have not typically provided confirmation for the field studies. For example, power assertion may act to *suppress* pleasure-oriented response tendencies when it immediately follows the behavior to be suppressed and is administered at high intensity (p. 300).

Despite the foregoing, Hoffman concludes that there is some scattered support for the assumption that the field correlations indicate an effect of discipline on moral development, rather than the reverse. One of his arguments is as follows:

> a number of the findings reported . . . bear on the parent's reported use of discipline in the past when the child was very young. If these reports are assumed to be reasonably valid, to argue that the child's moral development elicits different discipline patterns (rather than the reverse) necessitates the further assumption that the child's morality has not changed basically from early childhood. This is an unlikely assumption, in view of common observations [e.g., about the child's changing acceptance of responsibility for transgression] and the findings about the developmental course of moral judgments obtained by Piaget and his followers [p. 325].

Hoffman's point fails to take into consideration the fact pointed out earlier in this chapter: A child–effect on parent discipline could be operative even if the nature of the effect itself changed over time. The child's earlier behavior that triggered disciplinary efforts may have been of a different moral nature than the later behavior, or even nonmoral. Hoffman's point also fails to take into consideration the well-known lack of reliability of parents' retrospective reports on child-rearing techniques (Yarrow, Campbell, & Burton, 1968).

Hoffman's second point is that "whereas the findings for power assertion are consistent across the entire age range studied and included children as young as four years of age, the findings for induction are not consistent until after the preschool years. This makes sense when we consider that a certain level of cognitive development is necessary for the child to respond appropriately to induction [p. 325]." This difference in the findings at the various ages actually provides no support for the exclusive action of a parent–effect and reveals an assumption that the child is merely a target on which parent actions are registered.

Hoffman's third point is "that the parent's discipline choice is influenced by relatively enduring characteristics of the parent and by the marital relation, neither of which can readily be derived from the child's behavior [p. 325]." Unfortunately, the correlations to which Hoffman refers are of such low order that they would in no sense rule out variance attributable to the controlling effect of child behavior. For example, one enduring characteristic, social class, only accounted for 2–4% of the variance in discipline in a major study (Erlanger, 1974). Thus, it is certainly possible that at least an equal part of the remaining variance could be accounted for by the child's behavior.

The fourth point raised by Hoffman: "In one of the studies reporting a positive relation between power assertion and the child's aggressive behavior toward peers . . . power assertion did not relate to the child's aggressiveness at home, nor was it used any more frequently in response to aggression than to other deviant behaviors, which suggests that power assertion leads to aggression, not the reverse [p. 325]." In terms of the general model for child–effects already elaborated in this chapter, it would not be surprising that deviant behaviors other than aggression would elicit upper-limit parent controls. Further, the findings from the study cited are in disagreement with other research reviewed in the same volume (e.g., Sears, Maccoby, & Levin, 1957). The low frequency of aggression with respect to adults (4% in data reported by Wright, 1967, Table 8.8) would make it very easy to obtain low order relationships and inconsistencies between studies, unless such studies used parent reports that in effect summarized a great deal of experience with the child or unless the observation covered a very extensive period.

Hoffman's fifth point is:

> the view that the parent's discipline choice results from the child's moral development rather than the reverse would still leave unanswered the question of what led to the moral development in the first place. One of the most plausible answers to this question is that the parent who uses induction discipline often expresses similar views in the child's presence outside the discipline situation; and the child's identification with the parent in these situations is the important factor, rather than the effects of the discipline [p. 325].

To encompass a child–effect on the process of moral development, it is not necessary to assume that the child's moral development produced the parental technique. Neither the parent's disciplinary techniques nor the child's moral development appear *de novo*. Neither precedes the other. As has already been elaborated in the section of this chapter concerned with the different ways children and parents control each other's behavior, it is likely that the parent does have long-term moral development goals for the child. However, the child's own characteristics affect not only the disciplinary techniques utilized but also the extent to which the parent's goals can be realized. Moral development is forged bit by bit in many specific situations out of the interaction of the child's short-term, and the parent's long-term, goals. Burton's example of Jennifer amply illustrates this point.

In a more recent statement of his position, Hoffman (1975) adds a new point to support his argument that the direction of effects in discipline encounters is from parent to child. Parents only rarely indicate in interviews that choice of discipline–technique was affected by the anticipation of whether the child would or would not comply. This argument assumes that a parent should be aware of the eliciting action of the child's behavior on the repertoire, or of reinforcement effects. The assumption runs counter to the common experience in operant conditioning experiments of subjects being conditioned with little or no awareness of what has been happening to their behavior.

Despite defects in these arguments advanced by Hoffman, it should be conceded that in interactions involving discipline, the greater resources of the parent, combined with long-range goals, are likely to lead to a situation in which the parent dominates the child much more than the child dominates the parent. In addition, it should be noted that in many cases the present author's explanation for the correlational findings does not give an exclusive role to child–effects. Power-assertion and induction may indeed be having the effects on guilt and internalization that are postulated. Many of the arguments that we have advanced simply place the effect within the context of a broader causal pattern and place it with an insistence that the actual links between parent behaviors and effects on children be demonstrated, one by one. All in all, the effect of giving more attention to the influence of children should be better-focused research and a more comprehensive theoretical approach.

Intellectual Development

In the author's previous review of this area, a study by Bing (1963) was cited, in which it had been found that mothers of children who showed higher verbal than spatial and numerical ability had a more close and demanding relationship with their children than mothers of children who showed higher spatial and numerical than verbal ability. Verbal ability has been found to be associated with a close affectional relationship between mother and son (Honzik, 1967, p. 358–359; Moss & Kagan, 1958, p. 660) and with maternal behavior that involves a positive evaluation of the son, equalitarianism, and expression of affection (Bayley & Schaefer, 1964). Because findings from only one study (Baer and Ragosta, 1966) are in disagreement, and because these findings were based on college students' retrospective perception of maternal child-rearing practices, the association of verbal ability with a close, demanding, and somewhat intrusive pattern of maternal behavior will be accepted on the basis of the present literature. An explanation in terms of child–effects has been offered previously (Bell, 1968, p. 90) and still appears to be applicable. This explanation is that the high-verbal children were high in person-orientation and low in assertiveness, a quite feasible combination of characteristics in terms of the three-dimensional models of behavior summarized in Figure 1. The combination of characteristics could well have congenital determinants, as documented earlier in this chapter, or could have developed out of previous interactions that had nothing to do with a currently close and demanding relationship. Whatever the origins, it is possible that the children who are high in person-orientation and low in assertiveness reinforced their mother's social responses and elicited nurturant behavior. The resultant interaction intensified verbal expression, because this is the primary channel of communication at the age level from which most of the findings were derived. The mother's demanding and intrusive characteristics could be seen, according to this child–effect interpretation, as lower-limit control behavior in response to the child's low assertiveness, possible dependence, and passivity. This latter interpretation is in line with the projections of dependency and passivity onto parental restrictiveness and intrusiveness in the three-dimensional model.

Although the foregoing explanation is sufficient to account for the data cited, there are other findings in the same vein indicating that the direction of influence could also be from parent to child. Father absence, which presumably intensifies the mother–child relationship, is also associated with higher verbal than quantitative ability in the child (Carlsmith, 1964). In this case, a child–effect seems unlikely, although there are many complications involved in a parent–effect interpretation. The problems involved in the research approach using father absence will be discussed in Chapter 5.

SUMMARY

Since the 1960s, students of socialization have been able to free themselves increasingly from ideological fetters whose origins reach back for centuries. These early influences led to the oversimplified view of the human parent as the initial agent of culture, and the infant or young child as the object of acculturation. The change has been brought about by a number of recent developments involving recognition that (1) the behavior and appearance of the young are a very compelling part of the stimulus field for the parent; (2) if parents are effective they must, in turn, be affected by the products of their tutelage; (3) we obtain misleading information if we overlook the process of socialization and attend only to the final outcome as seen in the association of child and parent characteristics; (4) the child's characteristics even play a role in such phenomena as nutritional marasmus and child battering; (5) parents do not have a uniform impact on all children in their family (and the differences are not merely a matter of sibling birth order and sex role); and (6) effects of the young on parents and adults can be demonstrated experimentally.

Because of the above, most reviewers of socialization research have become sensitized to child–effects, although many individual investigators still concentrate on the products of socialization. Also, some still offer interpretations of correlations between parent and child characteristics as indicating the effects of the parents on the child, not realizing that a correlation by itself does not indicate the direction of effects. To maintain vigilance concerning the equivocal nature of correlations, to caution those who still assume too readily that parent–effects are somehow more reasonable or parsimonious, and to consolidate fragmentary hypotheses about child–effects that have been enunciated in the last few years, this chapter has presented an explanatory model. The model attempts to account for the small number of associations between parent and child characteristics that recent reviews of socialization research have considered deserving of explanation on the basis of consistency of findings.

The first element in the explanatory model involves congenital contributors to child behavior. Although the demonstration of a child–effect does not require that we trace the child behavior to its ultimate origin, there is sufficient evidence that we can reasonably assume congenital contributions to impaired sensory–motor development, impulsiveness, assertiveness, and social response in children. These congenital contributions are used in conjunction with a control theory model in which it is assumed that excessive or inappropriate child be-havior induces upper-limit control behavior from parental repertoires, and by contrast, child behavior that is below parental standards induces lower-limit parent controls that act to stimulate behavior. Parental repertoires are hierarchi-cally and sequentially organized. Child behavior "keys in" specific responses or patterns from parental repertoires.

Studies are cited in which one or another aspect of the former model has been used to explain findings. The model is then brought to bear on the task of understanding the few consistent associations of parent and child characteristics cited in recent reviews of research. The association of parental permissiveness with child attributes, such as assertiveness, achievement, and independence, identified by the culture as "masculine," is interpreted as involving neither upper- nor lower-limit control behavior. The parent is presumably reacting to appropriate capability and self-sufficiency by giving the child free rein. The often cited association of parent restrictiveness and rejection with child depen-dence is assumed to be due to a lower-limit control reaction involving urging, prompting, and directing in response to the fact that the child's performance is below parental standards.

The association of rejection, inconsistency, and severe physical discipline with child aggression is interpreted as an upper-limit control reaction to ex-tremely aggressive child behavior. The association of parental power assertion and low guilt in the child is assumed to be due to congenital contributors to fast-moving, impulsive, situationally controlled behavior that induces more power assertion in the parent and does not favor internalization.

The association of affection and inductive parent techniques (versus power-assertion) with high guilt in the child is assumed to be a response to person-orientation and social responsiveness in the child.

The explanations that have been offered can all be supported with evidence of congenital contributors to child behavior, but it should be noted that the associa-tions reported in the literature could be due to child–effects on the parent even if the child behaviors originated out of prior interactions of a different nature with parents. That is, child behaviors that produce a current effect on parents could be emergents of the prior history of interaction with the parent.

5

Research Strategies

Richard Q. Bell

INTRODUCTION

It has become apparent from the previous chapter that there are few definitive research findings in studies of human socialization and that there is ambiguity in the interpretation of even these few findings that have some claim to generality. Obviously, there is a need for a basic change in research orientation. If further progress in socialization research requires that parent and child be considered as a true social system, with the responses of each serving as stimuli for the other (and changes in each having some likelihood of affecting the other), it will be necessary to consider all the problems involved in disentangling influences in social systems. This chapter reviews research strategies that can be used to isolate the effects of child and parent participants in the family social system, considers the special problems that each of these approaches entails, and evaluates these strategies against the background of a classification system especially applicable to child development and socialization within the family. Even though a bidirectional perspective is an expansion in scope over traditional studies, it is recognized that we are abstracting from a more complete system in treating only relations between parents and children, in omitting socialization by siblings and peers, and in simplifying exposition by primarily referring to maternal–infant or parent–child pairs.

The treatment will include but not be limited to approaches that attempt to disentangle the relative weights of organismic and environmental contributors to the system, because the stimulus effects of children on parents, and of the parents on children, deserve treatment regardless of the question of origin. As has been mentioned in the previous chapter, a child could process and integrate experience during one period and subsequently manifest new products of this integration that would affect parents at a later period, even if there were no maturational contributors to change in the child's behavior between the periods.

BASES FOR COMPARING STRATEGIES

Since each research strategy will be discussed in terms of multiple criteria, the question of the value of each becomes one of the pattern of advantages and disadvantages in the overall mosaic of research effort—the "cost–benefit" ratio. No comparison will be provided on grounds for which other reviews are available, such as the general problem of making inferences from nonexperimental data (Blalock, 1961), the problem of generalizing from observational studies of families and of matching children and parents in contrast groups (Fontana, 1966), or the problems of longitudinal versus cross-sectional and other types of studies (Baldwin, 1960; Baltes, 1968; Kessen, 1960). As will be seen, longitudinal studies provide information on sequences of events and life histories but not necessarily information on the direction of effects between parents and offspring, unless special conditions exist.

Table 3 summarizes the research strategies, classified into the experimental

Table 3
Effectiveness of Research Approaches by Four Criteria

Type of Approach	Isolation of Parent– or Child–Effects		General-ization	Range of Behavior
	Short-term	Long-term		
Nonexperimental Strategies				
Studies of Biological Pairs				
Congenital defects	Least	Inter	Inter	Least
Physiological disorders	Inter	Inter	Least	Inter
Sustained separation	Inter	Inter	Inter	Least
Twin studies	Most	Most	Inter	Least
Nursery studies	Inter	Least	Most	Inter
Longitudinal studies	Most	Inter	Most	Most
Interaction sequences	Most	Least	Most	Most
Studies of Functional Pairs				
Teacher–child interaction	Most	Most	Inter	Most
Adoption studies	Least	Most	Inter	Least
Foster-care studies	Most	Inter	Inter	Least
Experimental Strategies				
Studies of Biological Pairs				
Drug studies	Inter	Inter	Least	Inter
Brief separation	Most	Least	Most	Least
Altering perception	Most	Least	Most	Most
Altering behavior	Most	Inter	Most	Most
Studies of Functional Pairs				
Manipulating behavior in family-like settings	Most	Inter	Inter	Most
Contrived participants	Most	Least	Least	Most
Sample selection	Most	Least	Least	Most

and nonexperimental, and further subdivided into those using biological (parent–child) versus functional dyads (strangers, ad hoc pairs, adoptees). The term *pairs* is used because only a few studies have utilized triads, and still fewer have utilized entire families. The biological category subsumes units in which the members are related by reason of common heredity and have functioned together in a system that provides life support, protection, and guidance. As will be seen, the distinction between biological and functional is basic to the isolation of parent– or child–effects, because an empirical link uncovered between parent and child characteristics and presumed to be a result of a history of interaction may mask a genetic link due to similar inherited characteristics of each. Studies of nonbiological pairs, functioning in some way that approximates the basic parent–child dyad, make it possible to avoid this confusion of major influences.

The adjectives *most, inter,* (intermediate), and *least* indicate the judged effectiveness of each strategy in terms of its ability to (1) isolate the effects of one member of the pair from the other (in either short-term studies of a few days to a few months, or in long-term follow-ups); (2) permit generalization to biological pairs; and (3) encompass a wide range of child and parent behaviors. The three levels of effectiveness defined by the adjectives are neither absolute nor precise. The order merely recapitulates the arguments made in this chapter and places together, at any one of the three levels, those approaches that are difficult to differentiate. Greater precision is not possible because there are so many variations in specific research designs that may be pursued within a single research strategy.

At the end of each treatment of the four subheadings of Table 3, there will be a comparison on the three criteria of isolation, generalization, and range of behavior. At the end of the chapter, there will be further comparison on other grounds, such as ethical considerations, which are particularly applicable to only a subset of the approaches.

Isolation of influences.   The first basis for comparison concerns the extent to which the strategy isolates influences. The influence may be very general, such as the extent of parent versus child contributions to a life history, or it may be very specific, as in the question of whether the behavior of child or parent is responsible for a specific phenomenon occurring in one ongoing interaction sequence.

Generalization.   Some strategies make extrapolation to socialization within parent–child pairs reasonable. Others isolate influences at the expense of limiting generalization to very special populations, procedures, or settings. One of the major questions to be raised is whether findings from studies using adults and children who are strangers to each other can be generalized to the usual process of parent–child socialization.

Range of behavior.   While the primary interest is in the extent to which the independent variable indexes parent or child influences in a fashion that permits broad generalization, it is also of interest to consider whether the independent variables that can be manipulated in a research strategy limit the investigator to a narrow portion of the spectrum of behavior or permit study of a wide range of behaviors, as required for the development of a comprehensive theory. For example, does the strategy permit only gross effects, such as determining the effect of the presence or absence of a participant? Can only general classes of responses be identified, or fine details of behavior? Ultimately, theories of socialization must deal with the minute-to-minute flow of events in specific interaction sequences, as well as account for the movement of events over several years of development. Dependent variables are less of a problem, because in most approaches it is possible to measure either very detailed or very general effects.

NONEXPERIMENTAL STRATEGIES

Studies of Biological Pairs

The effects of congenital contributors may be analyzed by contrasting parents of congenitally handicapped children with parents of nonhandicapped children. One paper has reported a consistent tendency for parents of children with congenital handicaps, such as cerebral palsy, Down's syndrome, congenital heart defects, and congenital blindness, to score higher than parents of normals on a parent–attitude questionnaire measuring intrusiveness (Bell, 1964a). The independent variable in such studies is a condition in the child that presumably affects certain of the parent's behaviors. Only in a few cases (Waldrop & Halverson, 1971) has there been specific research directed to the question of the link between the child's clinical condition and his behavior. Where there are multiple handicaps, each linked to a different set of behaviors, the independent variable is burdened with considerable heterogeneity, even though the research strategy involves indexing one handicap all children share. Nor do we obtain any information at the time the handicap-linked behaviors first began to exert their effect on others in the family.

There is an important requirement to be met in studies of this kind. To indicate an effect of the child's condition on the parent, the congenital handicaps selected must show low intrafamily incidence. In the several studies already cited that demonstrated effects on maternal attitudes of various child conditions, the intrafamily incidence is 2% or less, indicating that very few children in the same family have the condition. If the incidence is low, it is less likely that some parent characteristic related to the production of fetal conditions would be mistakenly identified as an effect of the child's congenital handicap.

Congenital defects can also be used to create contrast groups in which parents differ. Lenneberg, Rebelsky, and Nichols (1965) compared vocalizations of infants born to congenitally deaf parents with vocalizations of infants born to normally hearing and speaking parents. There is one advantage in this form of approach. Parents with defects could be located before the birth of an infant so that one could study the ongoing process.

The effects of physiological disorders.   Some diseases create a quasi-experimental opportunity in a substantial proportion of the general population, because they flare up and recede within a short period of time in only one member of a family and thus permit studies of onset and termination effects on other members. Excessive night-crying of unexplained origin (colic) begins at the end of the first month and ends in the third or fourth month in approximately 20% of all infants (Shaver, 1973). One retrospective study and two prospective studies illustrate efforts to use this research opportunity in order to answer the question of which comes first. Do characteristics of the mother contribute to the colic, or does colic produce anxiety and feelings of helplessness in the mother? From retrospective data gathered after the occurrence of colic, Lakin (1957) concluded that anxious mothers transmit their feelings to their infants, who respond with colic. Paradise (1966) found in a prospective study that there was indeed a condition in the mother that existed prior to the occurrence of the infant's colic, namely, a worsening of emotional status during pregnancy. Shaver (1973) found in another prospective study that the subsequent colic was also capable of producing effects on the mother, which then disappeared as the colic ebbed.

The prospective studies were able to clarify the event sequence and made it appear likely that tension, anxiety, and inadequacy in the maternal role can be induced by excessive crying in the infant. However, the fact that an emotional condition in the mother during pregnancy was associated with the occurrence of later colic reminds us that this design cannot sort out and identify causal factors conclusively. The disadvantage of the natural experiment provided by colic is that a variety of unidentified factors determined which infants had colic, and thus the independent variable was not actually under the control of the experimenters. Nonetheless, the analysis of such "experiments in nature" can make a valuable contribution to our knowledge by (1) throwing light on the complexity of the developmental events; (2) making us less hasty in drawing conclusions about the direction of effects between parents and their young; and (3) pointing out the possiblity that crying and fussing within the normal range may also have effects on parents that should be taken into consideration.

In the present discussion of methods, the important point is that these three studies illustrate the possibility of a research strategy in which the independent variable consists of groups (infants and parents) that do or do not display a physiological condition. The dependent variable would be created by the corresponding contrast groups (parents or infants).

Sustained separation. One other approach takes advantage of natural experiments. In this case, one entire component of a family system is removed, as in (1) Carlsmith's (1964) studies of the long-term effects of father absence, in the early years of a child's life, on the relative verbal to quantitative aptitude during the child's high school and college years; and (2) Bowlby's (1960) study of separation incident to the hospitalization of infants and young children. These illustrative studies seem very different, but there is a common feature— presumably, the contribution of one component to the family system can be evaluated by noting the impact of its removal.

The separation approach is valuable in that it approximates an experimental manipulation of a family system in otherwise intact families, and it rules out child–effects in most studies, because it is very unlikely that differences in children produced the father absence. Unfortunately, it is quite difficult to establish a parent–effect by ruling out other factors in the environment or to determine which parent is producing the effect. Because the experimenter does not select the families in which separation is going to occur, there should be careful matching of comparison cases and several checks on uncontrolled variables. For example, in studies of father absence during the World War II period, one subgroup consisted of doctors who tended to leave their homes early in the war and remain away longer because of the war-time demands for the occupational specialty.

Short-term studies of the events occurring while separation is in process, as in Bowlby's (1960) study, could overcome some of the problems of retrospective separation studies. For example, in the long-term father–separation studies, it is not known to what extent the effect on a child is mediated by an effect on the mother of the father's absence. Nor does this method separate the effect of the return of the father from that of his absence, but this latter is not in any event a child–effect. Bowlby's study of the ongoing process was able to differentiate initial and later effects of the separation, as well as the effects of the return of the parent. In addition, this general approach could be broadened to include children who remain in familiar contexts when parents are separated from them, rather than children who are removed from their home and placed in strange new situations such as a hospital.

Up to the present, the separation situation has been seen as a means of testing effects of parental absence on infants and children, but it is obvious that the same situation is also a means of testing the effect on a parent of removal from a child. It is common observation that some young mothers are very reluctant to leave their babies, even with caregivers who have a great deal of experience. They may be tense during the entire period of separation, and their conversation may focus on their babies. More systematic observation of this commonplace occurrence could tell us much about the mother–infant system at various phases, from the standpoint of the mother as well as the infant. Separation of a mother from her newborn during the nursery stay, versus rooming-in or provision of supplementary contacts for mothers of prematures, are variants of this procedure. In these comparisons, the formation of the relationship is the primary issue instead of the effects of interrupting an established relationship.

Twin studies. Leach and Costello (1972) have reported a unique effort to apply the classic twin-study approach to the problem of determining effects of infants on their mothers. Within-pair differences in infant behavior and maternal handling were to be contrasted for monozygotic and dizygotic pairs on the assumption that monozygotic twins behave more similarly to each other and thus will be treated more similarly by their mothers. The investigators have advised the present author that problems in automation of behavior recording have delayed the study, but the design is still of interest. It called for weekly visual observation and electronic recording of behavior in the first six months of life. From this kind of data, it should be possible to determine the sequence of events in which specific infant behaviors emerge followed by alterations in maternal behavior, and vice-versa. Long-term changes in more molar variables may also be uncovered in this kind of study, because it can be extended beyond the early months of life.

One concern with this application of twin studies is that mothers' more similar treatment of monozygotic twins might be due to knowledge of their zygosity rather than a response to behavioral similarity. This concern is allayed somewhat by the findings of one study (Scarr, 1968), which showed that mothers who were wrong about the zygosity of their twins reported neither greater nor smaller differences.

It appears that the use of the mother as her own control in the Leach and Costello study should make this line of investigation very sensitive to subtle differences in behavior that otherwise might not be detected. Differences in socioeconomic position, the mother's environment, marital situation, child-rearing experience, attitudes, and feelings and fantasies specific to each birth, operate to produce considerable variable error that could only be controlled less precisely by matching and randomization, were it not for the twin approach.

The Leach and Costello study offers an important advantage over other twin studies that have customarily contrasted twin pairs at a much later point in development. Tendencies toward polarization of behavior within the twin pairs, or overly symbiotic behavior, create unusual interactions in twins not likely to be found within nontwin siblings in the normal family. Generalization to the nontwin family situation should be less limited in the case of a study of pairs at an early time before within-pair patterns of infant interaction begin to develop.

Nursery studies. Newborns and mothers are typically kept in separate hospital space in the immediate postpartum period, thus providing an opportunity to study the effects of specific infant and maternal behaviors in natural pairs. The period of hospitalization is as brief as 2 or 3 days in American hospitals but may last as long as 10 days in European hospitals. A study by Levy (1958, p. 8) of maternal greeting behavior when the newborn was brought from the nursery for feeding, illustrates the approach. States were determined for each infant in the nursery prior to interaction with the mother. Analysis of Levy's data by the present author (Bell, 1968) indicated that infants who were awake when brought from the nursery were greeted, whereas those who were asleep were not. This finding supported Levy's contention that specific maternal behavior could be accounted for more by the infant's behavior than by the mother's general maternal style or attitude, whether the latter was estimated from interview material or from naturalistic observation of behavior.

The occurrence of variation within each infant is critical for demonstration of effects in the nursery approach. Otherwise, the relation between infant state and maternal response might reflect a genetic similarity between mother and infant or a common condition induced by some perinatal factor. For an example of the latter, mothers who are given sedatives in the postnatal period and who are breast-feeding may transmit sedative effects to the infant through the milk, resulting in a misleading finding of lethargy in the infant associated with lack of maternal responsiveness.

Longitudinal studies.   Longitudinal studies are needed to identify developmental sequences in major phases of the life cycle. These sequences are some of the basic phenomena that socialization research should set out to explain. However, it is mistakenly assumed (Fontana, 1966) that data from such studies will, in addition, automatically provide definitive answers to questions about determinants. In some instances, the nature of the variables themselves points very strongly to a causal interpretation. Different social development patterns in early and late maturing males (Jones, 1965), the latter indexed by the emergence of secondary sex characteristics, is usually regarded as a relatively clear example of a maturational contributor. However, such examples are rare. More often, it is extremely difficult to tease out determinants. An appreciation of the difficulties in isolating effects in longitudinal studies, particularly those involving a long time span, can be gained from reading Eron, Lefkowitz, Huesmann, and Walder's (1972) report on analyses of data from a 10-year follow-up study started when the subjects were 8–9 years of age. Peer ratings of aggression and the child's preference for violent television during the early period were correlated with similar measures when the subjects were 19 years of age. The same problems would exist if the data involved, instead, the effects of early parent or child behavior on later outcome. (As a matter of fact, however, parental aggressiveness, rejection, and punishment did not contribute to later aggression, according to the analysis.)

It is instructive that in the study by Eron et al., it was necessary to use cross-lagged correlation, partial correlation, multiple regression, and path analyses to support the hypothesis that the early viewing of violent television shows contributed to later aggression. These analyses were the subject of several later critiques and a rebuttal (Huesmann, Eron, Lefkowitz, & Walder, 1973). From the basic report and these critiques, there are several implications for efforts to sort out parent– and child–effects in longitudinal studies. At best, isolation of parent– or child–effects must be tentative, being based on a combination of statistical techniques and complex logical inference. The outcome of the effort to isolate effects will often be very ambiguous. Interpretations of cross-lagged correlations will be difficult if there is a change in the nature of the parent or child measures between the two time periods or a change in the reliability of their assessment. Either condition could very well occur in studies attempting to cover several years of rapid growth.

In a short-term study, on the other hand, more defensible results may be obtained. as in Clarke–Stewart's (1973) cross-lagged correlational analysis of mutual influences between mother and infant during the period of 11 to 17 months of age. Figure 2, adapted from Clarke–Stewart, shows the types of correlations involved. Because the cross-lagged (i.e., diagonal) correlation of .42 was significant, and because the other cross-lagged correlation of − .09 was not, the authors concluded (after further analyses eliminated some alternative hypotheses) that the frequency of the infant's looking at the mother at 11 months of age led to their spending more time together at 17 months of age. The infant's smiling and vocalizing played a similar sequential role as looking.

Yee and Gage (1968) have summarized other statistical techniques not mentioned in Eron et al. (1972) that are applicable to the situation in which an investigator wishes to make an inference about causal relations in a sequence of behavior on the basis of the fact that a change occurred in the behavior of one participant toward or away from the level shown by the other. The present author could not locate any applications to changes in parent–child behavior, but it is well to keep such techniques in mind because they compensate for the loss of information (concerning change in absolute level of behavior in two time periods) that occurs when one restricts efforts to correlational statistics.

Study of interaction sequences.   Even in the short-term longitudinal study, the basic data being analyzed are the status characteristics of individuals at two or more time periods—these characteristics comprising summary information from direct observation, experimental procedures, tests, or other measurements. The process of change is inferred from the statistical links uncovered between the summary measures of status. The picture that emerges is like an artist's first sketch. Sequence analysis provides the fine detail that brings the picture to full life. The information from each approach is needed by the other. Furthermore, it is difficult to apply principles of learning theory to complex, long-term changes in the status of individuals, whereas application to actual behavior sequences, described in the following studies, appear to be quite fruitful. Considerable space will be devoted to this topic, because it is an area of rapidly

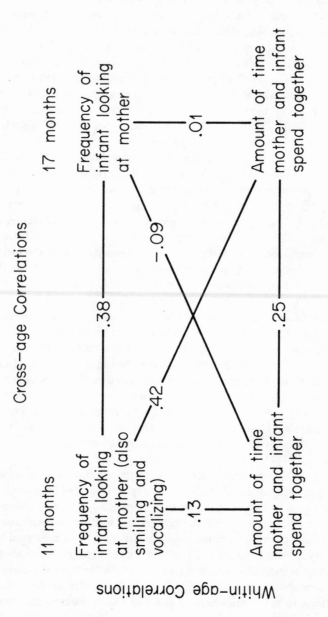

FIGURE 2 Cross-lagged correlation analysis of mother–infant interaction data. (Adapted from Clarke–Stewart, 1973. Copyright © 1973 by the Society for Research in Child Development, Inc.)

expanding interest, and we may be on the threshold of uncovering some new information on the direction of effects.

The data of sequence analysis are second-to-second or minute-to-minute interactions. While this stream of behavior is, indeed, "where the action is," most investigators experience it as a flood of confusing information at all steps from recording through analysis. Even the investigator who has hypotheses that make it possible to single out a small number of events for attention may find that it is necessary to process thousands of interactions to uncover a sufficient number of relevant events. If the objective is purely description, the stream of behavior output may be manifested in so many ways that each category contains too few instances to be reliable (Bell, 1964b). In order to obtain sufficient frequencies in some categories, it may be necessary to structure the situation so as to limit the outlets for behavior or to accept the necessity of extensive periods of observation lasting much longer than those ordinarily carried out in socialization studies.

In the initial task of data reduction, the investigator is confronted with the fact that the stream of behavior contains some items that each participant is emitting as an individual without reference to the other, as well as behaviors that are truly interactive. How does one separate maternal behavior that occurs after infant behavior but appears to have nothing to do with the latter, from maternal behavior that follows infant behavior and appears to be meaningfully related? Computer programs can readily detect and print out vast arrays of sequential occurrence, but what can be done with many of these that appear to be senseless? On what grounds does one reject the apparently senseless?

It simplifies matters greatly if one knows what to look for. Experimental, longitudinal, and other field investigations of aggressive behavior, combined with principles derived from operant learning theory, led Patterson and his colleagues (Patterson, 1974; Patterson & Cobb, 1973) to look for behavior of other family members immediately preceding or following noxious responses of a child (such as negative commands, crying, excessive dependency, destructive behavior, negativism, etc.). The studies are models of attention to the special problems of sequence analysis, the careful retraining of observers to prevent drift over time, preclusion of observer bias with respect to knowledge of deviancy or treatment status, and ingenious solutions to many practical as well as technical scientific problems. Considering the unusually high quality of the basic data (home observations of children referred for clinical treatment) and the fact that the investigators had clear hypotheses to help focus the inquiry, it is instructive that 70 one-hour observation sessions were needed with one case, and many of these sessions were specially structured in order to generate enough data to make defensible analyses of antecedent–consequent relations. The investigators had turned to an intensive study of one case in order to escape the problem of having different subjects contribute different amounts of data to event samples. This latter problem arose when they found it necessary to collapse data across all family members in order to have a sufficient sample of relevant sequences, in spite of the fact that 60–100 minutes of interaction had been obtained for each case in a relatively large sample of problem boys.

The statistical procedure used to establish sequential dependency was that of computing conditional probabilities. For example, to determine whether disapproval from the father was a controlling prior stimulus for noxious behaviors by the child, Patterson compared two conditional probabilities; one was the number of noxious behaviors emitted by the child, expressed as a proportion of all sequences in which the father's disapproval preceded the child's noxious behavior; the other was the number of noxious behaviors emitted by the child, expressed as a proportion of all other categories of prior events. If a chi-square analysis indicated that the former proportion was significantly greater than the latter, it was provisionally concluded that instances of the father's disapproval constituted controlling prior stimuli for subsequent noxious behavior emitted by the child. Chi-square technique was only used empirically, along with other methods of analysis, because it is not possible to satisfy its key assumption that independence would hold for any row or column within a fourfold table of antecedent and consequent events.

Lytton and Zwirner (1975) summed data across subjects in order to achieve greater generality in a study of parental antecedents of compliance that followed Patterson's general approach. Additional statistical techniques are offered.

In another hypothesis-directed study, Stern (1974) had concluded from a review of the literature that the infant's gaze was a potent factor in affecting interrelated components of maternal behavior such as gaze, facial expression, and vocalization. From videotape records of 2–7 weekly play sessions in the home of 8 twin infants between 3 and 4 months of age, he obtained sequence data that made it possible to demonstrate that the conditional probability of a mother terminating her gaze when the infant was gazing at her was less than when the infant was not gazing at her. The two conditional probabilities were compared by chi-square and found significant for each infant. Again, although it would not be possible to satisfy the assumption of independence in this statistical test, the direction of the relation between the two probabilities was the same for all mother–infant dyads.

One other sequence analysis that is of interest because it involved hypothesis testing is contained in a report by Moss and Robson (1968). It seemed likely to these investigators that a large number of a mother's contacts with her infant are responses to the infant's state, rather than the opposite, in the period of 1–3 months postpartum. They simply tallied the episodes of crying or fussing that preceded maternal contact in each of 54 mother–infant pairs and found that the average was significantly higher than for episodes in which the crying and fussing followed maternal contact. Individual cases followed the direction of the means. The data base consisted of two 6-hour observations at 1 month of age and one at 3 months of age.

The techniques developed by Newtson (1976) to detect "break points" or transitions in behavior sequences of individuals may be applicable to parent–child interactions. Newtson has found that either large or small units may be marked off reliably, that these transitions contain much more information than non-break points, and that there is considerable invariance of the judgmental process across judges and types of material. Ratings or subjective judgments of the interaction units themselves (as in the data cited from Schoggen, 1963) are also a valuable supplement to the quantitative analyses.

Turning to descriptive studies, a criticism that is frequently directed at psychology is that the basic stage of description has been omitted in many areas, and investigators move too rapidly in the direction of hypothetical models that have no correspondence to reality. A good case could be made for purely descriptive studies of event sequences in parent–child interactions. Until very recently, very few investigators other than Roger Barker and his colleagues have been interested in full and complete recording. Also, computer technology has only very recently been available to assist in the laborious task of data reduction.

Even in a purely descriptive approach, the selection of observation codes and categories of variables indicates the investigator's ideas about the importance of certain phenomenon. In the following studies, the investigators have selected some area of interaction as relevant to their interests, at the same time attempting to be comprehensive in terms of current interests manifest in the field at large. Lewis and Freedle (1973) analyzed 16 categories obtained from observation of 80 mother–infant pairs in a naturalistic setting when the infants were approximately 3 months old. The investigators were primarily interested in infant and maternal vocalizations, in the context of the infant's state, and in the general caregiving situation. One analysis and finding illustrates the way the sequence data and conditional probabilities were treated. The authors used a sign test to compare the conditional probabilities for male versus female infants vocalizing in response to maternal vocalization directed to them, in contrast with vocalization directed to another. Female infants showed a significantly greater tendency to vocalize more when the mother vocalized to them rather than to another. In general, the data indicated that females showed more advanced development of vocalization even at 3 months of age.

A method of grouping interactions into two- to four-part segments is illustrated in a report by Gewirtz and Gewirtz (1965) on 110 2- to 8-month-old infants from four different environments in Israel, each observed for approximately 12 hours. Two infants were selected from each environment, one an "only" infant, the other a "youngest." An effort was made to delineate "bouts" of interaction varying in complexity and in which one or the other participant was responsible for initiation or termination. An example of a complex, four-position bout is: infant fusses—mother picks up—infant quiets down—mother hugs. Expected differences between the two infants in the complexity of the bouts did not appear, but the analysis did reveal a much larger number of overall interactions for the "only" infant. Further analysis involving conditional probabilities for the same data have been reported (Gewirtz & Gewirtz, 1969). No statistical comparison of conditional probabilities was offered, but the authors' impression, based on records of one 8-month-old infant from each of the four caregiving environments, was that the infant's most frequent response to various adult initiations was smiling, regardless of whether the adult was approaching, smiling, talking, or hugging. On the other hand, the adult's predominant response to infant initiations was more likely to match these, especially with respect to the infant's smiles and vocalizations.

Sackett (1975) has recently reported a method of analysis that offers some promise of reducing the task of sequential analysis in descriptive studies. In this approach, the computer counts the number of times that each of several behaviors follows each occurrence of a given criterion behavior as the very next, second next, etc. Applied to observational data on rhesus mother–infant interaction, it yielded some very prominent departures from expected rectangular distributions for certain categories, without overly complicated computer programming. Statistical methods for treating the data are also suggested.

From the descriptive studies summarized up to this point, it is evident that the task of data reduction and analysis is formidable even with the help of the most advanced computer methods. In the descriptive studies we have described, either a small number of variables or a small number of cases have been selected for attention. Furthermore, many other kinds of analyses that are logically conceivable have not even been attempted yet (see Gewirtz & Gewirtz, 1965, p. 265, and Lewis & Lee–Painter, 1974). Obviously, for large samples on whom as many as 115 categories of behavioral information have been recorded, it is unlikely that a single investigator or team could ferret out all the complex information that is in the data, even when using the kinds of analyses that are conceivable at present.

Fortunately, data that are of high quality eventually come to serve as a resource for others attempting analyses going beyond those contemplated in the original study. For example, the present author turned to data recorded by Schoggen (1963) to answer the question of the relative proportion of interaction bouts started by children or parents. From 18 specimen records available for three mother–toddler pairs, each covering a period of at least 11 hours, it was possible to determine that from 49% to 61% of the bouts of interaction had been initiated by the child. The bouts, termed *environmental force units,* had been delineated as a sequence of interaction in which an action of the child or parent was directed toward a recognizable end state and was identified as such by the other. A similar estimate of child initiations emerged from the data of Wright (1967) and 11 children covering the age range from 1 year and 2 months to 10 years and 9 months. From further data available in Schoggen, these data on the percentages of child initiations appeared to be an underestimate of the intensity of child–effects. Observers had judged the goal of the mothers; in all but one of the 18 specimen records, it was considered that the mother's goal was to get the toddler to cease demands on her such as bothering her, questioning her, staying with her, pressing requests, and *attacking!* However, Hoffman (1975) turned to other analyses of the same data to test the hypothesis that in discipline encounters (that is, interactions in which the parent wishes to change the child's behavior against the child's will), the parent's greater power should lead to the parent determining the outcome of an interaction segment more often than the child, regardless of who initiated the segment. In disciplinary encounters (that occurred on the average of one every 6–9 minutes of the day), children were found to submit to instances of parent pressure 2/3 of the time. Thus from this analysis, it would be concluded that the initiation of an interaction sequence is not definitive in determining the outcome of a power conflict. Apparently, children may start about as many interactions as parents, but if a conflict exists between parent and child, the outcome may more often reflect the fact that the parent's potential as a reinforcing agent far exceeds that of the child.

Comparison of Biological Pair Approaches

In Table 3, three approaches are rated most effective in isolating short-term effects—the twin, longitudinal, and interaction sequence studies. The short-term longitudinal study is rated more effective than the long-term study, because it should be possible to isolate effects better using such statistical techniques as cross-lagged correlation. Changes in basic parent or child characteristics should not be so great as to violate the assumptions of these statistical techniques. Of course, even if the effects are not isolated, either the short- or the long-term study can identify *event sequences* in important phases of the life cycle within the family. These sequences are the basic data against which many explanations of the socialization processes should be checked, particularly explanations based on methods that merely approximate developmental history.

The lack of appropriate inferential statistics and the fact that different conclusions about the direction of effects can be obtained by focusing on one aspect versus another, may raise some questions as to whether the interaction sequence approach should be described as most effective in Table 3. However, in studies that have been cited to provide examples of application, it is evident that investigators have found ways of treating conditional probabilities with inferential statistics originally developed for other uses and that the inability to satisfy the key assumption of chi-square need not be a bar to adequate statistical evaluation. Furthermore, as in the case of the study by Eron et al. (1972), investigators can use a variety of analytic techniques in order to see whether a convergence of evidence exists for one direction of effects versus the other. In addition, they can compare results from initiation, maintenance, and termination of interaction bouts. The interaction sequence approach in Table 3 is rated least effective as a long-term strategy, but such a microanalytic approach is inapplicable rather than ineffective in isolating effects in a long-term study (the research of Patterson did involve processes lasting at least several weeks).

The approaches involving physiological disorders and congenital handicaps are somewhat similar relative to isolating effects, although it is usually more difficult in the case of the latter to separate out events in the developmental sequence, and there is a relatively small number of congenital handicaps linked to behavior. The congenital handicap approach is rated least effective in isolating short-term effects, because it generally lends itself better to long-term processes. There are exceptions, such as the study by Lenneberg, Rebelsky, and Nichols (1965) that covered a few months of early development.

The nursery, longitudinal, and interaction sequence approaches are most effective when it comes to generalization, because they can sample representative and broad segments of the child-bearing and child-rearing population. As far as longitudinal studies are concerned, the intensive study will subject its sample to the biasing effects of frequent contact, but the less intensive long-term study may suffer greater sample loss. However, these sources of error can be assessed with samples set aside for infrequent contact and by comparing initial and final sample characteristics. Cohort differences can be determined by including samples for whom data collection is started for similar age groups at different time periods (Baltes, 1968). Statistical allowances can be made for various sources of bias when they are uncovered. Accordingly, there is nothing in a well-planned longitudinal study that inherently limits generalization.

The interaction sequence approach has most often used small samples, but automation of recording or analysis may lead to much larger samples, and thus it is not basically limited in generalization.

The approach utilizing physiological disorders is rated least effective relative to generalization, because the samples of individuals selected for study differ from the general population in that they have certain physiological disorders.

Longitudinal and interaction sequence studies are again amongst the most effective considering the range of behavior to which they can be applied. Though the large-scale follow-up studies launched in the 1930s tended toward global characteristics of their subjects, simply because of the interest in such variables that existed at that time, there is no necessary limitation in a longitudinal study relative to the range of behaviors that can be studied. Twin and sustained separation approaches are rated least effective relative to range of behavior for different reasons than the congenital handicaps approach. In the case of the latter, the independent variable is restricted in range, because it is limited to handicap-related behavior. The dependent variable need not be restricted to molar variables or to measures such as attitudes, however. There is no reason why a very fine-grained analysis of behavior could not be carried out in families whose members have congenital handicaps. Experimental situations could be arranged in the laboratory to test the effects of specific handicaps. Thus, the dependent variable can be clearly focused although the independent variable is likely to be diffuse. The other approaches are rated least effective because the independent variable being manipulated is very global or general.

Studies of Functional Pairs

Teacher–child interaction.   Studies of interaction in school settings make it possible to identify sequential change free of the possible linking influence of common genetic background in parent and child. An example is a study by Yarrow, Waxler, and Scott (1971). Although the study involved the manipulation of the roles of teachers, the analyses of change pertinent to the present interest were a byproduct of experimental treatments and are thus classified under the present heading. The study reported that the more a child made bids for help on the first day of interacting with an adult caregiver while in a group situation, the more the adult initiated negative interactions on the following 3 days. In another analysis, the children's responses following any adult-initiated contact were classified into those that were positively reinforcing (in the sense of showing interest or compliance) versus nonreinforcing. It was then found that the adults invariably returned more quickly to initiate a positive contact with children following a reinforcement than a nonreinforcement. The study shows how a sequence analysis of short-term change, supported by knowledge of learning principles, can lend credibility to a directional interpretation of change involving the effects of children on adults. Long-term changes could also be studied because in many schools a teacher may be with her children for as long as a year.

Adoption and foster-care studies.   Investigators accustomed to studying intact biological human families need to be reminded of the power of cross-fostering studies in lower animals to differentiate (1) maternal responsiveness associated with hormonal factors at the termination of pregnancy (Rosenblatt, 1969); (2) effects of the mere presence of offspring; (3) strain differences in the stimulation afforded by offspring (Ressler, 1962); and (4) different aspects of the stimulation provided by the young, such as amount of motility (Rosenblatt, 1969). Furthermore, there are opportunities to pursue this approach at the human level while exercising statistical controls for some of the selective factors in adoption placement that plagued early studies carried out in the 1930s. For example, Rosenthal (1971) is studying genetic versus experiential contributors to schizophrenia in an adoption study in Denmark. This study utilizes family history data on both the adopted child and the adopting parents, made possible by the excellent national health and family records maintained in Denmark.

In the present context, the most important point is that adoption and foster-care situations have a scientific application other than to estimate the influence of genetic and experience factors—they can be used to separate effects of children and caregivers on each other. Yarrow (1963) carried out a study that took advantage of the fact that in several agencies infants who were candidates for adoption were routinely placed in foster homes soon after birth, where they remained for several months until they were placed for adoption. Since the foster care was temporary, it was less likely that the agencies would make efforts to match the infant and biological parents with foster parents. An infant was often merely assigned to the foster parents available to the agency at the time of the infant's birth. One foster mother may have three or four different infants within a year and may occasionally have two infants at the same time. It is possible to study the effects of several kinds of foster-care mothers on infants assigned to them by carrying out neonatal pretesting to establish pretest characteristics of infants and post-foster-care testing for effects of caregiving practices.

The foster-care approach can (1) preclude genetic mediators of any association found between parent and child behaviors, just as the adoption approach; (2) avoid selective placement procedures encountered in adoption studies; and (3) use the foster mother as her own control in studying the effect of different infants on her relationship with each. These are very valuable attributes of the approach.

Administrative problems involving agencies and families are difficult to overcome in foster care or adoption studies and are likely to be especially difficult in the case of the latter. It is not surprising that there have been so few studies of adoption. It is logically possible to overcome these problems and to carry out short-term studies of the early months of adoption or of some other short segment, but, as a practical matter, it seems unlikely that such studies will be carried out very often. Most adoption studies have been *ex post facto* in nature and simply utilize the child's status at a particular time to capture the results of several years of development. Thus, the important question for the adoption strategy is how well effects are isolated in the long-term study. In this case, the key problem is that of selective placement, which may produce an association between adoptive parents and the adoptee similar to the association between the biological parent and child. For example, if a social worker were successful in matching intelligence of biological and adopting parents, the genetic contribution of the biological parents could not be separately identified in a study of contributors to later intellectual development.

Without checks on possible selective factors the adoption approach could very well yield confusing data, but matching of cases in contrast groups, or statistical checks made possible by study of family histories in *ex post facto* studies, have made it possible to somewhat offset selective factors. If the checks are rigorous, as in Rosenthal's study (1971), the strategy is relatively unique in capability of separating effects accumulating over years of development. There are few other approaches that can lay any claims to isolating effects over a period of several years. There is also a possibility that adoption studies that are less subject to problems of selective placement may be possible in the future, because many agencies are placing less emphasis on matching biological and adoptive parents.

Comparison of Functional Pair Approaches

The teacher–child interaction approach can isolate both short- and long-term effects, because in many schools a teacher may be with her children for as long as a year. The foster-care approach is one of the most effective in isolating short-term effects, and can be considered intermediate in effectiveness relative to long-term interactions, considering the fact that developmental processes can be studied over a period of several months. In contrast, the adoption approach is rated as one of the least effective in isolating effects during short-term studies but most effective in long-term studies. The latter rating is given because in the case of the long-term studies it is likely that both the administrative problems involving agencies and families can be worked out, and the elaborate statistical checks on selective factors can be carried out. However, even with careful checks on selective placement in the adoption approach, and even though the foster-care approach is relatively free from the problems we would expect from a design not under the control of the experimenter, both of these "natural experiments" are labeled nonexperimental in Table 3, because the assignments are carried out by agencies rather than by the investigators and thus are not under experimental control.

All the approaches involving functional pairs are considered intermediate relative to generalization. The school setting utilized in the teacher–child interaction approach is an increasingly important area of socialization as the child grows older, but the criterion for generalization in this particular review is socialization within parent–child dyads. The processes that it might be possible to identify with this very flexible approach need to be checked further before assuming that they also exist in parent–child pairs. There are a number of reasons why generalization from adoption studies must be restricted. Adoptive mothers who subsequently have a baby of their own often comment on the difference between the two experiences. Adoptive parents are a special subgroup in that they have been selected by agency staff workers out of a larger sample of applicants for adoption. The commitment of the adopted parent to the adoptee may be greater than that of the average biological parent, for many of whom the decision to have a baby is less explicit. The motivation of adoptive parents is also seen in their efforts to overcome the usual legal and administrative problems. In all of these respects, adoptive parents are unusual. Adoptive and foster parents have in common the fact that they are most often selected by agency staff, but generalizations from foster-rearing is further limited by the short-term commitment. Thus, while both are rated intermediate with respect to generalization, the adoption study has a clear advantage over the foster-care study in this one respect.

With respect to range of behavior, the teacher–child interaction approach must be considered one of the most effective, because it places very few limits on the kinds of behavior that can be studied. The investigator can focus on minute aspects of behavior sequences, in contrast to the foster-care and adoption processes that are so molar in nature. In the latter, the independent variable being manipulated by placement of an infant or child is the complete set of characteristics of that child. Individuals as a whole, not traits or behaviors, are placed or fostered.

EXPERIMENTAL STRATEGIES

Studies of Biological Pairs

Drug studies.   By adding pre- and post-medication measures of parent–child interaction to double-blind placebo studies of the physiological effectiveness of drugs, an opportunity is available to isolate parent– or child–effects. Paxton (1971) took advantage of such an opportunity presented by a study of the effects of drugs on hyperactivity in children. The findings and problems encountered in carrying out the study can guide further efforts to incorporate a "piggyback" study of socialization in a project primarily designed to test drugs. First, it is important to consider that individual differences in physiology may result in only a subgroup of the treated cases reacting to the medication. In the case of Paxton's study, this meant that parent attitudes and self-report data could not be contrasted between the placebo and experimental groups, the latter being those for which the child received medication for hyperactivity. Thus an *ex post facto* analysis of the "reactors" versus the "nonreactors" is necessary, and the investigator must be prepared to have a substantially reduced sample available from the original contrast groups.

In the Paxton study, it was not administratively possible to arrange for direct observation of parent–child interaction before and after medication of the child, but an informal observation communicated to the present author may be of value in future drug studies if such measurements were possible. Paxton had the impression that the mother's behavior with the child may persist for some time due to her expectations based on past performance. Despite a change in the child's behavior that is very evident to the experimenter, the mother may show a period of disruption and reorganization before stabilizing at a new level. The observation schedule could easily result in negative or misleading results if not adjusted to the sequence of changes in maternal behavior, but with foreknowledge of the lag effect, an interesting phenomenon could be studied.

Brief parent–child separation.   The separation approach, discussed earlier, is not limited to absence of a parent for periods of weeks or months but can also be applied to very brief separations as in the studies by Gardner and Pease (1958) and Ainsworth and Bell (1970). In the latter studies, the parent is merely asked to leave the room briefly while the effects on the child's behavior are noted. In effect, parent behavior is changed by the instructional technique of the investigator. This brief separation also involves separation of the child from the mother, but it is interesting that studies of the effect on the mother could not be located in the research literature. There are many other occasions, such as pediatric examinations, when the infants are removed from their mothers' arms, that would permit observation of maternal reactions.

Altering perception.   One example of an experimental manipulation of behavior in natural pairs can be seen in a study by Hilton (1967). Following a brief period in which mothers of 4-year-olds observed their children doing puzzles, half of the mothers were led to believe that their child had not done as well as the other children; then all were observed in a repetition of the initial situation with the child working on puzzles. In a final situation, all children had a success experience. Mothers of firstborns and only children were more extreme than mothers of children from other birth orders in (1) the provision of support when the child succeeded; and (2) withdrawal of the support when the child was represented to her as failing. The research design followed that of the classic study by Merrill (1946).

The Hilton and Merrill studies primarily tested the effects on the mother of altered perceptions of the child's behavior in the laboratory. There is no logical reason why the design could not be reversed and the children be led to expect altered behavior from parents, although it has not been possible to locate any examples of such a study. Further, the procedures could be carried out in the home in order to improve ecological validity if circumstances in the home made the control of environmental circumstances possible. Hypothetically, this general strategy would make it possible to test the effects of each member of a parent–child pair on the other without the necessity of actually altering the overt behavior of either. There is a definite advantage in one respect over experimental studies with stranger pairs, because the effects of "ownness" may be missing in the latter.

To be successful, it is necessary that the altered perception approach obtain differences in behavior despite the fact that the instructions may run counter to the past experience of the mother or child with each other. When differences are obtained, however, it is clear that one has identified the direction of effects, because the children or parents are assigned to experimental groups at random or on the basis of some matching variable. The fact that a perception is being altered rather than a directly observable behavior (as in strategies to be discussed below) should not be considered an especially damaging drawback, because even effects of alterations in behavior must be mediated through perception.

Altering behavior.   In the nursery strategy discussed earlier in the chapter, the experimenter capitalizes on the occurrence of variation within infant behavior recorded before interaction with the mother. It is possible to translate this into an experimental approach by manipulating the infant's state with mild stimulation of the kind frequently but not systematically provided by nurses while bringing infants to the mothers for feeding. The infant may be used as its own control by inducing variations in such states as quiet–attentive versus fussing behavior, according to the experimental design. In case the infant is not used as its own control, mother–infant pairs should be assigned to different experimental treatment groups on a random basis or by matching in order to remove as a possible contributor to experimental differences even the minimal experience that the mother has had with her infant in the first few postnatal days. If these requirements are met, and if variation in the infant's state is systematically associated with alterations in maternal behavior, an infant effect on the mother would be demonstrated.

Gewirtz and Boyd (1976) have been exploring the possibility of using a contrived experimental interaction procedure with biological pairs to demonstrate conditioning of the mother's talking and smiling to her infant. The pair are separated by a screen. The mother perceives the infant as emitting vocalizations and as orienting toward her (head turning), although the information that these events have occurred is supplied by the experimenter contingent on the mother's behavior. Reliable conditioning of maternal talking and smiling to her infant has been achieved in six pairs. Mothers are apparently unaware of the contingency or of the fact that learning has occurred.

Two studies illustrate applications of the general strategy (not conditioning of parents) in older children. In a study by Rosen and D'Andrade (1959), parents of 10-year-old boys were studied in structured situations in which they could observe differences in problem solving efforts of their children. Parents of boys who were high achievers encouraged their sons more and interfered less than parents of low achievers in the very difficult tasks that had been selected so as to make most children struggle. Osofsky and O'Connell (1972) used a similar approach but with the specific objective of manipulating child behaviors (by giving difficult puzzles and telling children in advance to ask for or not ask for help) so as to demonstrate an effect of the manipulation on the parents. They found that fathers and mothers controlled more and physically and verbally interacted more when children acted dependent.

Returning to the nursery studies, the mother's behavior rather than the infant's could be manipulated by providing direct instruction as to what she should do or by influencing her attitudes and then noting the effect on the infant. The range of behavior that can be studied would be limited by the neonate's repertoire and by the ethics of influencing maternal behavior during this early, possibly very formative period. However, if we consider the application of this approach to parents with older children, it immediately becomes apparent that this is a highly promising line of study, having all the advantages of generalization inherent in the use of parent–child pairs, at the same time permitting experimental manipulation of the behavior of one participant. One only needs to think of all the studies of socialization that have been done by experimenters with children that could have been carried out using the parent as the experimenter. Of course, to offset the advantage of having parents functioning with their own children, there would be some loss in precision and uniformity of the experimental variable due to differences in the ability of parents to carry out instructions.

Studies of attachment behavior in young infants and preschoolers have quite often used the mother as an experimenter. For example, the mother is asked to go to a certain area of the room and remain quiet. The experimenter then notes how far the infant will crawl from her when attracted by novel toys. Mothers have been used to carry out a wide variety of experimental instructions with apparent success, as in the studies of Maccoby and Feldman (1972) and Coates, Anderson, and Hartup (1972). Another line of current research that uses this approach is exemplified in the behavior modification studies carried out in family settings by Patterson and Cobb (1973); parents are instructed to obtain pre- and post-baseline behavior data on child behavior problems, as well as carry out the intervening operant conditioning techniques intended to reduce the frequency of the behavior. The procedures may even be carried out over a period of several months.

Comparison of Biological Pair Approaches

With one exception, these experimental strategies are highly effective in isolating short-term effects. Administration of a drug can serve as an experimental manipulation in a short-term study, but that approach is only intermediate in effectiveness because of the variability of individual responses to drugs. Although drugs may alter behaviors that cannot easily be affected otherwise, behavior modification techniques or instructions to subjects are generally more efficient. None of the approaches are particularly effective in isolating long-term effects. Drugs are administered to some individuals for many years, but the effects could be difficult to identify after an initial reaction. Nor would it be easy to locate untreated clinical cases for a control group in a long-term study. The approach involving altering behavior could be used in studies going beyond the brief laboratory manipulations and even over a relatively long time within a family unit in the home, but it is certainly not as well adapted to the study of long-term effects as many of the other approaches already discussed.

It is particularly fortunate that three of the four approaches that we have been considering under this heading are highly effective in isolating short-term effects, as well as having clear advantages relative to generalization. Practically any sample can be used that is accessible to study. In the case of drug studies, of course, generalization is limited more than any other approach because of the very special samples required—populations with physiological or behavioral disorders.

It is also particularly fortunate that two of the research approaches that are highly effective in isolating short-term effects and that place few limits on generalization, make a wide range of behaviors accessible to study. These are the approaches involving altering perception and behavior. Of the four approaches, brief separation most limits the range of behavior that is studied. Although considerable variation could be introduced in how the absence of a participant comes about, the independent variable is basically gross in nature as it involves only the presence or absence of a person.

Studies of Functional Pairs

Family-like systems.   Some studies of functional pairs deserve separate identification, because the subjects are in settings that provide some of the emotional support and continued contact with adult figures present in family units. Bandura, Ross, and Ross (1963) introduced experimenters who, acting in parental roles, controlled or did not control access to food or toy resources. They found that children imitated the experimental "parents" who controlled resources. This experiment effectively isolated the effects of the experimenters on children, because the children were assigned at random to experimental groups receiving different treatment. Another example of a study in the same vein is that of Yarrow et al. (1971) to which we have already referred; in one phase of this study, the adult caregivers played high and low nurturant roles in a nursery school setting.

To extend the approach used by Bandura and colleagues to caregivers and teachers in the usual child-care situations, it would be advantageous to have male and female caregivers, as in some preschool studies (Waldrop, Pedersen, & Bell, 1968), or to introduce experimenters into the caregiving system for a sufficient period that the children would be accustomed to them prior to the enactment of experimental roles.

In the research of Etzel and Gewirtz (1967), there is a remarkable example of the opposite research approach, manipulating the functioning of infants so as to affect the behavior of adults acting as parents in a caregiving setting. They experimentally modified the behavior of infants in a nursery by conditioning. The resultant alteration of the infants' responses changed the behavior of their caretakers. Nurses who previously spent little time with an infant interacted considerably more after experimental procedures (carried out in a separate room) had extinguished crying and reinforced eye contact and smiling. Unlike other studies that we have discussed in which manipulations of behavior and subsequent effects occurred in close temporal proximity, the conditioning procedure in this case required several days, and the effects were detected several days later. It was not possible to locate any examples of this approach carried out with children.

Because the general strategy discussed in this section can be carried out in day-care, nursery school, and other caregiving settings, the studies could be extended over considerable time periods, even if not for the several years involved in some longitudinal studies.

Contrived participants.   In contrast to the previous approach, other studies of functional pairs retain only certain elements ordinarily found in parent–child interaction. Osofsky (1971) trained four 10- to 12-year-old children to ask for help, be independent, or to be uncooperative in several tasks involving object assembly, picture arrangement, and block design tasks, while being supervised by women who themselves had one daughter in the same age range. There was no effort to make mothers feel ''parental'' responsibility for children assigned to them. The independent variable was created by differences in the roles of the children, the dependent variable being the behavior of the adult women in response to the role-playing of the children. The findings were novel but too complex to summarize here. The role-playing strategy has also been used (Bates, 1975) to show that college undergraduates who were attempting to teach basketball maneuvers or mathematical principles evaluated their pupils more positively and showed more positive verbal and nonverbal responses when the 11- to 13-year-old confederates of the experimenter imitated them, showed face-to-face observation, and smiled frequently.

Although classroom behavior lies outside the realm of this text, it is worth noting that in some respects the relation of a teacher to the class is similar to the relation of parents to children. Jenkins and Deno (1969) used the role-playing of student confederates as an independent variable, obtaining striking effects on behavior and self-evaluations of teacher trainees.

It could be expected that sooner or later some investigator would realize that, strictly speaking, it is not necessary to actually use a child in an interaction situation in order to induce parent-like behavior from an adult. Berberich (1971) observed seven adult women who were led to believe that they were teaching a child a marble-sorting task. Trial-to-trial feedback from the experimenter to the adult concerning correct performance had the effect of controlling the adult's motor behavior and use of tangible reinforcers, verbal rewards, and punishments. The adults were only introduced to a child at the end of the experiment.

In the Berberich and Osofsky studies, the independent variable consisted of variations in actual or perceived child behavior. This same approach could be used with experimental manipulation of parent behavior constituting the independent variable and variations in child behavior constituting the dependent variable.

Variations in behavior produced by sample selection.   Siegel (1963) has summarized a series of studies that illustrate the possibility of creating variation in child behavior as an independent variable by selecting children from groups known to differ in behavior, then placing individuals from these groups in interaction situations with adults with whom they have had no previous contact. Siegel's studies involved retardates in the age range of 10–15 years of age, who were classified into high- and low-verbal ability groups. It was found that adults who had been asked to assist children in learning how to assemble a puzzle responded more frequently but more briefly and more redundantly to low-verbal children.

In trying to determine whether parents of schizophrenic children provide ambiguous communications, Haley (1968) found that there was no difference between two groups of normal children in accuracy of arranging picture theme cards—one group having listened to tape recorded instructions that parents of schizophrenics had given to their own children in a previous study, the other having listened to tape recorded instructions from normal parents who were strangers to them. Haley studied the effects of variations in parent behavior in the form of tape recordings in order to detect the effect on children, and Siegel studied the effects of variations in child behavior by selecting children from different samples and observing the effect on adult behavior. The sample selection strategy, just as the role-playing approach to creating variation in child behavior, has also been used successfully in producing effects of students on teachers (Rathbone, 1971).

Comparison of Functional Pair Approaches

Isolation of effects. The three approaches that have been considered in this section are highly effective in isolating short-term effects, and at least one, the manipulation of behavior in family-like settings, could be considered intermediate in isolating long-term effects. As in the case of intervention research with infants and children from disadvantaged homes, effects of experimental treatments might become obscure over long time periods; the strategy could otherwise be considered more effective in isolating long-term effects.

Generalization. The manipulation of behavior in family-like settings also has advantages over the other two functional pair approaches, as far as generalization is concerned. The two illustrative studies that were discussed were created in a supportive, stable environment to which the infants, children, and caregivers were accustomed to each other. For this reason, and because the research could be carried out on many kinds of populations, the approach was rated intermediate in Table 3.

Generalization to parent–child functioning in the home appears to be least defensible in the case of the studies involving contrived participation and sample selection. These laboratory studies use deviant children or adults or focus on the interactions of adults and children who are strangers to each other. There is certainly a basis for caution in attempting to generalize from laboratory studies, because Schalock (1956) has shown that some categories of mother–child interaction show quite different frequencies in home versus laboratory observation, even in child–parent pairs.

Leik (1963) has reported his own and other findings indicating qualitatively different results from group dynamics studies that used groups of strangers versus those that used families. Leik placed members of mother–father–daughter triads in nonfamily groups (three mothers, three fathers, three daughters), pseudo-family groups (mother, father, and daughter, all from different families), and in own-family groups. All groups interacted in order to reach a concensus on various issues related to family patterns or goals. Instrumental, emotional, and task satisfaction measures were obtained from a modification of the Bales' observation system. Agreement between members was negatively correlated with emotionality and positively correlated with instrumentality in the own-family groups. In the other two groups, agreement was positively correlated with emotionally and unrelated with instrumentality.

Leik based his conclusions on interactions within families having college-age children. Three studies of younger children have compared results from stranger– and parent–child pairs. Stevenson, Keen, and Knights (1963) found that 3–5-year-olds showed higher baselines and greater increments in response to urging in the "marble-in-the-hole" task when strangers instead of parents served as experimenters. Halverson and Waldrop (1970) found some evidence of maternal consistency with own and other children but found considerable evidence of differences. Mothers used more positive, encouraging statements with other preschoolers, more negative sanctions with their own, when supervising the performance of various tasks. In a similar study of nursery school children, Landauer, Carlsmith, and Lepper (1970) found that most children were less obedient to their mothers, and they speculated that children adopt conservative strategies in response to strangers, with whom they are unsure of consequences.

The degree of "strangeness" of the experimenter affects the behavior of children even a week after an experiment (McCoy & Zigler, 1965). Rosenthal (1966) has reported data indicating that within the range of 3–5 years of age, the degree of anxiety produced by exposure to an experimental situation will differentially affect the ability of older versus younger children to relate to a stranger. In short, in the case of young children, the latter studies support Leik's conclusion drawn from college-age students. These studies also lead to a more complex and difficult implication relative to studies using strangers as experimenters: some results may generalize to familiar pairs, others may not, and the age of the child must be considered. It is clear that an investigator using a study of strangers must provide empirical support for any efforts to generalize a particular set of results to individuals who are familiar with each other. The issue in this context is familiarity, not whether there is a genetic relationship between participants as in a biological family unit. An adopted child and parents are familiar with each other although not a biological family.

A second ground for concern about generalizations on studies using the sample selection approach stems from the fact that deviant child and parent groups were used as a source of behavior variation. We do not know that variation in verbal behavior within the normal range, as opposed to that in retarded children, would induce the effects found by Siegel (1963). On the other hand, Haley (1968) reported no significant or substantial difference in accuracy of card-arranging between normal children who listened to tape recordings from schizophrenic parents and normal children who listened to tape-recorded instructions by normal parents who were strangers to the children. In this particular case, the reaction to the strange adult appeared to be paramount, the instructions of the deviant parent being nondifferentiating.

While there are many reasons to question generalization from the three approaches involving functional pairs, the ratings in Table 3 remind us that these approaches show a unique pattern of advantages with respect to isolation of short-term effects and flexibility. In the approach involving family-like settings, practically any kind of variation in adult behavior toward children, or interrelation between adult figures who are performing parent-type roles, can be created to serve as an independent variable within the limits set by possible adverse effects on the children. In the case of contrived participants, the range of parent and child variables that can be studied is only limited by the ability of role players, by the reality of "participants" whose nature is revealed primarily through experimental events, or by the ability of the experimenter to develop instructions that effectively substitute perceptions in one participant for directly observable behaviors in the other. The range of behavior that can be studied by sample selection is limited by the ability of the investigators to locate groups of children or adults whose behavior differs sufficiently to create experimental effects.

OTHER CRITERIA FOR COMPARISON

The problem of labeling. Table 3 does not contain comparisons on three other criteria that are of less general importance but that are particularly important with respect to certain strategies. The first of these criteria concerns labeling and expectancies. The question is whether participants are reacting on the basis of labels or to the actual ongoing behavior of the other individual.

Rubin, Provenzano, and Luria (1974) have reported results from "nature's first projective technique." Before they had anything more than minimal contact with their first newborns, mothers described male infants as cuddlier. Fathers described females as cuddlier and were also more extreme than mothers in attributing to females such characteristics as softness, finer features, less coordination, less attentiveness, weakness, and fragility, despite objective evidence of similarities in the two sex groups in birth condition and physical characteristics.

Two research approaches have been presented already that deliberately alter perceptions so as to test effects of a label. Garbarino (cited in Bronfenbrenner, 1971) has proposed temporarily giving female infants male names, and vice-versa, presumably in day-care and other institutional settings, to test for differences in reaction of volunteer caregivers on the basis of actual versus attributed sex differences. There is a similarity to the studies by Hilton (1967) and Merrill (1946) except that the latter labeled behaviors rather than persons. Garbarino's approach should produce some interesting data by pitting stereotypes against actual behavior, as well as by testing the combined effects of real differences in behavior acting in the same direction as a stereotype.

As an uncontrolled variable, labeling is a possible source of error in many studies. Haley was concerned about the problem of labeling in his studies. One contributor to deviant behavior often reported in the parents of schizophrenics might have been the fact that they knew their behavior was being studied because of the deviance of their child. Another example is the strategy that uses behavior linked to congenital defects as a means of isolating effects of children on parents. Parents may be reacting to a diagnosis communicated to them rather than to behavior shown by the child.

However, Guskin (1963) has shown that judgments relative to abnormality made by college students viewing films of children are affected only when the child presents cues to support the labeling process. One of Siegel's studies, in the series to which we have already referred, labeled children of the same level of ability as "high" or "low" verbal. The labeling did not affect the verbal behavior of adults interacting with the children. Rosenthal, Baratz, and Hall (1974) found improved intellectual performance in only one of several grade levels to whose teachers they identified randomly selected children as likely to gain in creativity during the school year. They also reported that significant effects of such experimentally created teacher expectancies had appeared in only about one-third of the studies they reviewed. In fact, one of the most interesting new developments in this very active research area of education involves the fact that experimental alteration of the child's expectancies relative to his own achievements had a greater effect in one study (Rappaport & Rappaport, 1975) than experimental alteration of the teacher's expectancy relative to the child. Apparently, teachers forget experimental interventions, but a real change in child behavior has a persistent effect.

Continuity with past experience.   Due to experimental manipulations in some research strategies, the behavior of a child or parent is made to appear quite different from what has occurred in the past history of interaction. The effect of the experimental manipulation could be due to the sudden change or violation of expectancies based on the past history, as has been mentioned in connection with drug studies. One effect of a sudden change of behavior in one participant is that the other participant may not respond to the new behavior until the surprise effect has worn off. The nursery studies would be relatively free of problems, in this respect, because the mothers would have had so little prior experience with their infants. On the other hand, some of the studies involving altered perception or behavior in natural pairs are vulnerable to the effects of discontinuities. In Hilton's study, differences between mothers who were told that their child had or had not done well in puzzle-solving may have been attenuated by the fact that the instructions ran counter to past experiences of some of the mothers with their child. In studies of attachment, mothers have followed instructions from the experimenter to increase their distance from the child or to remain passive and uncommunicative in a certain area while their children explored the room. Some children may have reacted more to the fact that this was unusual behavior for their mother than they reacted to the intended experimental situation. In such studies, differences between treatment groups are obtained in spite of rather than because of the problem of discontinuity. When differences are obtained, it is clear that the effect has been isolated. Of course, this latter conclusion assumes adequate experimental designs (e.g., mother–child pairs used as their own controls, or pairs assigned to experimental groups at random or on the basis of some matching variable.)

Practical problems. We would ordinarily consider the use of research strategies that allowed influences to be isolated, permitted broad generalizations from the findings, and were flexible relative to the kinds of behavior that could be studied. However, as a practical matter, some studies require complex administrative and institutional arrangements, whereas others can be carried out by any investigator who has access to adult and child subjects (altering perception or behavior, contrived participants, manipulation by sample selection). Adoption, foster care, and drug and nursery studies all require that the investigator work out complex arrangements with institutions, some of which have not accommodated research efforts readily in the past. The adoption and foster-care approaches require the full cooperation of the agencies and many difficult arrangements that make the behavior of the infants and parents accessible to study. Because of the sensitivity of the problems with which they are concerned, it is understandable that adoption agencies place restrictions on research efforts, even though this makes it difficult to utilize this otherwise fine research opportunity. It should be noted, however, that the foster-care approach requires less modification of agency procedures and thus is much more likely to be feasible.

Drug studies require considerable care in working out administrative arrangements, but investigators are often likely to be welcomed by medical staff planning the project because of the supplementary psychological measures that will be provided. The administrative arrangements with hospitals and clinics involved may not be as difficult as working with adoption agencies.

Ethical problems. This review has not attempted to discuss the problems of ethics involved in each research approach, because the issues depend in so many cases on the specific application of the approach. However, most applications of some approaches are more likely to raise problems relative to the protection of subjects. In these approaches, it is important to consider whether the benefit to the participant and society justifies the risk in a study of the direction of effects. Most of the nonexperimental approaches involve no physical risk, minimal emotional stress, and little likelihood that the status of the participants would be jeopardized. These studies usually merely add an observation or measurement system to an "experiment in nature" that is already under way and will continue whether the research is carried out or not. The investigator must merely observe the usual precautions relative to informed consent, inducements to participation, and confidentiality of records. In the case of adoption and foster-care studies, the investigator would, in addition, have to observe agency regulations concerning protection of identity of biological and adoptive parents because of the sensitive nature of this information. From the standpoint of ethical problems, even one of the experimental approaches could be considered along with the nonexperimental. If a drug study can itself be justified on medical and psychological grounds, the addition of a "piggyback" design should entail little increase in risk.

Ethical problems become more difficult in the case of experimental strategies that involve altering the behavior of the participants or exposing subjects to unusual interactions with strangers. In this context, we can only bring up these problems and some of the pertinent issues. It is not possible to provide resolutions. For example, research that brings children into interaction with strangers may cause little concern if the nature of the interactions are in line with family and subcultural norms or with generally accepted child-rearing practices. By way of contrast, if the parents would not want their children to model behavior shown by an adult in an experiment, the investigator would have to give more than the usual attention to the question of whether the research is necessary.

Depending on the age of the children, some might argue that the problems of protecting subjects are much less acute when children interact with adults that are strangers to them than when they interact with their own parents. It could be argued that during some phases of development (periods of intense attachment, for example), the experimental production of parent behavior that appears unpredictable and confusing to a child could have many more adverse effects than similar interactions with a stranger because of the need for basic trust in the continuing relationship with a parent. A possible counter-argument: other strange adults that a child would encounter in the normal course of events would not undo the negative effects of interactions occurring in an experiment. Parents on the other hand, following the end of the experimental procedure, would restore equilibrium by again acting in their usual fashion and restoring the child's confidence.

However the above issues may be resolved in a particular application, the reader needs to be reminded that research designs have been presented in this chapter in skeleton form—only the elements necessary to the isolation of effects are included. Because it would have been too cumbersome to discuss ethical problems of each approach, the investigator must add these considerations to the scientific issues that have been raised in this chapter. If it appears that the research is needed and that the gains to the participants and society outweigh possible negative effects, the investigator should supplement the "bare bones" designs we have described with features that would make the experiment enjoyable and positive in nature for the child, parent, or other participants. Note that Hilton (1967) incorporated a success experience for the mother–child pairs in her study of altered maternal perceptions of the child. Features should also be added to the designs that would make it possible to detect adverse effects, as in a debriefing period.

To protect subjects in socialization studies, pilot work must be directed not only to the question of whether the research is likely to yield useful information relative to an hypothesis, but also to the question of whether adverse effects to the subjects have been adequately anticipated. It is worth commenting that investigators could contact others who have carried out studies of the same kind to get information on the impact of experimental interventions on participants. We would do well to utilize as fully as possible the experience of past investigations.

ORDER OF APPROACHES WITHIN EACH CRITERION

Isolation of effects in short-term studies. Eleven approaches can be seen in Table 3 that clearly isolate effects in short-term studies. Four are ranked intermediate, because the independent variable is manipulated indirectly (e.g., the drug and physiological disorders approaches) or because they take advantage of natural experiments that may introduce some form of bias (e.g., sustained separation and nursery approaches). Two are least effective, because they cannot be readily adapted to studying short-term behavior changes (congenital defects; adoption studies).

Isolation of effects in long-term studies. Of the 11 strategies that are most effective in short-term studies, 2 are also most effective in long-term studies—twin and teacher–child interaction studies. Of the strategies that are most effective in short-term studies, 4 are intermediate in effectiveness in long-term studies. It may only be possible to identify event sequences, not separate parent- or child–effects in long-term follow-up studies. Effects may be isolated well in short-term studies of foster-care, altering behavior, or manipulations in family-like settings, but may be more obscure as the study is extended over a few months. Of the 11 strategies that are most effective in short-term studies, 5 are least effective, difficult, or inapplicable to long-term phenomena (study of interaction sequences, brief separation, altering perception, contrived participants, manipulation by sample selection).

Generalization.   Six lines of investigation clearly place few restrictions on the investigator's generalization to other samples (nursery studies, longitudinal studies; study of interaction sequences, brief separation, altering perception, and altering behavior). These can utilize practically any sample of parent–child pairs available for research. There are many studies that are intermediate in limits placed on generalization, because they (1) use children or caregivers in family-like settings; (2) use parent–child pairs that are in some cases subject to sample bias (congenital defects, sustained separation); (3) use functional pairs that serve in many respects as parent–child pairs (adoption, foster care); or (4) use parent–child pairs that are, nonetheless, a special subsample of the general population (twin studies). The four approaches that limit generalization the most and are thus ranked least effective on this criterion, either use samples in which there is a definite likelihood of bias (physiological disorders, drug studies) or use stranger pairs (contrived participants, manipulation by sample selection).

Range of behavior.   Five experimental and three nonexperimental approaches (longitudinal studies, studies of interaction sequences, teacher–child interaction) leave the investigator free to identify either very specific or molar independent variables. By way of contrast, there are six approaches that limit the investigator to independent variables consisting of entire clusters of behavior (congenital defects), to variables as gross as "inheritance" (twin studies), or to manipulating an entire individual (separation studies, adoption studies, foster-care studies).

GENERAL COMPARISONS

First, relative to criteria, it can be seen from Table 3 that there is a tendency for strategies that are highly effective in isolating effects in short-term studies to be among the least effective in isolating long-term effects. Twin studies are the most important of the exceptions to this tendency, because effects lasting over several years may be studied as well as those lasting a few minutes in an ongoing interaction situation. Also, there is a tendency for strategies that are highly effective in isolating effects in short-term studies to be unlimited in the range of variables that can be manipulated. There are exceptions to even these two interrelations between classification criteria, and thus the criteria of Table 3 are not interrelated sufficiently to permit a reduction to a smaller number.

Turning now to the classification of strategies, it should be observed that the separation of child– and parent–effects is not the exclusive property of experimental studies. In fact, several nonexperimental strategies separate effects by taking advantage of natural experiments or situations in society that can be utilized for experimental purposes. Further, one type of study that is highly effective is not experimental in the usual sense at all—manipulation by sample selection. Further, it is evident that the restriction of research efforts to the studies classified as experimental by the liberal criteria of this text would leave many important issues of long-term developmental processes untouched. Thus, while it is necessary for progress in socialization research that we move beyond one kind of nonexperimental approach (correlations between parent and child characteristics at a single time), it does not follow that the answer lies in an exclusive emphasis on an experimental approach in which the investigator manipulates or controls all variables.

The last general conclusion gains support when attention is directed to the two criteria other than effectiveness in isolating parent and child influences. Two of the three experimental approaches using functional pairs pose definite problems for an investigator wishing to generalize to parent–child pairs. It is not sufficient to have achieved a clear separation of effects if the findings are not applicable to socialization within parent–child pairs. Studies using stranger pairs require additional investigation designed specifically to show that generalization to parent–child pairs is justifiable.

Clinical studies. It is noteworthy that very few clinicians were among the investigators (see Chapter 4) who first began calling for more attention to child–effects (a notable exception is Erikson, 1950). There is nothing inherent in the clinical study of a family or parent–child pair that makes the difference between child– and parent–effects more visible. However, events may occur in the course of treatment, such as physiological disorders, separations, or drug treatment. Sequences of interactions may be observed. A clinician may also intervene directly to alter perceptions or behavior of participants. Providing the clinician has an adequate record of behavior in parent or child before, during, and after the events, some useful leads may be obtained relative to the direction of influences. More firm statements could not be made from the data unless the usual precautions of formal research were observed, such as independence of recording of independent and dependent variables, and, even in such a case, findings could be specific to the single pair or family being studied.

Need for patterns of research approaches. Because of the difficulty of replicating results with different types of measurements in different samples and settings, it is not too surprising that a single developmental study is seldom decisive in supporting a theory. In most instances, it is necessary to infer the direction of findings from common results in a number of studies. Because, in any event, most investigators will need to carry out a series of studies in order to establish a convincing trend of empirical results, it may be fruitful to adopt a cost–benefit attitude toward selecting different kinds of studies. An investigator would be well advised to select strategies from Table 3 that have differing patterns of advantages and disadvantages. For example, there should be an advantage in terms of ability to generalize, in combining any of the experimental studies of functional units with studies involving altering behavior in parent–child pairs. If a common line of findings can be developed across two or more of these research approaches, there would be considerable gain in credibility. Similarly, for research programs that could undertake more complicated studies, it would be advantageous to pursue adoption or twin studies along with studies that involve the manipulation of family-like systems. The inability of the latter strategy to develop propositions concerning etiology and life history would be offset by the capabilities of the adoption and twin studies. In other words, investigators pursuing a series of studies should select strategies with advantages and disadvantages that are complementary. It is evident from the large number of approaches available that the experimental and nonexperimental investigator, the student pursuing a series of limited objective studies, and a director of research programs, all can select combinations that will be of more value to the understanding of development than a single approach.

Patterns or combinations of research approaches that cut across customary research orientations (experimental–nonexperimental, natural–artificial, molar–specific) are most likely to comprise a flexible research program that can explore different issues, separate effects clearly, and bring forth findings with general value. However, it is worth noting that altering the behavior of one or the other participant in parent–child units is not only among the most effective approaches for three of the four criteria of Table 3, but can also be accomplished very readily by investigators who have limited means and objectives. More specifically, attention should be drawn to the possibilities inherent in one experimental approach under this rubric that involves the use of the parent rather than the experimenter to carry out manipulations intended to affect child behavior. More frequent use of this approach could increase generalization beyond the laboratory.

CONTINUATION OF INCONCLUSIVE RESEARCH

This chapter has drawn attention to some logical possibilities for improving research on socialization in the family. It has been pointed out that there are many research approaches that can isolate parent– and child–effects better than those most commonly used. However, the gap between logical possibilities and actualities can be illustrated by examining research collated in chapters on socialization in the recent Mussen edition of *Carmichael's Manual of Child Psychology* (Mischel, Maccoby & Masters, Feshbach, Hoffman; 1970). Correlational studies are by far the most frequently cited in sections on child-rearing practices in these chapters. There are a small number of experimental studies cited, but most of these involve interaction of children with experimenters who are strangers to them. With respect to the correlational studies, most authors of these review chapters clearly express the need for caution in interpreting the direction of effects. Some authors go beyond cautions and offer specific alternatives to the usual interpretation of a correlational study as indicating an effect of parents on children (Feshbach, 1970, p. 217; Maccoby & Masters, 1970, p. 141). Nonetheless, the amount of space devoted to interpretation in terms of the effects of children on parents is very small compared to the total interpretive space, considering that most studies cited in these sections on parental practices and influences are correlational.

The authors of the review chapters point to a number of methodological and design problems such as (1) the failure to get at the specific contingencies in parent and child interaction; (2) past reliance on retrospective interviews with parents for information on both parent and child behavior; (3) poor differentiation of the components of large classes of behavior such as dependency and aggression; and (4) unrepresentative samples. It is not recognized that most of these problems could be solved in future research, and it would still not be possible to draw conclusions relative to direction of effects if the customary correlational approach is used. The most basic and fundamental defect of past correlational studies is that they do not provide a sensible basis for sorting out the direction of effects. There is very little support in these reviews for any hopes that the defects in correlational studies may be offset by convergence with findings from experimental studies. Thus, in several major areas of research on socialization within the family that have seen intense research activity in recent years, data from correlational studies in which the direction of effects is not clear is being supplemented with noncomparable experimental findings in which the direction of effects is clear, but generalization to socialization within the parent–child unit is tenuous. The methodological recommendations offered by reviewers, if followed, would leave these two basic problems unaltered.

SUMMARY

Seventeen research strategies have been described that offer greater capability of isolating parent– and child–effects than the one which has been used most frequently in studies of socialization within the family (a nonexperimental study of the association of parent and child characteristics at a single time). While it is necessary for progress in socialization research that investigators move beyond correlational studies, it does not follow that the best alternative is an experimental study involving children and experimenters who are strangers to each other. The capability of a research strategy for isolating parent– and child–effects is by no means limited to such experimental studies. A "cost–benefit" attitude toward selection of research strategies is advocated, with particular attention to the combined use of approaches that have complementary advantages and disadvantages.

Two experimental approaches that have not been used frequently up to the present, and yet can be carried out readily with the resources available to most investigators, permit isolation of effects in ongoing interaction situations, make it possible to study a wide range of behaviors, and place few limits on the ability to generalize from findings.

ACKNOWLEDGMENT

The author is indebted to James M. Weifenbach for many very helpful comments and criticisms of a draft of this chapter.

6

Human Infant—Effects in the First Year

Richard Q. Bell

INTRODUCTION

In Chapter 4 we discussed some of the major hypotheses of socialization research, the few well-agreed-upon findings on which they were based, and alternative explanations in terms of the effects of children on parents. In the course of developing these explanations, the rudiments of a theory emerged, primarily in the context of empirical research involving relations of child and parent characteristics at a single time. The necessity of explaining nondevelopmental data set a limit on the quality of the hypotheses that could be developed, although many explanations that were offered had developmental implications. Chapter 5 then attempted to demonstrate research strategies that could be used to generate data on which more adequate theories could be built. If the reader is no longer content with existing theories of socialization, nor with the very limited research strategies that have been used to generate data, then what is needed next are the ideas to spark a new line of research—hopefully an empirical effort that will fill in the void left by four decades of almost exclusive attention to the effects of parents on children.

This chapter will concentrate on ideas about how infants can affect parents. Because the socialization system has its beginnings in the early months of life, and because it undergoes dramatic changes within the first year, it is appropriate to concentrate the theoretical undertaking on this period. Ultimately, the theory should then be expanded into a more complete explanatory structure that would accommodate the role of both parents and infants in this, the formative period of the socialization system. A previous review (Bell, 1974) of the many ways in which the effects of the young may be shown in early human development will be extended and brought up to date. Since that review, some additional data have been reported that will assist the effort considerably. It has been possible to align the conceptual elements more adequately and to introduce general propositions that strengthen the explanatory system. The studies to be reported indicate a strong surge of interest and a promise of an increasingly vigorous research effort on infant–effects, but there is still insufficient data to support a rigorous theory. In the absence of any extensive corpus of relevant data, much of the material to follow must still, of necessity, be quite speculative. The theory is still in the process of being developed from an expositional to an integrated structure.

MAJOR CHANGES IN THE FIRST YEAR

One often hears parents say, "I don't know what's happened, but my baby has changed quite a bit." During many phases of development, an infant's behavior alters the general nature of the relationship rather than simply providing stimuli that are important fuel for the interaction. For example, the onset of sitting up, crawling, standing up, and other motor behaviors, alters the basis on which the entire system is functioning. Because of the change in the infant, the system shifts from predictable interchange to a new and initially unpredictable level and then slowly stabilizes and emerges again as a predictable system (Sander, 1974). Evidence for the infant's contribution to this restructuring can be found in studies such as that of Lusk and Lewis (1972) in which it was found that patterns of caregiver interaction showed the strongest correlation with the age of the infant, in contrast with correlations involving characteristics of the parents and of the family as a whole. Korner (1974) and Sander (1974) have also supported the position that the caregivers' behavior is substantially determined by the infants' ontogenetic level of development. Changes in the infant often come about rapidly, within 1 month or 2 weeks, but in other cases, the shift in the nature of the system induced by these changes is a very gradual one that can only be seen from the perspective of the entire first year.

From activity to reactivity.   Much of neonatal behavior—the crying, mass movements, and recurrent startles during sleep—appears to arise from endogenous stimuli. Livingston (1967) has pointed out that from the standpoint of neuroanatomical development, infants are organized for activity before they become organized for reactivity. Early in the first year, the mother is acted upon by the infant, whose behavior plays a strong role in inducing caregiving and social interaction, as well as differentiating these modes of interaction. Toward the end of the first year, the infant's behavior has become highly reactive in many complex ways. This change does not occur in all areas in a single month but accrues steadily in each of the domains of development at different times. By this time, the mother has acquired the capability of managing the infant and influencing its behavior, so that to a much greater extent their interaction is reciprocal in nature.

From preformed organization to malleability.   Although it appears possible as a technical feat to demonstrate transitory conditioning in a few areas in the neonate, the normal neonate appears in general to be "all wound up" so as to run through a rather inflexible cycle of sleeping, waking, and feeding. There is considerable evidence for an initial underlying organization of behaviors associated with this cycle, such as the infant's states and its eating behavior (Wolff, 1966). In addition, the procession of many other emerging behaviors that are not related to the sleeping–waking–feeding cycle appears to issue from a maturational time schedule. Yet, within the first 10 days, some yielding of this inflexibility can be seen in the fact that (1) the cycle becomes partially entrained to the pattern of daily events in the infant's environment; and (2) behaviors that are not locked in to the cycle can be tuned to the caregiver's moment-to-moment behavior such as vocalizations (Condon & Sander, 1974). As each month passes beyond the neonatal period, it is still easier to alter infant behavior, and by the third month many investigators have no difficulty in demonstrating conditionability in a number of areas. Thus, the early socialization process starts with the infant imposing its own organization on its environment, and there is a continuing emergence of rudimentary, preformed organizations that affect the interpersonal and physical environment, but the direction of movement is increasingly toward malleability.

From stimulus reduction to stimulus seeking.   The very young infant moves back and forth between bouts of pain and avoidance of pain or discomfort to states of quiescence in which the external world is sealed off. A substantial part of the neonate's existence is spent asleep, a state in which there is either quiescence or minimal response to external stimulation. Within a few weeks, the infant begins to emerge from this cocoon and clearly shows behaviors that open it to the world of external stimulation. Later in the first year, the infant becomes proficient in producing stimulation from the environment as well as in maintaining certain types of stimulation in which there is an interest. From the standpoint of the parent, the neonate seems to be saying, "Leave me alone unless I yell for help," whereas the crawling infant seems to be saying "Keep out of my way; I want to be able to get at things, and only once in a while will I need your help."

Proximal–distal shift.   Three different lines of research have documented a shift from response to proximal stimuli, such as tactile and proprioceptive, in the early part of the first year toward response to auditory and visual stimuli in the latter part of the first year. Part of this shift is due to changes in the infant's posture in the early months. As the infant emerges from a predominately fetal position to spending much more time supine and elongated, it is possible on physical grounds alone for there to be an increased benefit from visual stimulation. In connection with research on intersensory integration, Birch and Lefford (1967, p. 110) have documented the proximal–distal shift as far as tactile and visual stimuli are concerned. Supporting Birch and Lefford's study of sensory–motor development, Ellingson (1964) has shown in studies of evoked potential on both human and infrahuman species that cortical response to tactile stimuli is relatively mature at first, whereas cortical response to visual and auditory stimulation shows mature form considerably later. Investigators concentrating on mother–infant interaction (Lewis & Ban, 1971; Lusk & Lewis, 1972; Moss, 1967) have reported that touching, a proximal behavior, decreases over age, and looking, the most distal, increases. Maternal behavior shifts in response to this proximal–distal change. Korner and Thoman (1972) have shown that proprioceptive stimulation quiets an infant best in very early development. Later, complex auditory and visual stimuli become effective soothers (Moss, 1974).

The proximal–distal shift is not a change from the exclusive use of one or two modalities to certain others, because it is evident from the first that the infant is responding to both proximal and distal sources of stimuli. The auditory and visual systems, although less mature than the proprioceptive and tactile, are much better developed subcortically in the neonatal period than had been thought prior to the last 10 years of research. (Later in the chapter, some of the research involved will be discussed in another connection.) In soothing neonates, some mothers rely from the first on combinations of distal and proximal stimuli. The shift involves the general emphasis in the infant's responsiveness, subcortical versus cortical maturity, and, in general, the way in which the infant uses the external world.

There are abundant indications in the references that have been cited that maturational factors make a strong contribution to the proximal–distal shift. In addition, the present author has not seen any theory advanced that would implicate parent behavior beyond its contribution to the general context of environmental stimulation. Regardless of origins, however, it is clear that the basis for the behavioral interaction of the infant with adults in its environment changes. As the shift occurs, interactions can occur at a distance as well as at close range, and thus the relationship is placed more on an adult basis.

DEVELOPMENT OF THREE SYSTEMS

The behavior interaction system.   The mother and infant have been in physiological interaction during the entire process of pregnancy and even in a limited behavioral interaction consisting of responding to the movements of each other. The latter is a very restricted exchange based on gross bodily movements. Its limitations can be seen in what happens almost immediately after delivery, when the parents can see the infant for the first time. There is a predictable and orderly progression in inspection and contacts—from fingertip touch on the extremities to massaging, encompassing, and palm contact on the trunk (Klaus, Kennell, Plumb, & Zuehlke, 1970). The orderly progression occurs despite wide differences in the mothers' past experience with babies, suggesting to these investigators that a species-specific pattern of behavior is involved.

Both mother and father are likely to inspect the baby in detail, amused as they touch the tiny hands and feet. They try to get it to open its eyes. They may try to distract it from crying. They may express sympathy for the infant's distress, but the caregiving relationship has not begun in earnest yet. The behavioral interaction system, one-sided as it is, *has* begun, and out of it will quickly develop another system, that of caregiving, and later, still another—social interaction. As is the case with many biological growth processes, each system comes into play and yields to the differentiation of other systems by receding into the background or by emerging functionally in the "seams" between the systems that are developed later.

The beginning of behavioral interaction does not mean that socialization has begun. As Korner (1974) puts it: "Immediately after birth, maternal ministrations are usually not as yet geared to socialize, educate, or stimulate the infant toward goals held desirable by the mother; instead, her interventions are evoked by the infant's discomfort, associated with his first attempt to function as an independent organism. It is the infant's crying and other signs of discomfort that dictate maternal actions [p. 114]." Even in later development, young infants and children provide what we might call "kicks" for their parents in situations in which the parents have no socialization objectives whatsoever in mind, and in which the stimuli from the infant simply provide sensual gratification, excitement, or relief from boredom, as would a book or television. The mother may turn to a small infant when she simply wants to have a little bit of fun. The soft, cooing vocalizations of infants may, indeed, be inherently reinforcing for parental behavior, but mothers may turn to their infants for other reasons than past reinforcement of their maternal behavior. They may turn to their infants for something to do and thus at times use them only for their own stimulation purposes. These efforts may turn into social interaction sequences and end up achieving socialization objectives. However, there is much of the interaction that does not have such objectives.

Caregiving and social interaction.   Elements of caregiving and social interaction are present at birth. Caregiving expands rapidly, but social interaction must await further development. From the standpoint of the infant, the caregiving system initially involves emission of signals at the time of discomfort or noxious stimulation, which is followed by quiescence as there is relief from the source of stimulation. The parent is often reducing stimulation to maintain the infant in an optimal state of arousal or is providing input such as rocking that competes with endogenous aversive stimuli. From the standpoint of the parent, this system might also be characterized as essentially aversive in nature, although in this instance the parent is behaving so as to avoid aversive signals such as the infant's fussing and crying, and it might be better to refer to the parent's aspect as aversive–preventive. While the parent is thus primarily behaving to avoid unde-sirable immediate or long-range outcomes, life support and protection are being afforded the infant.

Richards (1971) has drawn attention to the importance of distinguishing social interaction from other systems of interaction such as attachment. In contrast with the caregiving system, social interaction involves mutual, reciprocal exchanges. It may be characterized in similar fashion for both mother and infant, because both behave so as to produce or maintain the behavior of the other. Rather than one participant reducing the effect of aversive stimulation being received by the other, each is providing stimuli for the other. In so doing, they maintain each other's level of arousal in an optimal range. In the terminology of our control systems model, they exercise upper- and lower-limit control over each other. Later in the chapter, descriptions of gaze interactions from Stern (1974) will be cited in illustration.

Kohlberg (1969) has pointed out the importance of two elements in a social interaction system: "In general, even simple social play and games have the character of either complementarity, reciprocity, (I do this, then you do that, then I do this), or imitation (I do this, you do this too). In either case there is a shared pattern of behavior, since reciprocal play is a part of reciprocal imitation (you follow me, I'll follow you) [p. 463]."

The distinction between caregiving and social interaction is also important from the standpoint of the basic learning situation. Socialization that develops out of caregiving should primarily be a result of drive reduction. Socialization that emerges from social interaction involves learning at moderate levels of arousal. Good arguments have been made to the effect that development from interaction is best favored by moderate levels of arousal rather than the states in which primary drive reduction could be assumed to occur (Bowlby, 1969; Es-calona, 1968; Walters & Parke, 1965).

To recapitulate, during the first year, the behavioral, caregiving, and social interaction systems differentiate against the background of general changes in the infant from activity to reactivity, from preformed organization to malleability, from stimulus reduction to stimulus seeking, and from response to stimulation of the proximal, then distal receptors.

Periods of development.   Having established some general concepts and principles that will be useful throughout the first year, the discussion will turn to the infant's effects within each of three major periods. These periods have been selected from the perspective of the interaction system—not from the standpoint of sensory, perceptual, motor, or cognitive landmarks. The periods are based on data furnished in Emde, Gaensbauer, and Harmon (1976), which shows that changes in unexplained fussiness and wakefulness and in the emergence of infant social behaviors combine to separate three periods: (1) birth to the end of the second month; (2) the third to sixth month, and (3) the seventh through twelfth month. In Emde's sample, the average hours of daily wakefulness increased rapidly between the first day of life and the second month, remained relatively stable from the third through the fifth month, began to increase again rapidly between the sixth and seventh month, and then leveled off between the seventh and twelfth month. Decreases in ratings of unexplained fussiness roughly parallel these changes in wakefulness. The time of appearance of the social smile in most infants (3 months) and the emergence of reactions to strangers at seven months also confirms the utility of delineating these periods. There is a sequential relationship between the criteria. Increases in wakefulness were precursors of both onset of the social smile and of distress in response to strangers.

In addition to his own data, Emde cites a number of findings from other studies that point to the desirability of treating the period before and after the third month separately. Between the second and third months, there are especially rapid changes in the nature of reflexes, conditionability, habituation, orienting, visual accommodation, and effective expression. That these shifts bear some relationship to change in the functioning of the parent–infant system is shown in the report of Moss (1967): From the standpoint of behavioral interaction alone, a difference was detected in the way the mother functioned with the infant before and after the third month.

THE PRIMARY CAREGIVING PERIOD: THE NEWBORN PERIOD THROUGH THE SECOND MONTH

Starting the Behavior Interaction System

In Chapter 7, Harper brings together the findings from a number of studies indicating how the pregnancy itself, its physiological effects, and the social effects of the new role for the mother, create parental expectations. The latter are then activated by the birth of the infant. We have already mentioned the inspection phenomenon shown by parents on first viewing of their baby. It seems quite likely that this behavior is a response to the tinyness of the baby as well as qualitative features such as the shape of the head (a short face, large forehead, and protruding cheeks) and features that the human infant has in common with infants of several other species (Tinbergen, 1951). Fullard and Reiling (1976) report their own data and summarize the work of others showing that "babyness" in human and other animal figures is responded to discriminately and positively by human observers, especially females. Human females show a dramatic increase in preference for representations of infants around the onset of puberty, pointing to a biological contributor to responsiveness. In Chapter 10, Harper documents in a number of ways for many mammal groups how the distinctive appearance of the young produces differential response in adults.

Just as the human mother shows marked changes in response to the sight of her new baby, so is her physiology changing rapidly as a result of the processes set in motion by pregnancy and its termination. Rosenblatt (1969) has shown that maternal behavior in rats is enhanced by a pregnancy termination effect involving hormone changes. This could well be in existence at the human level as well (see Chapter 8).

The hypothesis that the first pregnancy constitutes a crisis for a young couple remains controversial. A recent study in this series (Ryder, 1973) provides references to this literature and a finding that at least supports the existence of a transition period in the marriage. A decline in marital satisfaction is reported by wives in young couples having their first baby. Ryder did not have data that would throw light on the events leading to the decline. One possibility is that in some marriages the mother may receive less attention from her husband as a result of her preoccupation with her own body during pregnancy and investment of interest in the new baby. There are other possible explanations, but for the present purpose it is sufficient to note that marriage itself is affected by the chain of events ensuing from the pregnancy.

We have mentioned that the infant's appearance by itself could have a considerable effect on parental responsiveness in the neonatal period. The behavior of the newborn has a further stimulating effect—the thrashing and apparently uncoordinated limb movements create an appearance of helplessness. In old Russia, the practice of swaddling was seen as necessary to prevent self-destructive and dangerous movements of the infant (Benedict, 1949). Other factors may well be involved in swaddling, of course, because the human parent would have had to discover sooner or later that holding an infant or wrapping it tightly would quiet it down, as research has demonstrated (Lipton, Steinschneider, & Richmond, 1960). Whatever the causes, whether it is the appearance or behavior of the infant, it is clear that exposure of a mother to her infant when introduced experimentally (approximately 16 hours in the first 4 days of life) enhances responsiveness and attentiveness to the infant 1 month later (Klaus, Jerauld, Kreger, McAlpine, Steffa, & Kennell, 1972).

The infant makes another kind of contribution to the initial functioning of the pair that is not easily appreciated by the casual observer. From the perspective of research on sensory processes, it is apparent that infants are tuned to mothers of their own species. One of the towering contributions of Darwin was to point out the "correlation of organisms," meaning that the sensory–motor and other complex behavior systems of organisms functioning together are mutually adjusted. Human parents rearing infants of other species become very aware of the *lack* of correlation, as in the reported experience that the clinging of a chimpanzee infant is so tight and close as to be oppressive (Hayes, 1951).

A series of studies summarized by Eisenberg (1975) and a study by Hutt, Hutt, Lenard, Bernuth, and Muntjewerff (1968) indicate that the newborn and very young infant is specifically coded so as to be responsive to human tonal patterns and speech-like signals. Richards (1971) has offered the interesting speculation that the infant's endogenous pattern of sucking (the fact that there are both short and long intervals between bursts of sucking) makes it possible for the mother to move and adjust her own position in the short intervals between bursts or to interact socially with the infant during the long intervals. Again, these reports point to the matching of mother and infant.

To summarize, the foregoing evidence supports the proposition that the pregnancy, the infant's appearance, its behavior, and the way its sensory and motor systems match those of the mother make their contribution to the formation of the early mother–infant subsystem of the family, just as does the mother's societal role proscription.

Starting the Caregiving System

There should be no question that the cry of an infant has a marked effect on the human adult. Scientists have now documented what most breast-feeding mothers already know, that the cry produces a sensation in the breasts, and even a let-down reflex. Vuorenkoski, Wasz–Höckert, Koivisto, and Lind (1969) have shown that even hearing tape-recordings of infant cries can result in an increase in breast temperature. The cry also produces something more than a physiological response—it is apparent to any observer that it has a high probability of bringing the caregiver to the proximity of the infant. The subjective response of most adults is "something has to be done about that." Once the caregiver is in the proximity of the infant, other mechanisms, which the neonate is well organized to bring into play, have their impact. Next, the infant's grimacing and apparently helpless thrashing movements take over the direction of the caregivers' response. The most frequent maternal response is holding, and it is the most effective in terminating the crying (Bell & Ainsworth, 1972) probably because of vestibular and kinesthetic stimulation (Korner & Thoman, 1972). If the sight or smell of a soiled diaper does not happen to lead the caregiver to further appropriate action, a desire to encompass the flailing limbs of the infant will. The sequence may not start with crying. The attractiveness of the soft, warm skin of the infant also readily leads to holding and handling.

Moss (1974) has pointed out that some mothers respond to the crying infant because they wish to provide comfort and relief; others may respond mainly because the cry is a noxious stimulus they wish to terminate. In either case, the infant's cry apparently leads to maternal behavior that removes the activating circumstances. But what about the tendency of some mothers to hover and be overly responsive to their infants? Couldn't this induce crying from the infant? It is an unsettled question at present (Gewirtz & Boyd, 1977; Bell & Ainsworth, 1972) whether alacrity in responding to the infant's cry in certain stages of development may have conditioning properties that increase the frequency of the crying, thereby offsetting the cry-reducing effects of relieving the source of the infant's distress. Moss and Robson (1968), in a sequence analysis of a relatively large sample studied at both 1 month and 3 months of age, reported that the infant's crying and fussing preceded maternal contact more often than followed it.

In addition to Moss and Robson's data from sequence analysis, there are indications of congenital contributors to characteristics of the infant such as sleep problems that induce caregiving (Moore & Ucko, 1957; Bernal, 1973). One other study has reported evidence of the infant's congenital contribution to the caregiving situation. Beckwith, Cohen, and Parmelee (1973) studied premature infants determined to be at high risk for the emergence of later developmental problems on the basis of perinatal complications, newborn behavior, sleep characteristics, and neurological status. One month after the neonatal assessment, mothers of high-risk infants were found to hold their infants for longer intervals than mothers of low-risk infants.

Although the cry has a high probability of bringing a caregiver to the vicinity of the infant and inducing appropriate action, the contribution of the infant's cry must be seen in the context of the social and cognitive life of the mother. It is possible to distinguish different kinds of infant crying, but mothers do not respond to each one of these cries in a mechanical and unthinking way. Bernal (1972) reports from diary data on English mothers that their knowledge of how long a time has elapsed from the last feeding and how adequate the feeding was, enter into the complex set of determinants of the mother's response. Mothers are in no sense puppets on a string, responding without a second thought to a particular kind of cry.

Maintaining the Caregiving System

Up to the present point in the discussion, the aversive nature of the infant's cry has been emphasized, but it must be kept in mind also that crying, just as smiling, is a proximity-producing behavior that may bond the mother to the infant in addition to serving as a specific trigger for her action at any moment. In other words, crying, just as smiling, is an attachment behavior. Of course, infants don't purposely set out to behave so that the caregiver remains in the situation and is responsive to them. Rather, the behavior of the average infant is such that it operates effectively to maintain adults with appropriate motivations in the caregiving situation. There are a number of other ways that will now be described in which the infant contributes to the maintenance of the caregiving system. Most of these primarily involve communicating its condition and not exceeding the tolerances of caregivers.

First of all, the infant contributes to caregiving by informing the caregiver about preferences and limits. After a mother has seen a few startles or sustained distress reactions, she is quite likely to take steps in the future to prevent exposure of her baby to sudden or excessive auditory stimulation, to excessive play in general, or to handling that does not take into consideration the peculiar sensitivities and motor skills of the infant. In the first two months, the infant is very well equipped with avoidance mechanisms. It can indicate what it will or will not inject by swallowing or spitting out items that are given to it, by turning its head away from strong odors, by rejecting solids and forcing the mother to return to bottle or breast-feedings, and by falling asleep during overly rigid feeding schedules. Responsiveness to repeated stimulation wanes, indicating that the infant has a "shut-off" mechanism. In fact, habituation can be observed very readily by anyone who has a few minutes to shake a rattle or shine a light on an infant, whereas demonstrations of conditioning can often be seen only in statistical comparisons over many trials.

The major task of the mother in the first few months is to manage the variety of states that her infant manifests. Most observers of the very young infant are aware that the states of some are difficult to assess, whereas others provide clear indications, whether it be an alert awake state, a drowsy awake state, or one of the sleep states. Surprisingly, some infants can sleep with their eyes open!

It is equally important that the infant provide clues to behavior that may follow later. The predictability of the infant behavior patterns permits the mother to respond to early events in a sequence in order to avert later events. If a mother hears a soft whispering and knows that this is usually followed by gentle movements, rhythmic kicking, then uncoordinated thrashing, and finally, fussing or spasmodic crying (Wolff, 1966), she may take action in response to a very moderate stimulus that is not even aversive and thus prevent an aversive outcome. In other words, behavior early in a predictable sequence provides discriminative stimuli for maternal interventions that act to arrest the full development of the sequence. If the mother is sufficiently sensitive to her infant, she may even come to recognize that frowns shown during active sleep will forecast awakening and signs of hunger (Emde et al., 1976).

During the early part of the first few months, most sequences or bouts of interaction are started by fussing or crying, because the mother is reluctant to do anything that may awaken the sleeping infant and is content to let the infant sleep and rest as much as possible so that she herself may rest. Thus, from the standpoint of the control system model of interaction, most of the examples that have been given involve behaviors of the infant that test the upper limits of parents. The lower limits of parents may also be tested, however, in the case of infants that sleep too long or are too lethargic in their waking periods. Most mothers have some expectations relative to how much their infants may be available to them in an awake state and how active they should be. When these norms are not reached, they may become active in trying to overcome the apparent lethargy. It is a common experience that mothers become uneasy, ask friends, and finally seek professional help if they find their infants sleep too long or are not sufficiently responsive when aroused.

Setting the Stage for the Social Interaction System

By necessity, social interaction must be limited during the early weeks if the infant is primarily sleeping, fussing, or feeding. Aside from the interaction that could occur during feeding, the primary requirement for social interaction is that the infant be available in awake states for a substantial portion of time without requiring caregiving. This necessary, although not sufficient, condition for socialization develops in most infants toward the end of the second month when there is a rapid increase in the amount of wakefulness (Emde et al., 1976). Among other things, the increased time awake exposes the mother to the infant's gazing behavior. Stern (1971) has drawn attention to the effect of the infant's pattern of gaze alternation on the mother and has concluded from several lines of evidence that this pattern is something that the infant brings to the social situation because of the way its central nervous system is set to function. Although the mother's speech and own gaze or gaze termination behavior may increase the probability of the infant gazing at her, the gaze-to-gaze intervals are unaffected by maternal behavior and thus appear to be a part of the infant's underlying biology.

A second feature of the infant's behavior during the first 2 months sets the stage for later social interaction. Although the full blown predictable social smile does not appear with high frequency for most infants until the third month, the mother may trigger smiles with auditory stimulation, and endogenous smiling associated with various sleep states appears earlier. Mothers appear to know that this smiling is not directed at them, but they nonetheless find themselves responding in an affectionate way nonetheless. The phenomenon is often described as "smiling at the angels."

Some infants fuss or cry very little from the first and show little changes in this aspect of their behavior in the first few months, but the average infant shows a considerable amount in the first month or two, much of it fussing for which there is no reason that is very obvious to the mother. A necessary but not sufficient condition for the emergence of the social interaction system is a drop in this unexplained fussiness that occurs before the third month, from a very high level shown in the first month (Emde et al., 1976). This change complements the change in the amount of time that the infant is in an awake alert state, releasing the mother's energies from caregiving so that she can take advantage of the opportunity to interact with the infant in an awake state.

It has already been mentioned that evidence of a congenital contributor to the amount of time the mother holds the infant was uncovered in a study of infants at high risk (Beckwith, Cohen, & Parmelee, 1973). One hypothesis from this study is of interest from the standpoint of the social interaction system. These authors speculated that the difficulty high-risk infants have (in contrast with the low-risk infants) in maintaining mutual gaze was a contributing factor to more frequent and longer holding; the mothers of high-risk babies compensated for their inability to maintain contact with the gaze by intensifying their holding.

Maintaining the Behavior Interaction System

Successive production of novelty.   Gewirtz (1961) has argued that many of the behaviors of infants shown in early development are inherently reinforcing for parents. In addition, the successive emergence of new behaviors, regardless of the specific behaviors involved, is exciting and interesting to the parent. If something new is happening each week or so, the caregiver's motivation to remain in the behavior interaction system with the infant receives general strengthening. It has already been mentioned that the attentive mother may notice strange but fascinating smiles appearing at certain phases of sleep. Later, she may induce these smiles herself by talking to the baby or by making noises. Changes continue to occur. Soon the smile appears when the infant is open-eyed, following a feeding. Then the mother may notice that the smile appears more in response to her voice than to other sounds. Other changes such as an increase in attentive behavior, capability for quieting and looking bright-eyed when attending, and an increase in general activity in connection with attentive behavior, all emerge during this first period of 3 weeks.

The kaleidoscope of novelty continues to spill out its fascination in the fourth and fifth weeks. Now the baby focuses on the mother's face, there is increasing eye-to-eye contact, the mother's face appears to be more effective than other stimuli, and by moving her head she seems to be able to elicit some smiles. The fifth through seventh weeks bring still more delightful changes, much more smiling, and the occurrence of soft cooing vocalizations accompanying attention. Mouth and head movements that were formerly seen in connection with attention are reduced in frequency. From the standpoint of a social system, one is beginning to see the emergence of complementarity and reciprocity in the interchange between mother and infant. The novelty of all these events contributes to the positive quality of the behavior interaction system and thus supports whatever other factors are operating to maintain the interaction of the mother and infant.

Modifiability.   Although it is difficult to demonstrate learning in the neonatal period, the mother learns that she can distract her infant and thus begin to bring behavior under her control. As the infant begins to fuss she may say "ah-ah-ah" and find that the infant stops fussing. She feels effective because the infant is doing what she wants it to do, even though she may not understand that it is ceasing the fussing for reasons other than her specific vocalization. Any kind of auditory or near-receptor stimulation such as movement of the infant by rocking and jiggling might achieve the same effect.

THE EMERGENCE OF SOCIAL INTERACTION: THE THIRD THROUGH THE SIXTH MONTH

The Caregiving System Subsides

Before detailing the many ways in which social interaction emerges, it is important to remind ourselves of the intensity of the demand for caregiving in the preceding period so that we can appreciate the change that mothers experience. From small normative samples in which crying has been studied intensively (Bell & Ainsworth, 1972; Parmelee, 1972), it appears that the infant's crying in the first month or so constitutes a stress experience for many mothers. The average duration of crying is 7.7 minutes/hour, ranging as high as 21 minutes, and no substantial reduction occurs until the period between 1½ and 4 months. However, the frequency distributions indicate that a small number of infants cry a great deal more than others. Considering some of the reports on extreme cases affords an insight into the subjective impact on mothers of infants who are not quite so extreme. The reports yield clear indications that the tolerance of parents can be exceeded. Robson and Moss (1970) found that in some mothers attachment decreased after the first month if crying, fussing, and other demands for caregiving did not ebb. They cite one particular case that rather dramatically showed the impact on the subjective aspects of the mother's affection of her infant's sustained fussing or caretaking demand, as well as a failure in the emergence of social responses. The mother in this pair reported that she felt strange and unloved and wanted nothing to do with her infant, even though during the pregnancy she was positive in orientation. The infant was later found to have suffered relatively serious brain damage as a result of perinatal complications.

In Chapter 4, we have already mentioned that parents who have assaulted their children report that *they* felt abused by their infant's constant fussing and unusual crying. (It can be speculated that such atypicality may have been one of the reasons infants were abandoned in early times.) Thus in two different studies, it is apparent that the tolerance of caregivers can be exceeded during the early months, whether this comes about because of their own ineffectiveness in reducing crying or because of some unusual characteristic of the infant. From the standpoint of infant effects on the maintenance of the caregiving system, the unusual cases point to the fact that for most infants, crying and fussing is within limits that can be tolerated by their parents, and there is a reduction that eases the caregiving burden substantially by the third or fourth month.

An Actual Caregiving Sequence

To make the infant's contribution to the initiation and maintenance of the caregiving system more meaningful, a sequence of mother–infant interaction that primarily involves caregiving will be reported. This sequence was recorded by Howard Moss of the Intramural Research Program, National Institute of Mental Health, who conducted a continuous 3-hour observation on a 3-month-old male infant and its mother. No more selection of the case was involved other than the fact that it was the first of a series of 14 for which other analyses have been carried out. Comments on the theoretical relevance of various parts of the sequence are interspersed with the running record (Bell, 1971):

> The infant had been alone in his crib, awake and quiet for a 13-minute period in which there was no interaction. The interaction was initiated by a 3½-minute period in which he changed to an awake fussing state. This oriented the mother to the infant but did not at that time disrupt other on-going activities or elicit approach. Presumably, the level of fussing was below a level which activates her soothing repertoire. This period was followed by 1½ minutes during which fussing progressed to full cyclic crying, and the latter did elicit the mother's approach. She looked and presumably saw grimacing and threshing—further stimuli from the infant which had the effect of keeping the mother in the immediate vicinity. The mother stood over him, since he continued to thrash and cry. She then talked. The crying continued. The mother then picked him up and cradled him in her arms. This part of her repertoire was reinforced by the infant, who reduced motor movement but continued crying. After about 8 seconds the mother again talked, but the crying continued, and another element was introduced from the maternal repertoire—she held him so his weight was partially on his legs. The crying was maintained, however, and the mother then showed another behavior: holding the infant up in the air in front of and above her. The crying continued. She then held him against her shoulder and patted his back. This was followed by rather massive tactile and kinesthetic stimulation, jiggling, rubbing, and patting, but, after a pause, the infant resumed crying. Continuation of the tactile stimulation by the mother was followed by a reduction of the crying to fussing. However, the infant started crying again. Then the infant opened his eyes and was quiet for several seconds. The mother talked again, and the infant provided reinforcement for this behavior by continuing to remain quietly awake for several seconds, then emitting a noncrying vocalization. This elicited responsive talking by the mother, who then placed her baby in an infant seat. He remained quiet and awake in his seat, smiled, and the mother left a few seconds later. The state of the infant apparently terminated the interaction sequence. The smile could have differentiated this unit into a reciprocal social interchange, but the mother at this time was apparently only set to quiet the infant. Eighteen minutes in which the infant remained quiet and awake elapsed before another unit of interaction.
>
> To recapitulate, in the absence of a change in stimulation from the mother, the infant showed a sequential repertoire in that he progressed from fussing through alternating fussing and crying to full crying. The fussing oriented the mother toward the infant, then the crying activated what may be described as a sequentially ordered quieting repertoire. The mother talked to the infant first; then, after trying different methods, including positioning him so that he partially supported his own weight and patting him on the back, she finally reached the stage of more

vigorous jiggling, rubbing, and patting. She reverted to talking when the infant quieted, and his resumption of crying was followed by a recycling of her ordered repertoire, though in short-ened form. She proceeded directly to points in the repertoire that were later in the order when first presented [pp. 67–68]. (Copyright 1971 by the American Psychological Association. Reprinted by permission.)

Emergence of the Social Interaction System

Although the reduction in the aversive stimulation of fussing and crying and the availability of the infant for interaction in the awake state are necessary condi-tions for optimal development of the social interaction system, the dynamics are provided by the appearance of exciting social behaviors at or about the third month (Moss, 1967). During this period the mother is also exposed increasingly to the infant's gaze. Stern (1974) has reminded us of an obvious but important fact, namely that the average mother's response to the infant's gaze and other social behaviors is a complete and bizarre departure from adult behavior patterns. The response is so ubiquitous that it appears to be a species–specific behavior that the adult brings to the social interaction situation with an infant. The moth-er's vocal response involves a higher pitch, longer vowels, a slowed tempo of speech, "speaking for two," mock surprise, and unusually long responsive gazes to the infant. It is evident that the infant's gaze in particular has a clear triggering effect on maternal behavior, as well as a likely role as an unlearned reinforcer.

Although there is no sharp transition point at which infants become eager and curious about the environment, it is certainly apparent by the fourth if not the third month that babies enjoy play and are fun to play with. They have become motorically capable of trying to sustain simple activities that interest them. They induce others to maintain or provide interesting spectacles, and they show by their smiles that they enjoy the world about them (Wolff, 1960).

To a considerable extent, the infant's transition (from insulation against stimuli to functioning so as to increase stimulation) shows itself in attention directed toward inanimate objects. However, the shift also represents a contribu-tion to the beginning of the social interaction system in that the parent is a mediator for many of the infant's efforts. The face of the parent is a beautiful, creative plaything. As Rheingold (1961, p. 168) has pointed out, it is rich and varied in stimulation and response, especially contingent response. Moss (1974) has reported a change in the nature of the interrelations between fussing and crying and maternal behavior between the first month and the third month that has implications for the interpersonal aspect of the infant's stimulus-increasing activities. At the first month, crying and fussing is correlated significantly with maternal attending, holding, burping, and rocking. At the third month, these correlations decrease, and there is an increase in those involving social and physical stimuli as a means of soothing. One other indication of the infant's stimulus-increasing activities comes from the work of Haaf and Brown (1975), who found that between the tenth and fifteenth week the number of fixations on visual stimuli increased, and the average duration decreased. The younger infant related to the stimulus field with a small number of sustained looks, the older infant with more frequent brief looks. In other words, the older infant was maximizing variety of input.

Emde et al. (1976, p. 87) contrast the message conveyed by crying ("come, change what's happening") with what is communicated by the smile ("Keep up with what you are doing. I like it."). By the third month, the infant's smiles have progressed from (1) associations with sleep states; to (2) occasional unpredictable and incomplete smiles in response to a variety of stimuli; through to (3) a predictable and complete response to social stimuli. To a mother, the smile of an infant that occurs during sleep processes is interesting. The subsequent appearance of wakeful smiling to a variety of nonsocial stimuli is confusing but entertaining to her. The social smile has an entirely different impact, as has been described so well by Emde et al. (1976):

> When the young infant begins to smile regularly in response to the moving face of another, his social life takes a leap forward. His mother, father, and other family members are delighted by his beaming response. He is shown off to friends of the family who no longer have to feel they always have to tiptoe in the house of a sleeping baby. Instead, he smiles engagingly to everyone with his eyes brightly fixated on those of the person who looks at him. . . . . His mother automatically experiences delight and a feeling that her infant is delighted. An often heard comment, especially by parents of a firstborn is that now they feel that their baby is human: Before, he was more of a doll-like object, to be protected and taken care of [p. 86]. (Copyright © 1976, International Universities Press, Inc.)

There has certainly been no dearth of studies demonstrating that smiling and other social responses can be modified by conditioning procedures from the third month on. However, the fact that a response can be modified carries no implication that this explains its origin. No very convincing explanations in terms of learning have been offered as to why the social smile should begin to appear in some infants by the second month and most by the third. There is considerable evidence of heritability for the tendency to smile (Kagan, 1974).

At approximately the same time as the social smile appears in most infants there is an increase in babbling (Moss, 1967). Again, these vocalizations appear to be a contribution of the infant to the interaction system, because they develop quite well in infants of deaf-mute parents (Lenneberg, Rebelsky, & Nichols, 1965). Infants during the third month often babble to themselves and even show a reduction in amount of babbling when the mother comes in to interact with them (Jones & Moss, 1971).

An increment in modifiability is another contribution of infant behavior to the social interaction that is shown increasingly from the third month on. Before this age period, efforts to modify infant behavior usually encounter maturational limits. White and Held (1966) found that training infants in eye–hand coordination by the provision of experimental stimulation led to little improvement before the second month and even some fussing and crying. After the second month, change in response to the experimental treatment could be seen increasingly. Much of the stimulation was in the visual modality, and it is worth noting that the change occurred at a time when there should have been postural changes in the infant, with more time being spent in the supine position. Also there should have been better control of neck musculature, as well as prehension movements. It is apparent that maturational processes were associated with the ability of the infants to take advantage of the increased stimulation and training.

Papousek (1967) has reported that an average of 177 trials were necessary to achieve a satisfactory criterion of conditioned head-turning when the process was started within the newborn period, and only 42 trials needed when the process was started in the third month. In addition, it is probably no accident that most studies of the conditioning of social responses have started around the third month, rather than earlier. Jones and Moss (1971) have reported a relevant finding—at the second week in an observational study, infant vocalizations were found to be associated with the total amount of maternal speech, and at the third month they were associated with only the amount of maternal speech that *followed* infant vocalizations.

The infant's increased conditionability may make a contribution to the occurrence of "contingency games" involving complementarity and reciprocity, one of the more pure forms of social interaction. Watson (1966) has described how these contingency games develop. Apparently, responses of the infant that follow quickly on parent behaviors can, by that contingency, acquire reward value, just as those of the parent can for the infant, leading to a social interchange system in which the responses of each are rewarding for the other. Thus, even if the responses of each do not have unlearned reinforcing value, they could acquire such value and contribute to the development of contingency games.

Further Changes in the Social Interaction System

After the third month, the infant demands more of the mother in their social interaction, showing this by being more responsive to novel stimuli. Lewis, Goldberg, and Rausch (1967) have reported an increase in habituation to unvarying stimuli between the third and sixth month that may in part contribute to the change. Cohen (1974) has reported another change that may be implicated in the infant's becoming more "choosy" in interactions. During approximately the same period as we have been discussing, she noted an increasing tendency toward longer fixations on novel versus familiar human figures to which they were exposed. Rubenstein (1974) has reported that novel objects are manipulated more and looked at more by the sixth month, supporting the same line of findings. The increasing responsiveness to novelty makes a special contribution to social interaction, because it facilitates the mother's play (Bruner, 1972). The mother can try novel and unusual things and be rewarded with a vocalization or a smile.

Still another change that appears to originate in the infant and leads to progress in the social interaction system is the ability of the infant to respond in kind. Increasingly from the third month on, the infant is able to respond to a smile with a smile and to vocalize in response to a vocalization, in contrast with earlier, more diffuse and less organized reaction.

Social Interaction Bouts

It has been mentioned that infants in the awake–active state tend to babble much more when they are by themselves than when the mother is present. The occurrence of these babbling episodes is one way in which the infant may start social interaction bouts. It is difficult for mothers who overhear these episodes to resist finding out what is going on. Thus, they come into the area where the infant is babbling to itself. For the mother, the autonomous babbling may acquire the value of a discriminative stimulus for reciprocal play or "games." After starting the interaction in these games, the infant may discontinue the vocalization and shift into an alternation of smiling and vocalization in response to the mother's contacts. Infants may also start bouts of interaction by remaining quiet longer than usual so that the mother comes into the area in order to see what the infant is up to.

The infant is active in terminating bouts as well as in initiating them. Stern (1974) has reported that the infant initiates or terminates 94% of all mutual gaze interactions. The applicability of the control system model described in Chapter 4 to the terminations and resumptions Stern reports will be seen if the reader recalls a basic feature of the model: Actions that redirect or reduce excessive or inappropriate behavior are shown by one participant when its upper limits are reached by the behavior of the other, and priming and stimulating actions are shown when the behavior of the other is insufficient. The following is the typical interaction bout described by Stern:

> It consists of the infant looking at the mother, smiling, vocalizing, and showing other signs of mounting arousal and positive affect, including increasing motor activity. As the intensity of his state increases, he begins to show signs of displeasure, momentary sobering, and a fleeting grimace, interspersed with smiling. The intensity of arousal continues to build until he suddenly averts gaze sharply with a quick but not extensive head turn which keeps the mother's face in good peripheral view, while his level of "excitement" clearly declines. He then returns gaze, bursting into a smile, and the level of arousal and affect build again. He again averts gaze, and so on. The infant gives a clear impression of modulating his state of arousal and affect within certain limits by regulating the amount of perceptual input [pp. 208–209].

Stern (1974) has also pointed out the intra- and inter-regulatory nature of the control system. He notes that the infant acquires experience in managing its level of arousal and emotional state on the basis of an interpersonal exchange. It learns to initiate and maintain contact at some times and to disengage at other times, depending on the effect of the mother's behavior at that time. Through the repetition of many such social interaction games, the infant experiences pleasurable excitement that can be managed by his own "turn on" and "turn off" mechanisms, and he gradually expands the range of activities within which pleasurable levels of arousal are experienced.

Bouts of mutual gaze and gaze aversion are difficult to detect without special observation techniques, but they offer a new glimpse into the visual interior of the interaction. Placed in the context of other events, they should give us a much more meaningful picture of the interchange. The broader context of events can be seen in the following example of a social interaction sequence taken from the record of the same mother–infant pair for whom a caregiving sequence was reported earlier in the chapter (Bell, 1971). This sequence occurred one hour and 50 minutes after the caregiving sequence.

> The baby had been placed in a seat after he was fed, and ingested air had been relieved. Throughout this period the mother had talked to him, held him in different positions, and wiped his face. He either looked directly at her, smiled, or both, when being wiped. There followed an essentially social interaction sequence, lasting 6 minutes, in which infant vocalized and mother talked alternately eight times during the first 3½ minutes. The infant then smiled for the first time in 4 minutes, and the mother's rate of talking increased from one utterance in the ½-minute period before, to one every 3 seconds in the ½-minute afterward. The infant's rate of vocalization in turn increased from one per 17 seconds to one every 4 seconds for the same period. There followed an interval of 2½ minutes in which the infant smiled no more and there were six alternations of infant vocalizing and mother talking. The infant maintained his rate of vocalization, though introducing no novel responses, while the mother's rate of talking declined to one every 7 seconds. This last rate of decline was superimposed on a more general response decrement for maternal talking over the entire 6 minutes. Finally, the mother abruptly picked up the infant, held him close upright, then at a distance, tickled him, and turned her attention away. This burst of maternal activity reduced the infant's vocalizations, but the mother's cessation of responding was followed by fussing, then crying. She repeated the physical contact, but the infant continued to cry, and the sequence was terminated by the mother leaving the immediate vicinity of the infant and remaining away for nearly 3 minutes [p. 68]. (Copyright 1971 by the American Psychological Association. Reprinted by permission.)

In contrast with the caregiving sequence, the social interaction portion of the foregoing record indicates alternation of a relatively limited response repertoire between both participants rather than sequentially ordered repertoires. Each participant provides one or two responses that serve as stimuli for the other's response. The control system aspects of interaction involve the effect of repetition and novelty on increments and decrements in responsiveness. For some time the interaction had the quality of a well-established game, mother and infant alternating in providing a response that maintained the response of the other. There is pleasure in the ritual just as in a card game, but the actual hands dealt out have to change, or the participants lose interest in the ritual. When the infant introduced a novel element relative to this segment of the interaction—a smile—

the mother increased her rate of talking. When there was a return to the simple alternation of infant vocalizing and mother talking, the mother responded to the repetition by losing interest and breaking off the interaction. Thus, the capability of the infant for introducing novelty is important, both within the larger pattern of changes over the first few months and within the fabric of a specific interaction sequence.

From this example, and from the previously described episode of the same mother–infant pair, it can be seen that the control systems model (used to explain associations of parent and child characteristics in Chapter 4) is particularly helpful in thinking about caregiving and social exchanges at the level of actual interaction sequences. However, it is also apparent that it is necessary to think about a control system of the individual existing within the control system of interaction. Both participants in the interaction are involved in self-regulation as well as interregulation. This is evident in early development, because the behavioral manifestations of physiological homeostatic processes in the infant are so visible, especially in caregiving sequences. In social interaction situations as well, one can see how an infant that is feeling uncomfortable because of excessive excitation may avert its head, frown, or in other ways put out signals to reduce the social stimulation coming from the mother in order to maintain its own internal bounds. On the other hand, an infant who has not found much excitement during the course of its waking period prior to an interaction with its mother may engage in vigorous striking of her hands or kicking to get her to repeat interesting stimulation and to keep the wanted new level of excitation from subsiding.

From the standpoint of the infant, it may be conjectured that social interaction involves cycling between stimulus hunger and pleasure with decreasing periods of unmanageable excitement, as development proceeds.

From the standpoint of the mother, social interaction involves finding the infant ready for play or inducing it to play and then managing the state of the play in order to continue her pleasure in the transaction. An overstimulated baby who becomes fussy, or an infant who becomes drowsy, will not be able to play with her. In contrast with her management of states in the caregiving situation, the outcome of successful management efforts is positive, and the opportunity to play is for mutual enjoyment rather than mere avoidance of the unpleasant.

Evidence of the mother's control system is less obvious, but the interaction equation is symmetrical in this respect. For example, a mother who is under stress from other sources may be especially apprehensive about prolonged crying because she feels limited in her capacity to restore the infant to an optimal state. On the opposite side, the gradual emergence of the social interaction exchanges can be an exhilarating experience after the prior background of the essentially aversive–preventive system. The infant takes its place among other sources of excitement and pleasure. When she is bored with other activities, she can turn to her infant for fun. When the infant's limited repertoire becomes a bit monotonous, she turns to other children, husband, her friends, or other activities for "kicks."

This discussion of social interaction brings out some points relative to animate and inanimate objects. Much of the research on early infancy concentrates on interaction of infants with toys. In studies inspired by Piaget's theories, adults exist only as shadowy figures in the background who provide and manipulate physical objects on which the infant is acting in order to develop its cognitive capacities. In such research, it might be overlooked that physical objects do not modulate themselves in keeping with the state of the infant. Also, as we have mentioned before, the most elaborate toys cannot compete for any sustained period with the mobility and variety of stimulation that an adult can provide. In fact, there is evidence that infants develop their perception of the stability and continuity of the inanimate world after and, possibly, as a result of achieving the same status relative to their mothers or significant caregivers (Bell & Ainsworth, 1970).

Maintaining the Behavior Interaction System

Successive production of novelty.   It is only necessary to mention a few of the many changes manifested by the infant during the third to sixth months to see how their novelty could have an effect on the mother's interest. She could hardly escape being affected by her offspring's increased capability for manipulating objects, goal-oriented reaching versus indiscriminate contacts, sitting up, and crawling. It is well to remind ourselves at this point that it is not necessary that we be able to ascertain the complete causal pattern for the emergence of the new behaviors. They may emerge on a developmental time schedule as long as there is an average expectable environment. Some novel behaviors may have emerged as a result of special stimulation provided by a caregiver in an earlier period. Whatever the origin, new behaviors emerge at certain times for most infants, and the mother who functions both as a caregiver as well as a partner in social interaction cannot help but notice and be affected by these changes.

Inducing a singular relationship.   Certain infant behaviors during this period convey the message to the mother that she has been selected for a singular relationship. By the fifth month, most mothers in one study (Emde et al., 1976) believed that their infants vocalized, smiled, and got more excited in response to them than in response to others. They also noticed that their infants showed an intense interest in strangers and compared their faces or figures to their own.

The mother's effectiveness.   There is abundant experimental evidence of learning capabilities in the infant by the third month. It seems reasonable that the mother experiences the infant's increasing modifiability in some way, probably as a subjective recognition that she can have an effect. Not only is she partially out from under control of the cry–sleep–feed cycle, she should now know that she has acquired reinforcement value. She is effective in managing the behavior of her infant. This shift in control from the infant to the mother, in this one aspect of interaction, emerges by inference from correlational data obtained in a longitudinal study started in the newlywed period and continued through early infancy. Moss (1974) reports that factor scores representing characteristics of the spouses and the way they interacted during the newlywed period showed only negligible correlations with indices of the mother's responsiveness to their infants at the third week postpartum, but these became significant by the third month. Presumably, not until the third month did the demand characteristics of their infants recede sufficiently that the parents' own peculiar styles of interaction could emerge.

THE PERIOD OF ATTACHMENT: SEVEN TO TWELVE MONTHS

The Caregiving System Differentiates

Data from Emde et al. (1976) indicate that primary caretaking demand subsides substantially again just before the period of attachment, as it did just before the period in which social interaction flowered. This second decrease to a new low in unexplained fussing occurs between the fifth and seventh months. The amount of crying then remains stable throughout the remainder of the year. This change provides further relief for the mother from the cycle of fussing, feeding, and sleeping. During this same period, the infant is seeing and grasping, crawling into things, and showing still more lively curiosity and exploratory behavior. Its motor capabilities and interests are advancing faster than the bases for caution. These changes set the stage for the emergence of a new caregiving system centered around controlling the infant's activities and protecting it against consequences of its own capabilities (as well as protecting objects in the home). The primary caregiving system recedes into the background and a new system of control and protection assumes a position of prominence in the life of the parents.

Although most infants show a great reduction in fussing by the seventh month, Emde et al. (1976) reports that a small number continued to fuss and be irritable. The latter would fit in with the conclusions of Bell and Ainsworth (1972) that for a portion of their sample, mother and infant got into a vicious cycle: the more the infant cried the more the mother withdrew from efforts to soothe, particularly in the last part of the first year.

A new form of infant control.   Just as most mothers are beginning to feel a release from "king baby's" tyrannical fuss–feed–sleep cycle, and just as they feel their increasing effectiveness as a reinforcer, their babies restrict them in a new way. What started as an interest in the faces and figures of strangers and then led to comparison of the mother's image with theirs, now appears as a sobering expression, gaze aversion, avoidance of being held by the stranger, and then, in some infants, frank distress at the sight of a stranger. Furthermore, even the small amount of crying that appears during this period is directed toward the mother or primary caregiver. It is directional crying: not merely crying to anyone. Some mothers react very positively to the combined indications of negative responses to strangers and being singled out for attachment, taking delight in the increasingly close relation; other show concern over the increasing dependence.

Emde et al. (1976) have summarized inductive and deductive evidence that stranger distress appears in a substantial number of infants and is under maturational control. Its frequency is minimized in reports coming out of cross-sectional studies but not in longitudinal studies, simply because the incidence of a phenomenon of this kind over a time interval should be greater than prevalence at a single time. The findings from the longitudinal studies will be accepted in the present treatment not only because incidence is more relevant to the understanding of a developmental process, but also because repeated observations in a longitudinal study provide an opportunity to adjust observation to the peculiarities of each infant and to judge each successive behavior against the background of the infant's own baseline.

The case for experiential determination of stranger distress and its precursors is not strong, except insofar as specific triggering of responses is concerned. It is noteworthy that the schedule of appearance is similar in different countries showing a wide variety of child-rearing practices. There is not a gradual onset as would be expected if cumulative effects of learning were involved. Schaffer, Greenwood, and Parry (1972) report a stepwise progression of what they call wariness. Evidence for the heritability of stranger distress appears in the similarity of developmental curves for monozygotic twins, compared with the dissimilarity for dizygotic twins (Freedman, 1965). Accordingly, stranger distress is regarded as essentially a contribution of the infant.

Separation reactions.   Although this behavior shows a different developmental course from stranger reactions, building up steadily in intensity throughout the last part of the first year and increasing further in the months beyond (Emde et al., 1976), the effect on the parent of the increasing intensity of reaction is similar in one important sense to the effect of stranger distress. The singular relationship becomes a restricting bond that locks the mother into a new caregiving system. She feels that she and she alone has been selected to help the infant face the world and provide protection. She will share this responsibility for protection with others, but the message from her infant is that it feels its security only in her.

The Social Interaction System

It has been mentioned that the proximity of mother and infant engendered by the process of attachment is necessary but not sufficient for social interaction. Fortunately, smiles and vocalizations are both attachment mechanisms as well as stimuli to social interaction. During the seventh to twelfth month, these highly effective social responses are increasingly brought into play at a greater distance and from the foundation of a much more complete image of the mother. The infant can integrate the visual and auditory aspects of the mother as a social object (Cohen, 1974). Now the mother may find herself greeted by a vocalization from another room when she returns from a trip and registers her presence by talking to some other member of the family. Others in the family may elicit a response, but it is likely to be a different one, so that she knows her infant's response is discriminative.

One practical joke played by tourists in scenic country is to stop their car, get out, then stare at a point in the distance, talking to each other in a very excited manner. Other cars stop and soon a crowd collects, all peering at nothing! From the sixth month on, the infant has the same power to attract the attention of others. The intensity of their interest in objects and people is sufficiently compelling that in a laboratory situation, the mother is drawn to peer at what the infant regards much more than the infant is drawn to peer at the mother's objects of interest (Collis & Schaffer, 1975).

In general, communication becomes more effective, and there are many more interactions at a distance, but there are warps in the general fabric of the proximal–distal shift. There is still close contact, but now the infant can bring it about by crawling to the mother and maintain it by clinging. Physical contact is still frequent, but increasingly as a part of social interaction rather than as a means of soothing (Moss, 1974). Along the same lines, we have mentioned that during this period crying occurs more frequently when the infant is in sight or earshot of the mother rather than when she is out of the range of awareness. This change is interpreted by Bell and Ainsworth (1972) as an increase in the use of the cry for communication. Earlier, the cry was an indiscriminant call for help to anyone within range. Those infants who cry very little show increasing competence in communication by more use of facial expressions and bodily gestures, again an exception to the general pattern of the proximal–distal shift.

Apropos the preceeding period in which social interaction emerged, experimental findings were cited indicating that infants could show response decrement if adults were too repetitive. During the present period, infants may become increasingly "choosy" in another way. Those whose mothers interact with them a great deal are most ignored by their infants (Beckwith, 1972). The ignoring infants spend less time in self stimulation, pointing to the probable role of homeostatic mechanisms. Presumably, the ignoring of a highly stimulating mother serves to keep the level of arousal and excitement down to tolerable limits, because the input is near the infants' upper limits, and they have little need for rocking themselves, sucking their hands, and other forms of self stimulation.

Whatever the origins, whether from endogenous maturational determinants of the proximal–distal shift, from the emergence of attachment mechanisms, from the steady acquisition of communication skills due to interaction with the mother, or from some complex interplay of maturation and daily interaction, the infant is increasingly showing changes from the seventh month on that give the social interaction new dimensions. Mother and infant can enjoy each other at a distance or together. Either can bring interactions about by going to the location of the other. Communication exchanges go far beyond smiling, vocalization, and touching. All of these changes take place against the background of a more intense and special relationship that the infant has created in the mind of the mother by responding differently to her than to others.

Maintaining the Behavior Interaction System

In the period of attachment, the infant's ability to maintain proximity or to communicate at a distance, and its ability to single out the mother for a special relationship, are such powerful forces in maintaining the behavior interaction system (apart from their special effects on the caregiving and social systems) that it seems superfluous to cite other probable ''binding'' effects. A few illustrations will be given merely to flesh out the otherwise abstract characterization of this period. The mother must notice with interest the efforts of the infant to get its way, first of all, by ''magical procedures'' such as kicking and head waving, then, by the more realistic procedure of physically removing obstacles to a desired toy, and, still later, by trying to push her hands into a desired action (Wolff, 1960). She can thus see the infant's steady progress toward managing causal relations.

SUMMARY

The activation of the behavior interaction system after the birth of the infant and its differentiation into caregiving and social components in the first year is associated with the initial appearance and behavior of the neonate or subsequent changes in infant behavior. The changes that are emphasized in this chapter are usually regarded as under maturational control or as being changes for which no plausible explanation has been advanced in terms of parent–effects.

The following changes alter the general basis for the behavioral interaction system within the first year: from activity to reactivity, from preformed organization to malleability, from stimulus reduction to stimulus seeking, from response to proximal versus distal stimuli. Throughout the first year, the control systems model of interregulation first discussed in Chapter 4, proves helpful in explaining not only associations of parent and infant characteristics, but also actual sequences of interaction.

Three periods can be marked off by specific age-associated changes in the infant. The first period is that of primary caregiving (birth to 2 months), in which the most powerful influence is the compelling, demanding characteristics of the infant's crying and the helpless thrashing movements that the parent sees once the cry has produced proximity. Clinical examples indicate that mothers subject to caregiving demand within the normal range are maintained in this somewhat stressful situation by the fact that the infant provides readable cues to its condition and does not exceed the mother's tolerance limits.

Social interaction emerges in the second period (3 to 6 months), presumably due to a substantial reduction in fussing or crying, an increase in wakefulness (that exposes the mother to another compelling although in this case positive effect—the infant's gaze behavior), an increase in noncrying vocalizations, the appearance of predictable social smiles, and an increase in the general modifiability of its behaviors.

Primary caregiving demand due to the infant's crying shows a second substantial reduction just before the period of attachment (7 to 12 months), but two new demands arise to take its place. One is the need for control and protection incident to increased motor capability and exploratory behavior. The other is the restriction of parental behavior due to distress reactions to strangers and separation. While the caregiving system is differentiating, social interaction is carried out increasingly at a distance. The infant becomes more selective in what it will respond to, and the infant can bring about interactions by going to the mother.

As the changes in caregiving and social interaction are occurring, the infant is contributing to maintaining the general behavioral interaction system by the successive production of novel responses, showing modifiability, and by inducing a singular relationship with the mother.

Part III

CONCEPTS AND FINDINGS—OTHER MAMMALS

7

Basic Features of the Caregiver-Offspring Relationship in Mammals

Lawrence V. Harper

INTRODUCTION

Contrary to naive, popular views of the "maternal instinct," caregiving is not a fixed entity, easily distinguished from other behaviors. In most mammals, parental behavior consists of a long-term, gradually changing pattern of responses that reoccurs cyclically during the adulthood of at least the female (Rosenblatt & Lehrman, 1963). The caregiving pattern, whether performed by the biological or a "foster" parent, consists of a number of discrete activities such as nursing, retrieving the young, and grooming them. These activities wax and wane independently within a single caregiving cycle, and performance during one cycle is not necessarily predictive of behavior in subsequent cycles (Noirot, 1969b; Wiesner & Sheard, 1933). In a number of species including man, many of the motor elements employed in parental care also appear in other functional contexts such as mating, fighting, or feeding (Wickler, 1972). Because the form and intensity of caregiving change as the young mature, and because many of the activities involved in parental behavior are often shared with other behavioral patterns, the apparent unity of caregiving derives largely from the fact that its components usually have a common referent—the young.

An experiment by Plume, Fogarty, Grota, and Ader (1968) illustrates this point. Noting that female rats often pick up and carry various objects about their cages in the same fashion that the mother retrieves her young, these investigators compared the responses of rats to a food pellet, a plastic toy, and a young rat pup. They tested four groups of animals: virgins, females at mid-pregnancy, pregnant females near term, and mothers with 2-day-old litters. The mothers retrieved pups more often than any other group and were the only ones to choose pups more frequently than other objects. Plume et al. concluded that maternal retrieving or, for that matter, maternal behavior can only be defined by the *selective* display of a response to offspring.

Although the following discussion will indicate that offspring of unrelated species affect their parents in quite similar ways, these similarities often reflect no more than common strategies for coping with comparable adaptations such as highly dependent young. Strategies that appear to be almost universal across mammals, or nearly identical in closely related species, frequently turn out to be regulated by different processes. For example, although sheep and goats are fairly closely related and although many aspects of their parent–offspring relationships seem similar, they differ in terms of the mechanisms underlying parturition (Klopper & Gardner, 1973) and the development of the mother–offspring bond (Hersher, Richmond, & Moore, 1963). Material on a variety of species is included only to indicate the generality and many possible forms of offspring–effects, not to suggest that the underlying processes are the same. Parallels in human behavior will be pointed out where they are interesting and potentially important. As indicated already, well-controlled animal studies often help in the development of conceptual models against which "natural" experiments with human subjects may be evaluated.

BEHAVIORAL MATCHING

James' lock-and-key analogy provides a remarkably accurate description of a basic feature of adaptive behavior. It takes only a little reflection to realize that a fundamental condition for successful reproduction in any species is that the characteristics and behavior of the parties involved complement each other. Research with fetuses and newborn animals shows that prenatal maturation endows the young with patterns of response fitting them to the environment into which they will be born—which for a mammal centers about the mother (cf. Anokhin, 1964). The nursing relationship is an obvious example of such a match. Vocal communication provides another illustration of the fit between infant and caregiver. In both rodents (Noirot, 1972b) and humans (Ostwald, 1963), the cries of the young let their parents know where they are and how they are doing, and the auditory sensitivities of their caregivers are greatest in precisely the same frequency-ranges as the infants' calls.

In addition, the parent–offspring relationship involves change in the caregiver as well as in the growing young. Changes in parental and filial behavior must be synchronized in time; the "match" is a dynamic one. For example, Leon and Moltz (1972) found that lactating female rats secrete an odorous substance that is attractive to suckling pups. They compared the responses of young differing in age to mothers at different points in the caregiving cycle. The onset of mothers' emission of the "maternal pheromone" and pups' responsiveness to it corresponded to the period at which the pups became able to leave the nest but prior to their being able to survive without maternal care. The decline in maternal pheromone production and pup responsiveness occurred when the young were capable of surviving on their own.

Despite a substantial match between caregiver and offspring, the degree of behavioral coordination is not absolute. The evolutionary process affects the fitness of a species to cope with the average, expectable environment; in unusual circumstances, mismatches may occur even in the higher primates. Two observations of chimpanzee mother–infant relations are illustrative: In the first instance, a mother whose infant has strayed unusually far away from her was observed to use only a "hoo" call in the attempt to locate her offspring—even though the range of this call was too limited to be effective. In the second case, an infant had suffered a severe injury to one arm; pressure caused the infant to scream in pain, yet the mother's only response to her offspring's cries was to clutch it more tightly (van Lawick–Goodall, 1968).

When the parent–offspring match is not so specific as to prevent cross-species fostering, interesting difficulties frequently occur. Asynchrony in such cases also demonstrates how precise the adjustment between natural parent and offspring can be. Beach's (1939) report of caregiving in a South American pouchless opossum shows how behavioral mismatches may occur when young emit stimuli that release caregiving in adults of other species. He observed that, shortly after birth, the young opossums maintained nearly continuous contact with their mother by means of strong suction on the teats and clinging reflexes of the feet. When Beach scattered the litter about the cage, the mother retrieved her young and carried them to the nestbox. In so doing, she approached the pups much like a rat and nosed them, but, unlike rats who pick up pups in their mouths, the opossum pushed her pups backward under her belly. The young immediately rolled on their backs, grasped the hair of the females' stomach, and propelled themselves backward toward her teats. As they moved back, they made side-to-side "rooting" movements with the snout until a nipple was found and grasped. In this manner, all the opossum young were retrieved. When rat pups were included with young opossums in subsequent tests, they also elicited intense retrieving behavior. But the mother opossum followed a single, stereotyped sequence; she approached, nosed, and pushed the rat pups under her belly in the same way that she treated her own offspring. However, the rat pups, lacking the opossum's complementary rolling-over-and-clinging responses, failed to attach to the opossum and were retrieved successfully less than half the time. The mother made numerous attempts to get the rat pups under her belly but never attempted to pick them up with her mouth or prehensile tail—despite the fact that she carried nesting material in this way.

Incompatibility of parental and filial responses might therefore be added to biologists' lists of mechanisms that serve to discourage interspecies hybridization during evolution.

BEHAVIORAL "BUFFERING"

The matching of offspring characteristics and behavior to parental anatomy and activity obviously cannot be so precise as to cover all possible contingencies. However, the parent–offspring relationship is robust enough that successful reproduction is accomplished in a wide range of situations. A margin of error develops in behavior patterns possessing high adaptive value; in other words, the behavior pattern is "buffered." Evidence from several mammalian species indicates that the young provide a variety of stimuli to which caregivers are sensitive. Parental responses may be elicited by stimulation of any one of several sensory systems. Impairment of one or more sources of input often does not prevent functionally adequate caregiving, although it may be quantitatively diminished.

A classic paper by Beach and Jaynes (1956b) provides experimental evidence for this point. They studied the retrieving of lactating female rats after surgically blocking different sensory receptors and found that despite the absence of sight, smell, or tactual sensations about the mouth, only the speed and efficiency of maternal performance suffered, according to the sensory avenue impaired. Even multiple blocking such as blinding combined with olfactory loss did not altogether prevent experienced females from locating scattered pups and returning them to the nest. Mothers with all three modalities impaired still attempted to retrieve pups, although often unsuccessfully.

This almost unbelievable hardiness of the rat's parent–offspring system has even been demonstrated in caesarean-delivered females. Herrenkohl and Rosenberg (1972a) removed the olfactory bulbs of first-time pregnant rats 2 days before caesarian delivery of their pups, or they blinded or deafened them surgically immediately after caesarean section. Two days after the operation, the animals were presented daily, for 3 consecutive days, with three 1-day-old foster pups for a 15-minute period. Certain components of caregiving were impaired when the operated subjects' performance was compared with that of sham-operated control animals. However, retrieving, sniffing, and licking the pups, and the assumption of the lactation posture, all were displayed by mothers in every experimental group. These results indicated that neither vision, audition, nor olfaction alone were essential for postdelivery responsiveness in rats; stimuli reaching the mothers through other sensory channels could elicit functionally adequate maternal behavior.[1]

[1] A possible exception to this principle has been suggested by Gandelman, Zarrow, and Denenberg (1971), who found that olfactory bulbectomy led to cannibalism in both naive and experienced mother mice. At this writing, their data suggest that olfactory cues may be essential for caregiving in the mouse. However, neural ablation often disturbs more than one sensory system (cf. Herrenkohl & Sachs, 1972), and Fleming and Rosenblatt (1974b) have shown that, whereas olfactory bulbectomy may lead to cannibalism in naive rats, local anesthesia of the olfactory tracts does not. Thus, the indispensibility of olfaction for caregiving in mice requires further demonstration.

Tactual stimuli from the mammary glands may also be dispensed with. Moltz, Geller, and Levin (1967) showed that female rats whose mammary glands and nipples had been removed when they were of weaning age displayed an essentially normal caregiving pattern as adults. They even assumed the lactation posture over their foster litters. Nontactual cues from pups can thus substitute for sensations normally occurring as a result of suckling. When (tactual) input to the hypothalamus was blocked by surgery extensive enough to inhibit milk-letdown, rat mothers still gave birth normally and displayed the full complement of maternal behavior toward their neonates (Herrenkohl & Rosenberg, 1972b). Such buffering is not peculiar to rats. The olfactory bulbs of mother sheep have been destroyed, and the vision and olfaction of mother goats have been reversibly blocked with the result that, although the mothers were unable to discriminate their own from other infants of the species, they still displayed caregiving behavior (Baldwin & Shillito, 1974; Klopfer & Klopfer, 1968).

Caregivers are not only responsive to a variety of cues from the young, but both mother and young are capable of considerable behavioral flexibility under unusual circumstances. Rosenblum and Youngstein (1974) manipulated mother–infant interactions within groups of captive bonnet macaques by anesthetizing either a mother or her infant. When one member of the pair was unconscious and thereby unable to complement the behavior of the conscious partner, the latter demonstrated a behavioral "compensatory potential." When an infant under the age of 4 months was returned to the group unconscious, the mother played a more active role in maintaining contact with it than she did when the offspring was capable of reciprocating. Similarly, when the mother was anesthetized, the infant managed to achieve sustained ventral contact despite the fact that the mother was unable to facilitate the process.

These studies demonstrate the margin of error built into the caregiver–offspring interaction system and indicate that parental behavior is controlled by a complex mosaic of offspring stimuli. However, this does not mean that single stimulus parameters are always sufficient to evoke completely adequate caregiving responses. Often, when stimulation through any one sense can elicit a response, the simultaneous and appropriate excitation of several receptors enhances the act. In fact, a single stimulus dimension frequently depends for its full effectiveness upon others to provide the requisite context. For example, Beach and Jaynes (1956b) found that with more widespread sensory impairment, the response latencies of mother rats increased, and the proportion of pups retrieved decreased. They also showed that, despite some degree of substitutability, different sensory modalities were not equally important for retrieving. The performance of females who were blinded and had no sense of touch about the mouth was only slightly inferior to that of females who were blinded alone, while mothers who could not smell or feel their young with their snouts had considerable difficulty in retrieving their pups. In sum, although it may be necessary to analyze various offspring stimulus dimensions separately, the elements ultimately must be recombined to fully understand the ways in which stimuli emitted by the young control caregiver behavior.

MODIFIABILITY

The fact that the evolutionary process has endowed mammalian caregivers with a certain degree of responsiveness to offspring stimuli does not mean that prior experience with young is without effect. The behavior of both parent and offspring, although adapted to average conditions, must change with the development of the young and varying external situations. Examples of the modification of offspring behavior as a consequence of caregiver activity are abundant. Less often considered—but no less substantiated—are the many ways in which the appearance or activities of the young modify subsequent caregiver behavior.

In rats, prior caregiving may affect a female's sensitivity to stimuli associated with offspring. Surgical removal of both olfactory bulbs caused naive female rats to eat pups that were placed in their cages. However, if the operation was performed in two stages with several days' recovery time, and if exposure to pups was allowed in between operations, cannibalism was reduced. Compared to two-stage-operated females who were not exposed to pups between operations, the pup-exposed females spent significantly more time in caregiving activities (Fleming & Rosenblatt, 1974a).

In rhesus monkeys, simply giving birth and being exposed to an infant may increase subsequent responsiveness even when the mothers fail to provide care for their firstborns. Of 20 isolation-reared females, 17 failed to respond to their first offspring with consistent caregiving responses. Subsequently, 7 of them became pregnant for a second time. Despite the fact that only 1 of these monkeys was rated as an "adequate" mother with her first offspring, she and 5 of the 6 remaining mothers (3 of whom were previously rated as "abusive" and 2 as "indifferent") all were judged to be adequate mothers to their second offspring. One of these reformed mothers had mistreated her first infant so badly that it had to be taken away from her after 2 weeks and subsequently died of its wounds. Although she had failed completely to care for her firstborn, she performed adequately with her second infant (Harlow, Harlow, Dodsworth, & Arling, 1966).

As one would expect, prior experience in caring for young also leads to improvement in the execution of subsequent performances. In retrieving experiments with mother ground squirrels, average latencies to return pups to the nest decreased across trials. This increased efficiency was largely due to a reduction of the mothers' lingering in the nest after retrieving the first pup. Delaying the beginning of testing for various periods of time showed that the more rapid performances were due to prior experience and not developmental changes in either the mothers or the offspring (Michener, 1971). When the retrieving performance of mother rats across their first and second litters was analyzed, Carlier and Noirot (1965) not only found an intertrial reduction in time to retrieve, but the young of the *second* litters were retrieved more quickly. These results were in part due to the fact that "extraneous" activity and latency to begin retrieving decreased over trials and, in addition, across pregnancies. Analysis of the way in which mothers grasped their pups—whether by a central part of the body or by the extremities—indicated that central grasps resulted in significantly fewer retrieving attempts being interrupted by the mother dropping a pup before reaching the nest. Central grasps not only occurred more frequently across trials within both caregiving cycles, but they were also more common during the second cycle. In sum, retrieving improved both in the short-term, from trial-to-trial, and over the long-term, from the first to the second litter.

Similar data have been reported for humans. In two studies, groups of mothers of premature infants were involved in their babies' care while the latter were in hospital incubators. Control groups were composed of mothers who had to follow a more typical procedure that minimized contact with infants while they were hospitalized. In both these studies, the mothers who were involved in the care of their infants, although limited to the incubator situation, were more confident and effective than were women following standard hospital routine (Barnett, Leiderman, Grobstein, & Klaus, 1970; Leifer, Leiderman, Barnett, & Williams, 1972). The breast-feeding behavior of mothers with their firstborns has been compared with that of mothers with their second infants in the hospital during the first day after birth. Compared with experienced mothers, new mothers were more "interfering" and did not respond as well to their babies' cues; they spent more time in extraneous activities such as talking to their infants, and they took longer to position their offspring at the breast so that sucking could begin (Thoman, Leiderman, & Olson, 1972).

Thus, although naive mammalian parents may be capable of responding with adequate care to the cues emitted by their offspring, experience in ministering to young may further refine caregiving in terms of (1) economy of effort expended; (2) the efficiency of particular components; and (3) in the case of "atypical" responsiveness, the likelihood of responding appropriately to subsequent young.

SUMMARY

Parental behavior involves a variety of responses not all of which are unique to caregiving. The behavior of both parent and offspring are matched to form a complementary series and are often buffered against physiological and environmental fluctuations. As the young mature, the match must be maintained, involving changes in both caregiver and young. Just as offspring behavior is modified by interaction with the parent, parental behavior changes as a result of caring for the young.

8

Effects of the Young on the Caregiving Cycle

Lawrence V. Harper

INTRODUCTION

Parental behavior involves a pattern of responses that is not closely related to any single, unitary "drive" (Noirot, 1969b; Slotnick, 1967). The kinds of care provided change over the course of the cycle, because both parent and young are changing physically and behaviorally as a result of their relationship (cf. Schneirla & Rosenblatt, 1963). Because maintenance of the species depends upon the young ultimately producing viable offspring themselves, the transition from filial dependence to adult reproductive status is the final measure of parental success. Therefore, mammalian parents are constrained to make a considerable investment in the development of their young. Granted that caregiving behavior is the resultant of an interaction between parent and offspring, this chapter focuses upon the role that the young play in determining the nature and timing of the care they receive.

INITIATION OF PARENTAL RESPONSIVENESS

Current evidence suggests that mammalian young begin to influence their mothers from the earliest stages of pregnancy. In some species, such as mice and dogs, adults are responsive to the young regardless of gender or reproductive condition. However, among the majority of mammals studied, mothers usually account for most of the caregiving behavior. Indeed, even in mice, lactating females are more responsive to young than inexperienced females (Noirot & Goyens, 1971; Voci & Carlson, 1973). Presumably, the mother's greater responsiveness stems from physiological changes resulting from pregnancy and parturition. Some of these changes may be influenced by the developing young.

Pregnancy and parturition.   The physiology of pregnancy in mammals is not completely understood. However, most investigators agree that fertilization must somehow initiate pregnancy. In rabbits, prior to implantation, the blastocyst may manufacture hormone-like material that readies the mother's uterus to accept it (Haour & Saxena, 1974). Although these data are the subject of debate (Sundaram, Connell, & Passantino, 1975), confirmation would indicate that mother and "offspring" are interacting from the very beginning.

A general rule among animals giving birth to several young is that the larger the litter, the shorter the gestation time. In man too, fetal mass is an important determinant of the duration of pregnancy (Bulmer, 1970). In addition to affecting fetal size, the genotype of the young appears to influence gestation time directly, particularly when the time deviates from the norm (Holm, 1967). In sheep, even the hormonal signal for the onset of labor may originate from the fetus. Clinical data suggest that the hormones produced by the human fetus also play an important role in initiating the birth process (Anderson & Turnbull, 1973; Chard, 1973), and recent research on the hormones produced by the fetal pituitary promises to illuminate the mechanisms involved (Silman, Chard, Lowry, Smith, & Young, 1976).

In addition to contributing to the duration of pregnancy, the fetus may affect the birth process. In rabbits, cervical dilation caused by passage of the young increases the intensity of uterine contractions (Cross, 1966), and in domestic dogs, the muscular tonus of the fetus affects the ease and speed of delivery (Naaktgeboren, 1964). In man, the fetus' position in the uterus (head- or breech-presentation) influences the difficulty and duration of labor (Peiper, 1963). Immediately after birth, the human neonate's sucking facilitates expulsion of the placenta (Caldeyro–Barcia, 1961).

In sum, the "offspring" are involved in determining the onset, duration, and termination of pregnancy.

Pregnancy-related behavioral changes.   During pregnancy, the mother's hormonal balance changes markedly. In man and several other mammals, the fetus or the fetus-and-placenta may account for some of these hormonal alterations (Klopper, 1973). If we assume that hormones affect maternal behavior, some pregnancy-related behavioral changes may be influenced by the fetus.

In a number of species, there is an increase in responsiveness to offspring stimuli toward the end of pregnancy; it is often especially noticeable just before the onset of labor. Some of these changes are related to blood-borne factors, probably hormonal, which appear to peak at the time of birth (Terkel & Rosenblatt, 1972). Thus, in species such as sheep, in which hormones originating from the fetus help to trigger the onset of labor and in which pregnant females display a marked interest in young immediately prior to giving birth (Hersher et al., 1963), the fetus may be thought to have "primed" its mother to receive it.

While cultural expectations or cognitive dissonance may be important in determining human responsiveness, it is still interesting to note that even when the pregnancy is unwelcome, mothers' attitudes become increasingly positive as gestation progresses (Hubert, 1974).

Some of the reported relationships between maternal anxieties and neonatal abnormalities in humans may represent effects of an abnormal fetus on the mother rather than effects of maternal emotional state on the unborn baby. For example, if the relationships between maternal emotionality during pregnancy and Down's syndrome in the offspring are confirmed, it would point to an offspring–effect, because Down's syndrome is the result of a genetic defect in the fetus (Gruenberg, 1967). It is also possible that some cases of postpartum depression among mothers who deliver in hospitals may be the result of their being denied access to the stimuli appropriate to their state, namely, their babies (Hannan, 1975).

Whatever the cause, the early lactation period in most mammals is one of heightened sensitivity to young. Observers have frequently remarked that animals who have just given birth appear to be especially responsive to offspring; some even utter "maternal calls" during labor (Collias, 1956). In flying squirrels (Muul, 1970) and rats (Wiesner & Sheard, 1933), lactating mothers appear to be indefatigable retrievers despite repeated performances. In primates, mothers' solicitude for dead young also indicates heightened sensitivity to offspring-related stimuli (Hall & DeVore, 1965; Kaplan, 1973).

Formation of the mother–young bond.   Many mammalian mothers form exclusive ties to their offspring and are unresponsive to other infants. This is particularly true among ungulates and pinnipeds (De Vos, Brokx, & Geist, 1967; Peterson, 1968). Research with sheep and goats indicates that there exists a critical period shortly after birth during which the mother is maximally sensitive to the stimuli presented by the young; the first infant with which she interacts defines an "acceptable" offspring, narrowing the field, as it were. Once the attachment process is complete, inducing the mother to accept an "alien" offspring is much more difficult.

Collias (1956) was one of the first to experimentally demonstrate the importance of contact between mothers and offspring in the period immediately following birth. He found that if group-penned sheep and goat mothers were denied access to their newborns for more than 2 hours after birth, they would subsequently reject them. In contrast, if the young were returned within 15 to 45 minutes, the mothers accepted them. Moreover, if mothers were allowed to interact with their offspring for 1–2 hours immediately following birth, subsequent separation for as long as 3½ hours did not affect their readiness to accept their own young. More recent experiments have further clarified this phenomenon. Smith, Van–Toller, and Boyes (1966) showed that the period of sensitivity in experienced sheep lasted for about 8 hours. In goats, the period during which mothers would become attached to their young appeared to be considerably more brief, probably less than 1 hour (Klopfer & Klopfer, 1968). In both species, however, alien young were rejected once a mother became attached to her own offspring.

Even when the mother–offspring bond is not so exclusive, the postnatal period is still important for the maintenance of responsiveness. Rat mothers who were denied contact with pups during the first 4 days after littering were much less solicitous of young than were mothers whose offspring were removed for comparable periods of time at other points in the caregiving cycle (Rosenblatt & Lehrman, 1963).

The first few days after birth may be a period of particular maternal sensitivity to stimulation from the young in man. Women in the study by Barnett et al. (1970) who were trained to participate in the hospital care of their premature offspring showed more attachment to their young when compared with mothers who were not allowed such early caregiving experience. In another study, 14 of 28 mothers of full-term firstborn infants were given a total of 16 hours of extra contact with their neonates between the third and seventy-second hours after birth. Interviews with these mothers and observations of their interactions with their infants 1 month later revealed that they were more solicitous of their babies than the controls. An intensive follow-up study at the end of the first year showed that the early-contact mothers, as a group, exceeded the controls in solicitude and apparent concern for their infants' welfare (Kennell, Jerauld, Wolfe, Chesler, Kreger, McAlpine, Steffa, & Klaus, 1974). Conversely, there is a suggestion that the incidence of child abuse may be greater where early mother–infant separation has occurred (Klein & Stern, 1971). Such data strongly argue for more careful research on the importance to the mother of stimuli coming from the infant in the first few days after birth.

Setting the "tone" of the early relationship.   This early postdelivery period may be important not only as the time during which the mother–offspring bond is established but also as a period in which the quality of future exchanges is determined.

Observations of mother–young interactions in goats just after birth suggest that if the mutual exchange of signals between mother and infant is not properly synchronized, the mother may butt the young away. As a result of the rebuff, the infant may subsequently approach the mother in a defensive posture and thereby elicit further maternal rejection (Klopfer & Gamble, 1966). In rats, response-patterns established by interactions with foster young may influence a female's subsequent response to her first litter. Whereas most rats whose olfactory bulbs were surgically removed just after giving birth would still rear their young, virgin females attacked and devoured test young postoperatively, and these same animals subsequently cannibalized their first litters (Fleming & Rosenblatt, 1974a).

Among humans in industrialized societies, breast-feeding is optional; the decision to try is subject to a number of considerations that usually do not relate to the infant itself. However, when a mother has decided to breast-feed, the first few mother–infant encounters may be critical in determining whether the attempt will be successful. Among the offspring-related conditions that appear to be important in this regard are whether the baby is sleepy or still satiated from a bottle-feeding when presented to the mother to nurse, and whether it has been affected by pain-relieving drugs administered to the mother during labor (Newton & Newton, 1972b; Wolff, 1971). These factors can reduce the infant's sucking response and thereby delay—or prevent—the mother's lactating. When the neonate has actively rejected the breast, mothers have reported feelings of inadequacy and strong aversion toward further attempts to nurse (Gunther, 1961). In some cases, failures to achieve successful breast-feeding may even cause maternal hostility toward the baby (Hubert, 1974).

The importance of infant responsiveness is not limited to sucking; independently derived measures of maternal stimulation and infant responsiveness are highly correlated, suggesting that infant reactivity can be a potent determinant of maternal stimulation (Osofsky & Danzger, 1973). As babies grow older, the amount of time 9- to 12-month-old infants spend looking and smiling at their mothers also can predict that amount of time their mothers will spend in contact with them later, when they are 16–18 months of age (Clarke–Stewart, 1973). In short, early experience with the young can shape subsequent maternal caregiving practices.

Artificially induced responsiveness.   The young of several species are capable of inducing solicitude in initially unresponsive adults. In their classic study of maternal behavior in rats, Wiesner and Sheard (1933) observed that virgin females who at first ignored pups began to display caregiving behavior after repeated and prolonged exposures to them. Rosenblatt (1967) replicated and extended these findings. He exposed naive adult rats to groups of five 5- to 10-day-pups for 10–15 days and tested them daily for retrieving, lactation posture, licking, and nest-building. He found that essentially all the females tested, including animals whose ovaries or pituitaries were removed, became responsive by the end of the exposure period. Even male rats, whether intact or castrated, showed responsiveness to pups as a result of prolonged exposure.

Subsequent research indicated that when previously unresponsive virgin females began to display parental behavior as a result of exposure to young, all the components of caregiving appeared at the same time. Once virgin females were induced to respond to pups, their caregiving performance over the next 10 days was nearly comparable to that of new mothers caring for their own offspring. The major differences between "induced" and natural mothers appeared to involve more rapid retrieving by the lactating females in the first 4 days after giving birth (postinduction) and more nest-building throughout the period of observation. The lactating rats also spent more time in the nursing posture—

probably because the induced virgins' nipples were not large enough to allow their foster litters to attach. The effects of induced caregiving appeared to be relatively permanent. Females who had been previously induced displayed caregiving after shorter periods of being caged with pups than did naive virgins. When previously induced virgins were compared with mothers who had had comparable caregiving time with their first litters, no difference was found (Fleming & Rosenblatt, 1974c).[1]

Contact-induced parental responsiveness has also been observed in ungulates. As indicated previously, mothers who are not allowed to interact with their newborns during the first few hours after birth often reject their young when reunited with them. However, in sheep and goats (Hersher et al., 1963) and domestic cattle (Hafez & Lineweaver, 1968), if a mother is physically restrained long enough to allow an infant to nurse, she will subsequently accept it.

Although they may reflect social expectations and cognitive factors rather than biological predispositions, comparable phenomena have been observed in man. High levels of personalized care have led to nurse–infant attachments in residential nurseries. Such attachments may sometimes be infant-initiated. In a center for unwanted and illegitimate infants, special caregiving relationships were most often the consequence of the babies' becoming attached to the nurses (David & Appell, 1961; Stevens, 1971).

Thus, in several mammalian species, prolonged exposure to stimuli emanating from the young can cause an increase in adults' responsiveness. Actual physical contact with young is not always necessary to achieve this effect. Herrenkohl and Lisk (1973) selected initially unresponsive virgin female rats and exposed half of them to rat pups enclosed in wire-mesh baskets affixed to an outside wall of their cages. The exposed females retrieved test pups more often and more consistently across test days than did nonexposed rats. Noirot (1972a) also reported that female rats housed in colony rooms where breeding and nursing occurred were more responsive to pups than were females housed in isolation. She suggested that the sounds of the young might account for this difference. Consistent with Noirot's interpretation, female rats who retrieved pups spontaneously on pretests were less likely to show caregiving after several days of social isolation (Herrenkohl & Lisk, 1973).

In naturally responsive animals, even brief contacts with young may sensitize potential caregivers. Noirot (1964a; 1964b) gave naive male and female mice 5-minute presentations of either a 1-day-old live pup or a drowned pup of the same age. Between 2 and 8 days later, the live-pup-exposed subjects were each given a comparable exposure to a 1-day-old drowned pup. In these retests, more

---

[1] In the home cage, sensitized female rats and mothers who had just littered appeared to be equally responsive to pups. However, when testing was conducted in a T-maze, Bridges, Zarrow, Gandelman, and Denenberg (1972) found that new mothers were more likely to retrieve than were induced females. Thus, induction may not achieve the same intensity of responsiveness as that which results from gestation and parturition.

of the mice initially exposed to live pups retrieved the dead pup than did those who were initially exposed to a dead pup. Presumably, prior exposure to a live pup sensitized the animals so that they responded more readily to the stimuli presented by a dead one. Practice effects were ruled out by a second experiment in which the live pup was placed directly in the nest for the initial exposure. Even under these conditions, which elicited only licking and the lactation posture, all the females subsequently retrieved a dead pup placed outside the nest. Noirot concluded that the effects of exposure to the "optimal" live pup caused a general heightening of responsiveness to a suboptimal stimulus. Comparable findings were obtained even when initial exposures were either to live or dead pups hidden in small, perforated metal containers (Noirot, 1969a).

Brief exposure to young can also sensitize adults in species that are not spontaneously responsive to offspring. In golden hamsters, virgin and nonpregnant adult females attack very young pups; only lactating females show solicitude. However, when naive females were first exposed to an optimal (9-day-old) pup, they were subsequently more solicitous of 5-day-old pups than females who were initially exposed to 1- or 5-day-old pups (Noirot & Richards, 1966).

Induction phenomena are not limited to strictly "psychological" responsiveness. The young can also cause physiological changes in potential caregivers. In mice (Selye & McKeown, 1934), rats (Ota & Yokoyama, 1967a), red kangaroos (Sharman, 1967), and rhesus monkeys (Harlow, Harlow, & Hansen, 1963), stimuli from nursing-age young can induce lactation in nonlactating females whose nipples are large enough to permit sucking. Similarly, nonlactating human females will produce milk in response to prolonged sucking by infants (Newton & Newton, 1972b). Moreover, in nearly all mammals, man included, nursing is required for the maintenance of milk production.

DIFFERENTIATION OF PARENTAL RESPONSIVENESS

Since continuation of the species requires that the young change physically and behaviorally, the nature of the caregiver–young relationship must differentiate over time. Within a single mammalian caregiving cycle, a number of changes in parental structure and functioning occur. Some of them result directly from stimulation by the young. The best known examples of offspring influence on caregiver anatomy and physiology involve the changes in mammary tissue and milk production during lactation (Meites, 1966).

Behaviorally, differentiation of the caregiving relationship ranges from gradual, quantitative shifts in the mother's frequency of contact with her offspring to quite marked qualitative shifts in the nature of the care given and the setting in which caregiving occurs. For example, in some seals, caregiving is largely confined to brief nursing bouts that gradually decline in frequency until weaning (Bartholomew, 1959). By contrast, in the lion, early postnatal care is given exclusively by the mother in a hiding spot away from the pride; when they are more mature, the young are introduced to the group. They then receive solicitude from most of the members while they develop hunting skills (Schenkel, 1966).

When one considers the changing needs of the developing young—especially of species giving birth to immature offspring—it becomes clear that qualitative changes in the caregiver–young relationship are inevitable. The match must be maintained despite the fact that the stimulus qualities of the offspring are changing.

Intracycle matching.   The intracycle match between parent and offspring can be illustrated by the following experiment. Caesarean-delivered rat pups were fostered on rat mothers who had littered either 1 or 10 days earlier. Whereas the 10-day lactating mothers tended to retrieve the subsequently offered foster pups more rapidly than the 1-day mothers, the latter group, who were better matched physiologically with young lacking locomotor capacities, achieved a higher rate of pup survival (Grota, 1968).

In Chapter 7, the maternal pheromone in rats was mentioned. It will be recalled that this scent is produced by the mother about midlactation and is attractive to pups who are old enough to leave the nest on their own. The timing of maternal pheromone production and the pups' sensitivity to it ensures that the litter continues to maintain contact with the mother while they remain dependent upon her care. In a follow-up experiment, Moltz and Leon (1973) compared the scent production of female rats rearing foster litters. The pups in these litters were maintained by daily replacement at the ages of 1 or 16 days or at an age appropriate to the time elapsed since the mother gave birth. They found that after 16 days, the mothers whose foster litters were composed of 1-day-old pups (who were incapable of locomotion) did not produce detectable amounts of pup-attractants (as measured by the responses of 16-day-old test pups). However, the mothers whose foster litters were maintained at an appropriate age did produce the attractant by the sixteenth day, when pups normally begin to stray from the nest. Mothers who were exposed to 16-day-old pups from the beginning appeared to release the pheromone slightly earlier than mothers rearing appropriately aged pups. Thus, pheromone production was in part a response to the stimulus qualities of the growing young.

Nursing.   Some of the first evidence for the role of offspring in the differentiation of caregiver responsiveness came from experiments in which the duration of lactation was extended artificially. By repeatedly replacing natural litters with offspring whose ages were typically within the first third of the lactation period, milk production has been extended well beyond the usual limits in opossums, mice, and rats (see Meites, 1966, for review). These observations lead to the inference that developmental changes in offspring characteristics can account for the changing milk output of mothers under natural conditions.

In most mammals, milk output varies with the demands of the young. Sharman (1967) has shown that even the quality of the milk given by the red kangaroo mother varies with the age and size of the offspring. In a single female, he found that the composition of the milk secreted from one nipple sucked by a "pouch-infant" differed markedly from that secreted by another nipple sucked concurrently by an older sibling.

It is a common observation that, as the young get older, the initiative for beginning or terminating a suckling bout may shift from infant to mother or vice versa. The amount of time spent nursing varies according to the age of the young in both man and other mammals. These trends often seem to be related to the size of the young or to their locomotor capacities (Gewirtz & Gewirtz, 1968; Rosenblatt & Lehrman, 1963; Schneirla, Rosenblatt, & Tobach, 1963).

Since the young must eventually forage for themselves, a significant change involves the shift to solid food. A variety of patterns can be observed from abrupt weaning without a transition to gradual weaning during which the mother shares her food with her offspring. In some species, other members of the group may aid by sharing the kill or by regurgitating food (Bartholomew, 1959; Estes & Goddard, 1967; Kruuk, 1972; Vandevere, 1972). Although the young must often play an important part in determining when such a transition will be made, we have little or no direct information concerning the ways in which they influence this change. One obvious hypothesis from human experience would be that the infant's tendency to bite and chew during the teething period causes the mother to avoid nursing and substitute solid food.

Caregiver–young proximity. In many mammals there is also a developmental change in the degree to which the parent or the young are responsible for maintaining contact. Indeed, a shift in responsibility for maintaining proximity from mother to offspring has been used as one objective criterion for determining stages in the caregiving cycle. For example, on the basis of radio tracking data of racoon mothers and their litters, Schneider, Mech, and Tester (1971) divided the caregiving cycle into phases corresponding to the degree to which the cubs followed their mothers' movements. Similarly, Rosenson (1972) divided the temporal course of infant–mother relations in two captive bushbabies (a "primitive" African primate species) according to infant– versus mother–initiative. Whereas in the first month the mother initiated the approaches and departures, by 5 to 6 weeks after birth, the infant was responsible for maintaining proximity.

Retrieving and transport provide other examples of how changes in proximity–maintenance may be affected by the young. It is likely that the infant's size and weight as well as its overall coordination are involved in the change from ventral to dorsal transport in monkeys and apes (De Vore, 1963; van Lawick–Goodall, 1968). In the bushbaby, one of the few primates in which the mother carries her offspring in her mouth, the portion of the infant's body grasped may be partially determined by its weight. Older, heavier infants are more often grasped toward the middle of the body, presumably because their greater weight requires that the load be more equitably balanced. The importance of the infant's size, as opposed to prior maternal experience, is inferred from the fact that the same relationship between weight and a centered grip is observed in experienced females (Doyle, Anderson, & Bearder, 1969).

In ground squirrels, mice, and bushbabies, the young begin to resist being carried as they become able to maintain proximity to their mothers and to regain the nest on their own. Comparisons of retrieving in mothers rearing their first litters and mothers rearing their second young suggest that the first litters "teach" mothers to give up retrieving after the offspring begin to leave the nest spontaneously (Michener, 1971; Noirot, 1964a; Sauer, 1967).

Similarly, in man, the developing locomotor capacities of the young are associated with changes in the parent–offspring relationship. Konner (1972) has noted that fear of strangers and separation protest, both of which affect parental behavior, are ontogenetically linked to the onset of independent locomotion. Locomotor development thus may be central in the shift of proximity–maintenance from caregiver to child (Bowlby, 1969).

Another change in proximity behavior often involves offspring curiosity or exploration. Several studies with human infants have related changes in the young child's proximity-seeking behavior to its interest in the inanimate environment (e.g., Maccoby & Feldman, 1972). Although Hinde 1974) has shown that changes in contact-maintaining behavior in monkeys cannot be explained on this basis alone, the young of many mammals do take an active role in separating themselves from their parents, particularly at younger ages, and experiments by Harlow and Harlow (1965) show that interest in the environment may be one of the causes. In view of the fact that maternal restraining attempts wane after the young begin persistent, independent sorties, it appears that some mothers may simply give up trying to keep their offspring in the nest or in physical contact (Noirot, 1972a; van Lawick–Goodall, 1968).

Caregiver responsiveness.   Changes in parental sensitivity occur in the course of continued interaction with the young. As Rheingold (1961) has shown, maintenance needs differ as the child matures, thereby requiring changes in the nature of the care provided—e.g., the frequency of feedings and restraint of locomotion. These basic changes occur even in busy institutional settings where the demands of many infants leave little time for other forms of solicitude. In nuclear family settings, the newly developing responsiveness and social skills of the infant and young child provide opportunities for parents to engage in more purely social interactions such as mutual smiling, reciprocal vocalizations, and peek-a-boo games with their offspring (Bell, 1971). Such exchanges may also influence subsequent interactions (Clarke–Stewart, 1973).

On the other hand, continued exposure to the young may lead to decrements in responsiveness. In nonhuman primates, reductions in parental solicitude as a result of offspring behavior may be obtained by modifying the setting or prior maternal experience. Restricted physical and social environments appear to increase offspring-initiated contacts with mothers and, as a result, accelerate the onset of maternal rejection or punishment (Jensen, Bobbitt, & Gordon, 1973). Among the motherless rhesus monkeys studied by Harlow and his associates at Wisconsin, increased maternal abuse of the young over time was attributed to the infants' developing motor skills, which allowed them to initiate contact more frequently and more persistently than previously (Harlow, Harlow, Dodsworth, & Arling, 1966).

In summary, the young can play an important role in changing the patterns of care provided. Furthermore, as indicated by the last example, conditions leading to the differentiation of parental responses may contain the seeds of the termination of caregiving.

TERMINATION OF THE CAREGIVING RELATIONSHIP

Some mammalian young maintain ties to their mothers as long as they live; nonetheless, they also establish reproductive relationships with other members of the species. In other forms, reproduction may depend upon the offspring founding their own home ranges or territories. In the latter cases, it is obvious that the young must cease to rely upon their parents for sustenance, shelter, and guidance within their physical and social environments (Brown, 1966; Carpenter, 1940). The termination of caregiving relationships usually results from a decline in the parent's solicitude. Such declines are often in response to change in the young.

Age-related changes.   Noirot (1964c) has demonstrated the importance of age-related changes in offspring–stimuli as determinants of declining caregiver solicitude in mice. She presented single pups between the ages of 1 and 20 days of age to naive, virgin females. Individual adults were exposed only once. For pups of each age, 10 females were tested for 5 minutes after initial contact with the young. As the age of the test pups increased, there was a progressive decline in the proportion of females retrieving, building nests, licking, and assuming a lactation position over the pups. She concluded that as young mice mature, they cease to emit stimuli that release caregiver behavior.

In other mammals, maturation of the young leads to the development of characteristics that elicit responses which are incompatible with caregiving

(Brown, 1966; Carpenter, 1940; Geist, 1971). These changes thereby contribute to the termination of the caregiving relationship. Analogously, among certain human groups, developmental milestones achieved by the young may serve as the basis for culturally defined changes in and the ultimate termination of the caregiving relationship (Mead & Newton, 1967; van den Berghe, 1973; van Gennep, 1960). Cases such as these often provide excellent examples of the ways in which parent and offspring affect each other: When parental care enhances the maturation of the young, it also hastens the development of offspring–stimuli that lead to the termination of the relationship.

Birth of subsequent offspring.   Among species in which mothers cease to care for older young when they again give birth, the offspring may be said to play a part in determining the duration of certain aspects of caregiving. In many mammals, sucking by the young keeps their mothers from conceiving again (the so-called "lactation diestrus," e.g., Bruce, 1961). To the extent that mothers who do not produce offspring in a subsequent birth season are the only ones that continue to be responsive to their yearlings, the offspring may affect parental sensitivity. Even when lactation diestrus is not involved, when maternal solicitude wanes or turns to overt rejection due to the impending birth of a new offspring, the next generation plays a role in terminating a previous relationship if declining solicitude for the yearling results from hormonal changes produced by the fetus.

Infant attraction to peers.   In several mammals, observational studies indicate that a reduction in mother–offspring bonds may result from the growing attraction of the young to their peers. For example, Rowell, Din, and Omar (1968) observed a steady increase in the amount of time young baboons spent in peer-directed play over their first 8 months of age. Similar changes in social interactions have been reported by Harlow and Harlow (1965) for rhesus monkeys. In some other primates, "play-groups" may become the focus of juvenile activity just as certain human cultures institutionalize a period during which the young reside with their age peers prior to achieving full adult status (Kummer, 1971; Mead & Newton, 1967; Money & Ehrhardt, 1972). Observers of modern Western cultures also suggest that adolescents' peer-group ties function as a prop for, if not a cause of, their autonomy-strivings (Mussen, Conger, & Kagan, 1974).

In mountain sheep, the transition from nursing to peer relationships may affect a complete termination of the parent–offspring bond. Geist (1971) observed that yearlings deserted maternal bands to join other groups well before their mothers sought seclusion to give birth again. There was little evidence that the transition was prompted by maternal rejection. As in the case of Harlow's rhesus monkeys (Harlow & Harlow, 1965), the shift seemed to occur despite parental efforts to discourage peer contacts.

In summary, it is likely that spontaneous attraction of the young to their peers often plays an important role in terminating the caregiving bond.

Stimulus satiation.   For many mammals there seems to be a period of intense mother–offspring contact immediately after birth that is followed by progressively declining solicitude and, finally, offspring independence. In some species, such changed parental responsiveness may be due to endogenous changes in the mother. However, in mice and rats, there is evidence that stimuli from the young trigger processes leading to the inhibition of maternal solicitude even while the young are still nursing.

Noirot (1964a) compared mother mice's treatment of their first and second litters (both adjusted to 6 pups). She found that, with their second litters, mothers ceased retrieving earlier, licked their pups less frequently, and engaged in less nest-building. To evaluate the effects of changing hormonal state, a group of virgin females of similar ages was subjected to the same regimen of testing as the mothers, each having her "own" foster litter for every test. The virgin animals showed essentially the same decline in responsiveness as the mothers with their first litters throughout the 20 days of testing. The data suggested that prolonged contact as well as the stimuli associated with pup age acted to reduce caregiver responsiveness.

Grosvenor and Mena (1973) investigated the conditions under which the hormone *prolactin* was released from the pituitary glands of female rats who were rearing their first litters. They also observed the effect of this hormone on milk production. Two groups of mothers were tested on the fourteenth or twenty-first days of lactation, after a 4-hour period of isolation. Within each of these groups, four subgroups were exposed to (1) suckling by their pups; or (2) exposure to the litter—without contact—through a wire-mesh cage floor; or (3) exposure to 25 to 30 nursing rat mothers and their litters in adjacent cages; or (4) exposure to their pups below the cage floor followed by exposure to lactating mothers. Analysis of the amounts of pituitary prolactin and mammary-gland-refilling after exposure indicated that the 14-day lactating group responded with hormone release to either suckling by or exposure to their litters but not to exposure to other mothers and their litters. The 21-day lactating groups showed prolactin release under all conditions, but, unlike the 14-day group, they did not show an elevation in milk secretion following prolactin release except when exposed to *other* mothers and their young. Furthermore, if exposure to their own 21-day-old young occurred immediately before exposure to other mothers, there was no rise in milk production in the 21-day group. These data suggested that for the older mothers, the presence of their own pups in some way blocked the action of prolactin on milk output. Experiments using drugs to neutralize the hypothesized inhibiting agents supported this interpretation. Thus, in addition to releasing hormones that stimulate milk production, sensory cues from older rat pups also activate inhibitory mechanisms preventing the prolactin from reaching or acting upon the mammary glands, thereby bringing the nursing period to a close.

SUMMARY

Examination of the mammalian parental cycle from conception through termination of the caregiving relationship reveals that the young play an important part in controlling caregiver behavior in every phase. This does not mean that the parent is simply the pawn of the young, nor does it imply that the offspring of every species play an equally important role in all aspects of the parent–offspring relationship. However, given the theoretical considerations outlined in the preceding chapter and the evidence reviewed here, it does mean that development of most aspects of the parent–offspring relationship depends upon input from the young.

9
Effects of the Young on Bouts of Interaction

Lawrence V. Harper

INTRODUCTION

In the same way that changes in caregiver state or behavior can reveal offspring–effects within the cycle, short-term variations can also be related to stimulation emitted by the young. As indicated in previous chapters, effective moment-to-moment care depends upon an exchange of signals between parent and offspring. From the standpoint of evolutionary theory, the young must play some part in regulating the timing and form of these encounters. Although there are surprisingly few quantitative data concerning the ways in which offspring signal changes in their momentary states, the evidence shows that the stimuli emitted by the young do play a role in initiating, maintaining, differentiating, and terminating bouts of interaction.

BOUT–INITIATION

An obvious example of bout–initiation in man is the child's asking for something. When 4- to 6-year-old middle-class girls asked for help solving puzzles, their mothers and fathers offered more verbal and physical assistance and were more controlling than when their children did not make such bids (Osofsky & O'Connell, 1972). The signals of preverbal infants may be equally effective. For example, Gewirtz and Gewirtz (1969) studied the interactions of infants and caregivers in four different settings in Israel. Across a residential institution, a kibbutz, a one-child home, and a multiple-child home, the probabilities that an infant's vocalization would be followed by a caregiver's smile ranged from .52 to .81, and when the infants smiled, the caregivers' smiles had probabilities of .46 to .88. Clearly, these human caregivers responded to their charges' signals.

172

Nursing.   In the nursing relationship, there is usually a regular rhythm of interaction, which may be initiated by either the mother or the infant. In many primates, where mother–infant contact is sustained, initiation of a nursing bout involves relatively minor adjustments. By contrast, in such species as the Alaska fur seal and the rabbit, the young are left alone in a "pup pod" or nest and are visited for brief nursing by the mother at intervals separated by a day or more. Whereas the young primate can easily initiate a feeding bout by simply reaching for the nipple, the seal or rabbit pup cannot nurse until the mother makes herself available. However, even in the latter cases, it is the presence of her offspring that accounts for the mother's repeated visits (Bartholomew, 1959; Zarrow, Denenberg, & Anderson, 1965).

Among a number of animals whose offspring can walk shortly after birth, the young may initiate nursing bouts by employing stereotyped responses. Nursing-age ungulates attempt to induce their mothers to suckle by crossing in front of them, thereby blocking their movement, before they seek the teat (Geist, 1971; Tyler, 1972). In guinea pigs (Harper, 1976) and bushbabies (Doyle et al., 1969), the young attempt to initiate nursing by crawling under the mother.

Even the neonate human has the means to initiate feedings. Sound–spectrographic studies have shown that infants' hunger cries differ from their pain cries and that adult caregivers can be trained to discriminate these signals (Wasz–Höckert, Partanen, Vuorenkoski, Valanne, & Michelsson, 1964). Thus, if its parents are aware of the meaning of a cry, the baby can communicate a need for food and thereby elicit an appropriate parental response.

Contact and retrieving.   Chapter 8 indicated that responsibility for main-taining proximity shifts from parent to offspring when the young develop locomotor skills. Prior to this period, the vocal behavior of the young can be an important contributor to proximity–maintenance. In several rodent species, the very high-pitched (ultrasonic) cries of pups elicit and orient maternal retrieving. Mother voles and field mice will run to the arm of a T-maze from which the calls of young are broadcast (Colvin, 1973; Sewell, 1970). Similarly, the recorded calls of infant marmosets and bushbabies will bring their mothers to the source (Epple, 1968; Sauer, 1967). In man, the infant's vocalizations often release adult approach and contact: Middle-class American mothers responded to over 75% of more than 2,000 recorded bouts of "fussing" (Moss & Robson, 1968). The latter observations have been confirmed by Lewis and Lee–Painter (1974), who categorized the human infant's "fret/cry behavior" as an "initiator" of care-giving behavior.

Responses to exploration and play.   In most mammals, the young are responsible for the initiation of play–bouts with adults. In affluent human societies, the inquisitiveness of the young frequently accounts for parental pro-hibitions or discipline. Newson and Newson (1974) observed that about one quarter of the disciplinary "smacks" delivered to 1-year-old Nottingham children were in response to the destruction or unauthorized manipulation of household furnishings. Similar findings have been reported for older children in the United States (Minton, Kagan, & Levine, 1971; Rebelsky, Seavey, & Blotner, 1971).

Clearly then, the young can initiate bouts of caregiver activity. From a theoretical standpoint and from the limited data available to date, it seems that this will be a fruitful field for further inquiry.

BOUT–MAINTENANCE

At the minimum, maintaining an interaction requires that one actor passively tolerate the activity of the other. For example, Hinde and Spencer–Booth (1967) suggested that when rhesus monkey mothers were weaning their offspring, the infants could cling to their mothers as long as they did not move about. When more active participation is required of the respondent, the situation becomes more complex and theoretically important. Many students of child development have attempted to rate the quality of mother–offspring relations. Unfortunately, the bases for judgments of "maternal sensitivity" have not always been entirely clear to others.

Perhaps part of the problem has been a traditional failure to give offspring their full due; once the importance of offspring–signals is recognized, naturalistic observations can provide easily quantifiable indices of maternal (and offspring) responsiveness. For instance, 1-year-old children almost always respond to maternal overtures for interaction. In contrast, offspring overtures are frequently ignored by mothers (David & Appell, 1971).

If one defines a bout of interaction in terms of the function achieved, such as nursing, bout–maintenance may depend upon specific activities of the offspring. When a mother cat lies on her side, extending her legs to form a "functional U" around her litter, the kittens' approach, rooting, and nipple-attachment maintain her in that position. Moreover, the total duration of the nursing bout depends upon the number of kittens sucking (Schneirla et al., 1963). Careful observation of interactions between mother caribou and their offspring indicated that 87% of the nursing bouts in which the calf approached the mother from the side or diagonally resulted in maternal acceptance. In contrast, only slightly over half of all the other approaches met with success. Furthermore, successful nursing approaches in which the young took a side approach lasted almost three times longer than bouts initiated by a different approach. Thus, it seems that the calf must follow the "proper form" in order to induce the cow to permit the initiation as well as to maintain a nursing bout (Lent, 1966).

Recent research on human caregiver–young relationships shows that the infant may be involved in maintaining bouts of "social" interaction. Brazelton, Koslowski, and Main (1974) described how mothers needed to carefully respond to signs of excitement from their 2- to 20-week-old infants; they had to provide their babies with periods of reduced stimulation in order to sustain playful, "social" exchanges. As indicated in the introduction to this chapter, infant smiles and vocalizations also elicit reciprocal responses from adult caregivers, thereby maintaining social interactions. The infant's gaze may even hold his mother's visual attention for durations that far exceed mutual gazing among adults in the same culture (Gewirtz & Gewirtz, 1969; Stern, 1974).

Much has been written about the ways in which caregiver responses modify the frequency and duration of infant behavior (e.g., Rheingold, Gewirtz, & Ross, 1959). We are now discovering that feedback from the infant is also important in sustaining parental involvement. Among others, Robson (1967) and Wolff (1971) have described the importance of the infant's eye-to-eye contact and smiling in the maintaining of maternal interest. Perhaps one of the best examples of the power of the smile is provided by Fraiberg's (1974) description of the almost frantic lengths to which parents would go in order to elicit smiling from their blind offspring. These infants seemed to smile most regularly when bounced, tickled, or jiggled vigorously. As a result, they received much more tactile–kinesthetic stimulation than sighted infants. From this, it seems fair to conclude that the smile of the infant was acting to maintain an extreme form of parental behavior.

In short, the evidence indicates that acceptance of a bid for interaction and the signals that lead to the prolongation of a particular exchange can emanate from either parent or offspring and that the young can—and do—play an important role in determining the duration of interactions.

BOUT–DIFFERENTIATION

In short-term exchanges, one aspect of the interaction, such as suckling, may be maintained while another, such as maternal grooming, may be initiated. According to Collias (1956), the tail-wagging of the nursing lamb not only maintains the suckling bout by facilitating maternal recognition, but it also elicits maternal grooming of the lamb's anogenital region. In humans, the feeding behavior of new mothers provides an example of the ways in which offspring may cause their caregivers to employ various means to attain the "same" functional end. Kaye and Brazelton (1971) observed feedings in the first month after birth. They found that as long as the infant was sucking, there were few if any attempts to stimulate feeding; the mothers simply concentrated on holding the infant and keeping the bottle in place. However, when the infants *paused* at the end of a sucking burst, their mothers began to stroke their babies' cheeks and move the nipple, in attempts to get their offspring to continue sucking.

Another kind of differentiation involves a qualitative shift in caregiving. For example, in their first few weeks, rhesus monkey infants moved away from their mothers toward objects in the environment. These exploratory sorties precipitated maternal restraining or hovering behavior, thus differentiating the bout from infant—contact to maternal following—restraining (Hinde & Spencer—Booth, 1967). Time-sampled observations of mother—infant interactions during feedings show how the human infant can cause changes in the quality of care within a bout. In one study, four of the six most common shifts from feeding activities were in response to infant behaviors. Infant vocalizations and looking at the mother appeared to be among the most potent stimuli for the mothers to temporarily cease feeding activities and engage in more purely social exchanges (Olley, 1973).

Differentiation within bouts may also result from the chaining of caregiving components; enactment of an earlier response can increase the probability of attention to stimuli eliciting subsequent actions. Noirot (1969b) analyzed the sequential patterning of naive mice's retrieving, licking, nest-building, and crouching over 1- to 2-day-old pups. Two basic orders of the four responses emerged. All bouts began with retrieving. All but 3 of 45 animals who performed each of the four responses ended with the lactation posture. Within these bounds, nest-building usually preceded licking. Thus, of the 24 possible serial orders, only two were frequently observed. Similar stereotyped chaining typified the behavior of animals displaying only three responses. (Here, the lactation posture was the most frequently omitted response.) Because retrieving is usually elicited by ultrasonic calls, and because the nature and frequency of these calls varies when the young are picked up, the pups probably had some effect in determining the sequences (cf. Noirot, 1972b).

Comparable findings have been reported for pinnipeds. Ono (1972) analyzed 125 instances in which mother Steller sea lions rejoined their pups after having gone to sea to feed. The data revealed a stereotyped sequence of mother—pup interactions. In 85% of the 60 reunions that ended with nursing, the sequence was (1) mother vocalize and then pup vocalize; and (2) mother nose pup and then pup locate and attach to teat. In Chapter 10, it will be shown that individual recognition in this species is mediated through auditory and olfactory means. Thus, given that mother sea lions allow only their own pups to nurse, it would seem that this pattern also depended upon a sequential exchange of stimulation between mother and offspring.

In summary, although research in this realm has just begun, the evidence suggests that the young play a role in determining the variability of caregiver responses during the course of bouts of interaction.

BOUT—TERMINATION

Among species in which parent—offspring contact or proximity is almost continuous, the distinction between differentiation and termination depends upon the level of analysis. However, bout termination is easy to identify when physical proximity occurs only intermittently. For example, when young deer and goats are satiated, they end nursing bouts by seeking a hiding place and lying down, away from the mother (e.g., Collias, 1956; Linsdale & Tomich, 1953). Among rabbits, it is the mother who actively separates herself from the litter to terminate nursing. However, in this case too, the young influence timing of the mother's departure. Does, whose mammaries were emptied by foster litters while they were under general anesthesia, would "nurse" their own litters as early as 2 hours later. Mothers whose teats were under local anesthesia during a first encounter nursed even their own litters again in the same day. In contrast, if mothers nursed their offspring normally, they would not accept their young within a 2-hour period. Some kind of refractory state appeared to build as a result of tactual stimulation by the pups. This refractoriness could not be explained entirely by the effects of mammary emptying, because mothers who were unconscious while their glands were emptied nonetheless permitted their litters to suck within 2 hours when conscious (Findlay, 1969).

In humans, feedback from the nursing infant also affects the termination of feeding bouts. Olley (1973) observed that inexperienced mothers actively sought cues from their babies as to whether they had had enough milk. Similarly, Hubert (1974) reported that one of the major sources of concern for mothers who had elected to breast-feed their firstborn infants was that they had no obvious cues as to how much milk their babies had consumed. In contrast, mothers who employed bottle-feeding obtained immediate visual information by observing the amount of milk drained from the bottle, and they were much less hesitant to terminate a feeding.

Performing certain forms of caregiving in response to a particular individual may reduce the probability that the same pattern will be repeated after a brief interval. Naive, virgin female mice were presented with a 1- or 2-day-old pup for ten consecutive 5-minute trials. The number of animals assuming the lactation position increased, and the number retrieving remained maximal across trials. However, the proportion who licked the pup and built nests declined with successive presentations of pups. This decline in licking and nest-building appeared to represent some form of transient inhibition, because, 1 day later, the mice reacted to a single presentation of a similar test pup with baseline-level responses. Motor fatigue was ruled out as an explanation in a further experiment. Nine successive trials with a 1-day-old pup were immediately followed with a (less attractive) 10-day-old pup. As before, licking and nest-building declined over the first nine trials, but when the stimulus pup was changed on the next trial, the percent of the group responding returned to baseline. A process similar to habituation seemed to be operative, because a single presentation of a 10-day-old pup on the following day did not elicit as much responsiveness as did a single presentation of a 1- to 2-day-old pup (Noirot, 1965).

These data indicate that the young may terminate bouts of interactions in several ways: directly, by removing themselves from the situation, or indirectly, either by signalling the caregiver that they "have had enough" or by providing sufficient stimulation to habituate responsiveness.

SUMMARY

The control of short-term interactions between parent and offspring involves a mutual exchange of stimulation. Depending upon the species and the nature of the exchange, either party may make the first move to initiate, maintain, differentiate, or terminate a bout of interaction. Available data strongly suggest that few behaviorally significant exchanges between mammalian caregivers and young will fail to involve reciprocal stimulation. In view of frequent, clinically oriented studies in humans that report relationships between global measures of maternal sensitivity and later offspring behavior, it seems imperative that students of human development intensify their efforts to identify and describe the precise form and meaning of various offspring signals.

10

The Nature of Offspring-Stimuli

Lawrence V. Harper

INTRODUCTION

The foregoing sections showed how the young influence both the caregiving cycle and bouts of interaction within it. This chapter is concerned with identifying the specific offspring stimuli that affect caregiver behavior. In addition to experimental findings, stimulus dimensions that seem to be promising candidates for analysis will also be pointed out.

AGE DIFFERENCES

In all mammals, the young possess qualities distinguishing them from other age classes simply by virtue of the physical constraints imposed by the birth process. From the theoretical considerations presented in preceding chapters, we can expect that as a result of natural selection, adults will have a tendency to be sensitive to these cues and to respond to species-mates according to their ages. This is most obvious when one considers the life history of so-called solitary mammals. In the nutria, interadult contacts are limited to brief mating encounters; adults otherwise avoid one another. Nevertheless, mothers maintain prolonged physical contact with their young (Ryszkowski, 1966). Similarly, except for brief periods during the mating season, female golden hamsters are territorial, and other adults are attacked when they encroach upon a resident's domain. However, if 2-day lactating females are presented with foster litters of various ages, no pups under 14 days of age will be attacked as if they were territorial rivals, although a number of them may be treated as prey. Pups over the age of 14 days will be treated as territorial rivals, but they will not be devoured. Although "parental" solicitude occurs infrequently in response to alien young in hamsters, 7- to 10-day-old pups most often receive care (Rowell, 1960).

Age-related phenomena can also be observed in more gregarious species. In Chapter 8, we saw that adult mice displayed maximal responsiveness to relatively young pups. Similar observations have been made with lactating females of other species. Wiesner and Sheard (1933) and Rosenblatt and Lehrman (1963) found that rat pups between 5 and 10 days of age received the greatest amount of care from foster mothers. Among primates, too, abundant data attest to the attractiveness of the young. In a multiple-choice apparatus, jungle-reared rhesus monkey mothers spent more time near neonates than near juveniles or adults. Although they spent more time near adults overall, laboratory-reared adult females also spent longer periods with neonates than older infants and juveniles. In a later experiment, experienced, wild-trapped pigtail monkey mothers were separated from their offspring at birth and tested in the same apparatus. They too showed clear preferences for neonates over juveniles or adults during the first 2 weeks after giving birth (Sackett, Griffin, Pratt, Joslyn, & Ruppenthal, 1967; Sackett & Ruppenthal, 1974).

In man as in other mammals, the quality of caregiving varies with the age of the young. Rheingold (1961) and Brody (1956) have shown that the young infant "demands" particular kinds of care. The fact that all human societies use age as a criterion for ascribed status indicates just how salient this dimension is for human beings (van den Berghe, 1973).

A number of studies demonstrate that adult mammals often react to the young with responses (or tolerance) shown to no other age–sex class. For example, in one study, unfamiliar animals of different ages were introduced to a wild troop of rhesus monkeys. Whereas introduced adults and juveniles were chased, threatened, and even attacked by troop-members, infants were not (Southwick, Pal, & Siddiqi, 1972). Olympic marmots are also more tolerant of younger animals. Extended "greetings" between adults and juveniles result in adult "reprimands" to the latter. However, when weanlings engage in such behavior, adults respond negatively much less often (Barash, 1973).

Thus we can conclude that the young possess characteristics that can elicit a unique set of responses from adults (cf. Harper, 1971).

INDIVIDUAL DIFFERENCES

In addition to age-related characteristics, there exist individual differences in the stimulus qualities of young that are independent of age.

Gender. Several studies indicate that offspring gender affects caregiving behavior in nonhuman primates. By the fifth week after birth, wild-reared pigtail monkey mothers who were caged with only their male offspring carried their infants less often than did mothers of females. The mothers of males were also more "punitive" to their infants and more "oriented to the environment." Among laboratory-housed rhesus monkeys, mothers of female infants restrained their young more than did mothers of males during the first 3 months. During the following 3 months, male infants were groomed less, played with more, and were more often presented to by their mothers than were the females. Like the pigtails, the female rhesus monkey infants received more nonspecific contact, clasping, and embracing, and were withdrawn from less often than were males. Among captive lowland gorillas, mothers subjected male infants to more intense genital inspection and manipulation than female infants (Jensen & Bobbitt, 1968; Mitchell, 1968; Hess, 1973).

The apparent gender of a human child is clearly an important determinant of caregiver attitudes and provides the cues for implementing many culturally de-termined patterns of child-rearing behavior. This extends beyond the parent–child relationship. Across 15 preschool settings, teachers reacted more often when boys were aggressive or destructive than when girls behaved in the same way. Teachers were also more likely to respond to boys' rather than girls' bids for attention with directions or explanations emphasizing problem-solving. Boys received more approval and attention than girls for participating in class ac-tivities, and girls received more attention than boys when simply hovering near the teacher (Serbin, O'Leary, Kent, & Tonick, 1973). Although social expecta-tions obviously are involved in such gender-specific responsiveness, it is still the child who is the "discriminant stimulus" to which the caregiver reacts.

Congenital factors.   Even though adult laboratory mice are generally so-licitous of young, the congenital endowment of pups can be related to variations in caregiver responsiveness (Ressler, 1962). Congenital peculiarities of offspring behavior color caregiver responsiveness in primates as well. Young monkeys who do not respond typically to social signals receive less adult solicitude than to more "normal" animals, and mothers of brain-damaged human infants tend to be more ambivalent and negative toward their offspring (whose states change unpredictably) than are mothers of apparently normal newborns (Mitchell & Schroers, 1973; Prechtl, 1963). Thus we must be alert to the contribution of individual differences in the make-up of the young to the development of parent–offspring relationships in man (cf. Chess, 1971).

Several studies demonstrated differences in the "open field" behavior of rat mothers whose litters were either from different strains or subjected to handling in early infancy (Hudgens, Chilgren, & Palardy, 1972; Joffe, 1965). This latter finding again reminds us that we are dealing with an interaction: Given the fact that maternal behavior can be affected by treatments given to the young, some effects of early handling may represent maternal responses to alterations in pup behavior rather than direct consequences of handling per se (Barnett & Burn, 1967; Bell, Nitschke, Gorry, & Zachman, 1971).

Analysis of Offspring Stimuli

The foregoing studies demonstrate age-related and individual differences in the ability of offspring to stimulate caregiver behavior. Now it is time to turn to an analysis of the cues that serve as the bases for such discriminations and the stimuli involved in the subsequent elicitation of caregiving responses. Evolutionary theory suggests that natural selection will favor the utilization and even the intensification of age-specific attributes to the extent that they facilitate recognition of reproductive status (Wynne–Edwards, 1962). Because systematic study of these attributes as stimuli for caregiving behavior has only begun, possible leads will be suggested along with a review of established phenomena. Offspring stimulus dimensions will be examined according to the sense modalities by which they are perceived.

Visual stimuli.   Physical size is one of the more obvious attributes distinguishing the young; the anatomical constraints of reproduction require that mammalian offspring be smaller than their mothers. However, in most species, size is also related to viability so that it is difficult to isolate for study without the use of artificial stimuli. However, body conformation also is correlated with age. Lorenz and his students (e.g., Eibl–Eibesfeldt, 1970) have suggested that the newborn's large forehead relative to its muzzle, its large head-to-body-size ratio, and its frequently encountered "awkwardness" may be common features that serve to stimulate parental responsiveness. Studies by ethologists indicate that humans respond positively to: (1) a comparatively thick head; (2) a prominent forehead in which the brow area is greater than the face; (3) relatively large eyes set below the middle of the skull; (4) short, thick limbs with pudgy hands and feet; (5) rounded body form; (6) a soft, elastic surface texture; and (7) round, "chubby" cheeks (Wickler, 1972).

Some of these stimulus attributes have been studied in the laboratory. Adult subjects rated the "cuteness" of simple line drawings of babies' faces that differed only with respect to eye-height and frontal location (forward or back in profile view). As suggested by the ethologists, the position of the eye relative to the rest of the face affected judgments of cuteness. In another experiment, a series of silhouette heads was generated on the basis of features empirically distinguishing six infants from six adults. Adult subjects made paired-comparison judgments of whether the heads were "adult" or "infantile." Even when the stimuli represented gross exaggerations of the critical features, the two classes could be identified. "First order" exaggerations tended to be judged more "babyish" and more "real" than silhouettes of actual babies' heads. The distinguishing features of babyishness were a short, wide head with small features and a small chin (Brooks & Hochberg, 1960; Gardner & Wallach, 1965; see Fullard & Reiling, 1976, for further review).

Distinctive coloration has been reported for the young (especially the neonate) of at least eight mammalian orders.[1] Among many primate species in which the newborn's coat is different, adults and juveniles often show particular interest in

---

[1] Tenerecs (Gould & Eisenberg, 1966); bats (Nelson, 1965); rodents (Eisenberg, 1963), lagomorphs (Ross et al., 1963); canids (Snow, 1967); pinnipeds (Orr & Poulter, 1967); cetacians (McBride & Kritzler, 1951); artiodactyls (Schaller, 1967); primates (De Vore, 1965).

them. For example, wariness or hostility characterizes adult interactions in inter-troop encounters among Hamadryas baboons. However, adults generally show positive reactions toward any infant in the natal coat (Kummer, 1968). Booth (1962) has provided direct evidence for the importance of the natal coat for several old-world monkeys. While making field observation of wild troops of *Cercopithecus* monkeys, she sometimes took hand-reared infants along with her. When she was accompanied by an infant in the natal coat, adults of both sexes who observed the infant became agitated and made threatening approaches to her—much closer than if she were alone or accompanied by an older juvenile. Experiments with stuffed infants indicated that the critical feature was indeed the coloration of the stimulus object—combined with movement.

As the foregoing observation suggests, movement of the young also affects potential caregivers. The young of many species appear to move in special ways or to have distinctive gaits. On the basis of field observations of free-ranging langurs, Jay (1963) suggested that the quality of movement may be infant–specific and serve as a stimulus for maternal solicitude. The unique features of children's locomotion, from the first days of independent walking, have been documented at length (Bernstein, 1967), but there have been no studies of how adults react to these features.

Observational reports of birth in a variety of species suggest that the motor activity of the young may be an element in orienting the mother to her neonate. The importance of the infant's later activity is suggested by the observation that the mother baboon and her infant were the "center of interest" for a captive group only when the baby was awake (Rowell et al., 1968). Similarly, Doyle et al. (1969) reported that both proximity and activity of the young were stimuli promoting adult grooming of offspring among captive bushbabies. In humans, the infants' movement also seems to be important in eliciting caregiver attention (Clarke–Stewart, 1973; Lewis & Lee–Painter, 1974).

Observational studies suggest that stereotyped displays by the young may release specific caregiving responses. For example, infant bushbabies and young jackals roll over on their backs to elicit adults' grooming (Sauer, 1967; van Lawick–Goodall & van Lawick–Goodall, 1971). In Chapter 8, we saw how the young caribou crosses in front of its mother when attempting to initiate a nursing bout. A somewhat similar pattern occurs in human children who wish to be picked up. When the young child wants to be held, it steps directly in front of the adult and raises its arms up and toward the caregiver. This response is almost invariably followed by the adult's picking up the child (Anderson, 1972; Bowlby, 1969). The smile provides another well-documented example of the ways in which a stereotyped motor pattern affects caregiver behavior in man (e.g., Gewirtz & Gewirtz, 1969).

Tactual stimuli. In several species that give birth to very immature off-spring the young are born with little or no hair on their bodies; their coats develop during the litter period. As one might expect, experimental studies show that the presence of hair on the young affects caregiving. The olfactory bulbs of mother mice were removed within 3 days of the birth of their young. Subsequently, 80% of these mothers cannibalized their young upon recovery from the operation. However, only 55% of a group of mothers who were subjected to the same operation on Day 7, and none of those operated on Day 14 did so. Females who were bulbectomized on Day 3 were then presented with 1-, 3-, 7-, and 14-day-old pups. Here too, the older the pup, the less likely the mother was to eat it. A comparison of bulbectomized females' responses to 1-day-old pups, normal 14-day-old pups, and hairless (depilated) 14-day-old pups indicated that the presence of body hair inhibited cannibalism. Thus, even though bulbectomy had rendered their behavior atypical, the operated mice were still responding to cues emitted by the young. In a later experiment, mother mice who had 2-day-old litters were presented with 14-day-old pups that were either normal or depilated. The mothers attacked the normal test pups more frequently than the hairless ones; the latter received more parental care. These results implied that the presence of body hair helped the intact mouse mothers to discriminate the "intruders" from their own pups (Gandelman, Zarrow, & Denenberg, 1971; Svare & Gandelman, 1973).

Schneirla, Rosenblatt, and Tobach (1963) suggested that the warmth of the young contribute to the formation of the parent–offspring bond in domestic cats, and Beach and Jaynes (1956a) indicated that thermal cues may be a stimulus for retrieving in laboratory rats. It seems likely that temperature senses may also be important when physical contact between caregiver and young is intense and prolonged, as in the case of primates.

Primate young cling to their mothers for transport and when frightened, as well as when nursing. Whether or not thermoreceptors are involved, the clinging young must provide a good deal of tactual stimulation. Hinde, Rowell, and Spencer–Booth (1964) hypothesized that much of the cradling and supportive posturing of mother rhesus monkeys represented efforts to maximize physical contact with infants rather than attempts to carry them in a particular position. Harlow et al. (1963) also suggested that the infants' clinging may be important in arousing and maintaining maternal responsiveness in this species. They found that the only failure to foster an infant to a nonlactating female occurred when the infant did not maintain a ventral clinging posture—despite frequent attempts by the foster mother to bring it to that position. The female gave every indication of being attracted to the infant initially; however, she eventually seemed to lose interest after the youngster repeatedly failed to respond appropriately to her bids for contact.

On the other hand, certain kinds of tactual stimulation appear to have aversive qualities. Mother–offspring pairs of pigtail monkeys were placed in cages that either lacked or provided apparatus for play and exploratory behavior. Infants who were reared in the barren cages were about as active as the other group, but they climbed on their mothers more often. In consequence, they received more maternal punishment than did the infants who could do their climbing on the play equipment (Jensen & Bobbitt, 1968).

The effects of suckling on maternal physiology and responsiveness already have been mentioned in several contexts. In some species, the young also stimulate the entire mammary by kneading or butting it during bouts of nursing. For example, litters of domestic pigs were reduced to eight piglets each and were housed separately from the sow save for regular nursing at 90-minute intervals. Under these conditions, the more time the litters spent "massaging" the sow's udders, the greater the weight gain of the young, and presumably, the greater the mother's milk production (Gill & Thompson, 1956).

Olfactory–gustatory stimuli.   Of the several senses, our knowledge of taste and smell is the least extensive, partly because of the difficulties involved in isolating and analyzing the effective substances. However, work by Müller–Schwartze (1971) indicates that certain glandular secretions of black-tailed deer are age– and sex–specific. To date, this study is the only one known to the writer in which systematic attempts have been made to isolate and analyze pheromones peculiar to young mammals.

On the other hand, field reports of maternal behavior in seals, bushbabies, feral ponies, and sheep and goats suggest strongly that olfactory stimulation from the young plays an important role in the mother's recognition. For example, just after giving birth, sheep and goat mothers will follow a rag soaked in the fluids rubbed from their young (Hersher et al., 1963). A common observation is that new mothers are highly attracted to the fluids associated with birth (cf. Nadler, 1974; Rheingold, 1963; Tyler, 1972). Because it is difficult to control natural odors, most experimenters have either interfered with the caregivers's olfactory receptors or artificially altered the olfactory qualities of the young.

In Chapter 8, we saw that the period just after birth is an especially important time for the formation of mother–offspring bonds in sheep and goats. Several studies have shown that olfactory–gustatory cues are involved in this "maternal imprinting." In one such study, the nasal passages of pregnant goats were sprayed with a cocaine-based anesthetic immediately before they gave birth. This treatment caused a temporary blocking of the female's sense of smell. While thus anosmic, the mothers were allowed 5 minutes with their first kids, and then the young were removed. After a booster treatment, about 2½ hours after birth, the mothers were presented with their first kid. Of 9 mothers, 8 accepted their own kids. Of these 8, 6 were also presented with an alien neonate; every one accepted the alien as well. These data contrast sharply with evidence already reviewed indicating that a brief period of early contact with own young causes normal mother goats to reject other kids (Klopfer & Gamble, 1966).

Somewhat similar observations have been reported for sheep. The olfactory bulbs of 8 ewes were removed when they were about 3 months pregnant (see Chapter 7, Footnote 1, for same procedure with mice). At birth, half of the mothers failed to lick dry their neonates; nonetheless, all but one subsequently performed adequately in rearing their lambs. However, unlike normal sheep, but like Klopfer and Gamble's goats, 6 of the 8 anosmic ewes also nursed alien lambs in addition to their own offspring (Baldwin & Shillito, 1974). Because the blocking of maternal olfactory sensitivity, even after the mother–infant bond has been established, also tends to disturb recognition of offspring in both sheep (Pfeffer, 1967) and goats, we may conclude that olfactory cues from the young are important for the mothers' developing of an exclusive attachment to their offspring and for subsequent recognition of offspring.

Among species in which the mother–young bond is not so exclusive, experiments show that olfactory cues still may be the basis for a mother's identifying her own young. Lactating female rats were observed to retrieve their own before alien pups. Although desensitization of the mothers' snouts did not affect their pup recognition, when females who previously had discriminated their own pups were rendered anosmic by surgery, they failed to display selective retrieving (Beach & Jaynes, 1956a).

The foregoing studies suggest that olfactory cues facilitate caregiver responsiveness. However, there is also evidence that the *absence* of olfactory stimulation from young may enhance the development of female rats' solicitude for pups under certain conditions. Although virgin female rats whose olfactory bulbs had been surgically removed usually cannibalized pups placed in their cages, a small percentage of these subjects showed "induced" responsiveness and did so in about one-third the time usually required to induce intact animals. A further experiment indicated that the effect was due to impaired olfaction rather than damage to the nervous system. The sense of smell of 12 virgin females was blocked by injecting zinc sulfate into their nasal cavities. None of these females cannibalized their foster young, and 11 of the 12 adopted a nursing posture over the pups within 24 hours of presentation. These findings suggest that olfactory cues peculiar to the young may initially elicit avoidance responses from inexperienced rats (Fleming & Rosenblatt, 1974a; 1974b).

In summary, the data indicate that olfactory cues can be important stimuli for caregiver behavior in mammals. Indeed, it would not be too surprising to find that the human neonate possesses a distinctive odor, perhaps a result of secretions from the scalp region.[2]

Auditory stimuli.   In contrast to the study of olfaction, the physical nature of auditory stimuli is known, and sounds can be easily recorded and analyzed. Field observers of parent–offspring relations suggest that vocal exchanges are important in the postpartum period in sheep and goats (Collias, 1956), and experiments show that sounds made by the young affect their caregivers later on

---

[2] We are indebted to Valerie Horowitz and her son Michael for suggesting the scalp as a possible source of the distinctive odor of human infants.

in the cycle. For example, mother rats who were separated from their litters and were later exposed to the sounds of other mothers suckling their young showed hormonal changes typical of nursing (prolactin release from the pituitary). The same stimuli elicited greater milk production in intact mothers than in deafened mothers, thus confirming the role of audition (Deis, 1968; Deis & Orias, 1968). As we have seen in Chapter 9, the recorded ultrasonic vocalizations of young mice and field voles elicit and direct maze-running in lactating females.

On the basis of experiments in which mothers of chilled (and thereby more vocal) rat pups appeared to be more "agitated" than mothers of less vocal young, R. W. Bell (1974) suggested that ultrasound acted simply to increase maternal responsiveness or alertness. However, the ultrasonic cries of young mice may have more specific effects. Naive females were placed in a large cage containing a smaller one in which there was either a virgin female or a mother and her litter. The naive females built nests closer to the small cage if it contained a mother and litter than if it held a virgin female. To test the effect of specific auditory cues, litters were subjected to chilling or rough handling, which affected the rates and characteristics of pup vocalization. The quality of the pups' calls were indeed important: Naive adult females exposed to calls from chilled pups built heavier nests, whereas those exposed to calls from roughly handled pups built more finely shredded (softer) nests. Thus, not only did the calls elicit caregiving responses, but they affected the quality of the responses shown (Noirot, 1974). Recalling that the newborn human's cries convey information about its state, we must conclude that the calls of some young mammals can do more than simply "arouse" potential caregivers.

Other studies indicate that offspring vocalizations may in fact convey additional information. Analysis of sound spectrograms of infant field voles' vocalizations indicated both species and age differences in the form of distress calling (Colvin, 1973). With respect to cues indicative of the caller's age, the vocalizations of young mammals often have a higher pitch than those of adults, even when their form appears to be the same. Such field impressions have been verified by sound–spectrograms for at least 12 species.[3] The higher pitch of the human child's voice is a matter of common experience. Moreover, among several other mammals, the form of the calls may be unique to particular age classes.[4]

In addition to the foregoing, the vocalizations of *individual* young may also be distinctive. In species in which the mother–offspring bond is exclusive, mothers often can identify their offspring by the quality of their calls. An experimental

[3] Lemmings (Brooks & Banks, 1973); voles (Colvin, 1973); bats (Gould, 1971); field mice (Hart & King, 1966); rats and mice (Noirot, 1966; 1968); Australian flying fox (Nelson, 1964); beaver (Novakowski, 1969); titi monkeys (Moynihan, 1966); sea lions (Orr & Poulter, 1967; Peterson & Bartholomew, 1969); elk (Struhsaker, 1967a).

[4] Monkeys (Epple, 1968; Grimm, 1967; Rowell & Hinde, 1962; Struhsaker, 1967b); rodents (Noirot, 1972b); bats (Nelson, 1964); elephant seals (Le Boeuf, Whiting, & Gantt, 1972).

example is provided by research on the behavior of semidomesticated reindeer. Like most large, hooved animals, the mother reindeer cares for only her own calf. In this study, the calls that calves emitted when separated from their mothers were recorded, and spectrographic analyses of the vocalizations revealed stable, individual differences in the characteristics of the calls of both adults and young. When a calf was removed from the herd, its calls were broadcast over a loudspeaker. Out of 8 trials, 7 of the 8 absent calves' mothers called or moved and vocalized to the loudspeakers; in only one instance did another calf's mother show any reaction at all (Espmark, 1971). Similar findings have been reported for northern elephant seals, another species in which the mother–offspring bond is exclusive. In this study, pups were separated from their mothers and their distress cries recorded. After the pups had rejoined their mothers and had settled down, pup calls were broadcast. Eleven of the 14 mothers who were exposed to at least one call of both their own and an alien pup responded more frequently to own-pup vocalizations. Overall, 45 of 92 own-pup calls were answered. Free observations at another rookery where mothers and pups were individually identified supported the above findings (Petrinovich, 1974).

Human mothers also rapidly learn to identify their own infants' voices. Formby (1967) tape-recorded the cries of infants whose mothers had chosen to "room-in" with their infant during their hospital stay. Within 48 hours of giving birth, 20 of the 31 mothers reliably distinguished their own infants' crying from that of other newborns. A second group of mothers who roomed-in in three-bed wards were asked to record for whom they had awakened during the night. By the fourth night of their confinement, the 10 mothers as a group recorded only one "mistake" in 23 awakenings to an infant's crying. Similarly, in another study, a group of 10 infant cries was played for 35 mothers who had just given birth to their second child. Among the 10 cries, 2 were from each mother's own infant. By the second day after birth, 11 of the 35 mothers consistently discriminated their own offsprings' vocalizations from those of other infants (Valanne, Vuorenkoski, Partanen, Lind, & Wasz–Hockert, 1967).

In summary, the calls of the young can alert the caregiver, influence the form of the response given, direct the respondent in space, or serve as the basis for individual recognition. In some species, offspring calls may influence parental behavior in several, or even all, of these ways.

INTENSITY OF STIMULATION

As we have seen, the young must emit the appropriate cues and possess the necessary response capabilities to insure that caregiving is released and is functional. Furthermore, they must provide an adequate level of stimulation. Despite the fact that parental and filial behaviors are buffered, there exist upper and lower bounds of stimulation beyond which caregiving becomes less frequent or breaks down altogether.

Too much stimulation can cause reduced responsiveness. In a now-classic study, mother rats who were rearing larger litters tended to be less "maternal" than females rearing smaller litters (Seitz, 1958). Subsequent research replicated these findings in several species. In rats, mothers reared litters in two-compartment cages constructed so that pups could not follow them from one compartment to the other. They raised four or eight pups for the first 9 days after littering; on the tenth day, they were presented with foster litters of four or eight 10-day-old pups. Mothers who had been rearing four pups spent more time with their foster young than did mothers whose initial litters numbered eight pups. Furthermore, there was a tendency for the smaller foster litters to receive more attention than the larger ones. This was particularly true when either 4- or 8-pup litters of 1-day-old young were offered on the tenth day (Grota, 1973).

Similar data have been obtained with laboratory mice. Priestnall (1973) recorded the amount of time that mothers spent with their second litters, which had been adjusted to 2, or 5, or 8 pups. Throughout a 20-day observation period, females who were rearing smaller litters spent more time inside the nest with their pups than did females rearing larger litters. Mice rearing larger litters spent more time out of the nest, away from the pups, eating and drinking. The greater metabolic demands made on the mothers by the larger litters could have caused the mothers to spend more time out of the nest feeding. Thus Priestnall repeated the experiment with litters of 2 or 8 pups and with food and water supplied directly over the nest. Although time in the nest increased for all the mothers, those rearing litters of 2 still spent more time with pups than did mothers of 8. Thus it was litter size per se that governed time in the nest.

The foregoing experiments indicated that exposure to greater numbers of young can induce caregiver refractoriness. In species that normally bear only single young, additional offspring may constitute an almost unmanageable burden even under laboratory conditions. In rhesus monkeys, single births are the norm. In one experiment, the natural offspring of rhesus monkey mothers were removed within 12 days of birth. The mothers were then presented with either one or two foster young under 9 days of age. Mothers presented with single foster infants accepted their charges and cared for them without incident. However, those receiving two young all displayed ambivalent and rejecting behavior toward one of the two fostered infants. On at least one occasion, this maternal agitation led to debilitation of the rejected youngster. The mothers' behavior suggested that their difficulties stemmed in part from an inability to "arrange" both infants so that they could simultaneously cling to their bellies. Presumably, then, the females' caregiving repertoires were biased toward caring for a single infant so that the burden of attempting to transport two youngsters would not normally be accepted in the wild (Deets & Harlow, 1974).

On the other hand, there may be a threshold that must be exceeded before otherwise adequate stimuli will prove effective. Studies of nursing behavior show relationships between the degree of parental response and the regularity, quantity, and/or intensity of offspring stimulation. For example, mother rats were allowed unrestricted access to their litters of six pups for the first 8 days after littering. At that point, the litters were removed permanently, or were returned to their mothers for nursing once, or twice, or four times daily for one hour, or the litters were returned permanently. Litters that had only limited access to their mothers were kept healthy by fostering them on other lactating females. One nursing period per day was inadequate to prevent mammary regression comparable to that of the mothers whose litters were permanently removed. Only the mothers who nursed four times per day showed mammary development comparable to the unrestricted mothers and produced enough milk to maintain offspring survival (Tucker, Paape, Sinha, Pritchard, & Thatcher, 1967). In man, the importance of frequent sucking stimulation for establishing and maintaining lactation is well documented (Newton & Newton, 1972b).

Although regular nursing is a vital factor in maintaining lactation, for many species frequency alone is not sufficient. Tucker and Thatcher (1968) allowed rats 2 days' undisturbed contact with their first litters; on the third day, they adjusted litter size to 0, 2, 6, or 12 pups and allowed unrestricted nursing. Daily litter weight gains between Days 7 and 16 showed that total milk yield increased with the number of pups suckling. In rats, a positive correlation also exists between litter size and prolactin release in reponse to unrestricted suckling, and between the number of functioning mammary glands and the number of nursing pups (Mena & Grosvenor, 1968). Similar relationships between number of young nursing and milk output have been found in rabbits and Virginia opossums (Findlay, 1969; Reynolds, 1952).

The induction of caregiver responsiveness is also affected by the quantity of stimulation received. Terkel and Rosenblatt (1971) exposed naive, unresponsive, female rats to four 5- to 10-day-old rat pups in cages varying from 36 to 468 square inches of floor space. The smaller the cage, the sooner the females began to retrieve and display caregiving responses. Thus, sheer proximity, and presumably, the intensity of stimulation afforded by the young, influenced the rapidity with which females became solicitous. In another study, two groups of virgin adult females who had failed to display caregiving in pretests were housed with five 10-day-old pups. For one group, the pups were free in the cage; for the other, the pups were placed in a wire basket next to the female. A third group was caged alone. The females who had physical contact with the pups were subsequently more likely to retrieve, lick, or assume the nursing posture over test young than were females in the other two groups (Herrenkohl & Lisk, 1973).

SUMMARY

Both quantity and quality of offspring stimulation are important determinants of the quality, amount, and duration of caregiver response. Moreover, as indicated in Chapter 7, the total pattern of stimuli must be considered. In order to fully appreciate the complexity, subtlety, and robustness of the caregiver–offspring relationship, the investigator cannot stop with simply "disecting" limited facets of the relationship; he or she must then reconstruct the whole.

11

Beyond Caregiving:
Range of Effects of the Young

Lawrence V. Harper

INTRODUCTION

This book is predicated upon the fact that the parent–offspring relationship is reciprocal. The focus upon offspring–effects is deliberate, intended to emphasize the seriousness of neglecting the effects of the young. Although animal behaviorists were the first to systematically explore offspring–effects in the caregiving context, even they have not entirely avoided the image of the young as passive recipients of adult tutelage. Thus, this chapter continues to emphasize the importance of the young while turning from the caregiving relationship to examine a variety of behavior patterns.

Just as traditional models of human socialization have underestimated the importance of offspring in shaping the caregiving relationship, most students of mammalian behavior have failed to systematically consider the full range of effects of the young. The evidence to follow will show that offspring affect their caregivers and the wider group in precisely those areas in which adults exert a major influence on the development of offspring behavior. In short, it is suggested that, in order to understand the behavior and evolution of man and other mammals, the entire spectrum of ''socialization'' should be approached as an interactive process in which all parties undergo change as a result of their participation.

EFFECTS ON THE BEHAVIOR OF THE PARENT

The effects of the young on the parent's caregiving behavior have been outlined in some detail. Available evidence indicates that a number of additional facets of the adult's behavior are influenced by the young, either directly or indirectly.

Emotional state.   The unidirectional view emphasizes how parental behavior influences the emotional state of the young. However, in Chapter 8 we saw that a variety of hormonal adjustments occur in the mother as a result of conception. These changes represent only "the tip of the iceberg;" many areas of biological function are altered as a result of pregnancy (Eichorn, 1970). Given such far-reaching alterations in maternal physiology, related changes in behavior are not hard to find.

Among human beings, a frequently encountered concomitant of pregnancy is an altered sense of well-being. Sometimes the feelings are positive; all too often they are negative as a result of such phenomena as painful sensitivity in the nipple area and nausea. However, the mother is not always the only one to be so affected. The custom of ritual couvade is geographically worldwide, the only possible exception being inhabitants of Australia. Even in so-called advanced societies, the father may suffer symptoms apparently associated with his wife's pregnancy. In the United States, self-reported physical symptoms of 327 expectant fathers were compared with similar data from 220 otherwise comparable married men whose wives had not been pregnant in the preceding 9 months. More expectant fathers experienced physical symptoms than did the controls. Furthermore, these men reported more appetite loss, nausea, toothache, and sickness—all symptoms that often occur during pregnancy. It was estimated that 20–25% of all expectant fathers suffer from some kind of psychosomatic symptoms that disappear after the wife gives birth (Trethowan, 1972).

Many observers of animal behavior have been struck by the apparently greater wariness or agitation of pregnant and newly delivered females. Observers of human parturition (especially in hospital settings) have remarked on the fear and confusion that is displayed by new mothers *after* delivery (cf. Hubert, 1974). These responses doubtlessly reflect the tremendous physical effort and stress involved in giving birth; they complement the more often-mentioned adaptations required of the neonate. For a mother, adjusting to these changes and coping with the responsibilities of caring for her young can have far-reaching consequences. According to Kaij and Nilsson (1972), whereas the incidence of psychotic complications of pregnancy is only about .1 or .2%, major psychiatric illnesses follow parturition at a rate of between 20 and 25%. They suggest that the onset of postpartum disorder tends to occur between the first and fourth weeks after delivery.

In animals who have already established a relationship with their offspring, experimental alterations of the cues emitted by the young may precipitate agitated behavior on the part of caregivers. In rats and mice, some of the behavior patterns so affected seem to be unrelated to caregiving, suggesting more generalized changes in the caregiver's responsiveness (R. W. Bell et al., 1974; Sherrod, Connor, & Meier, 1974). Similarly, among humans, women who have difficult infants often report feeling panicked and powerless. Mothers who have given birth to damaged or malformed infants often suffer from loss of self-esteem (Morris, 1972; Richards, 1974).

Of course, the picture is not all negative; caregiving can have a very positive effect. Chappell and Meier (1974) observed a female rhesus monkey who had been reared in social isolation and whose adult behavior was characterized by bizarre, repetitious responses. When caring for her firstborn, she displayed significantly fewer stereotyped and atypical behaviors. For some animals, simply being exposed to the young may have beneficial effects. Rhesus monkeys who were isolated for their first 6 months of life showed only limited rehabilitation if subsequently allowed to interact with isolated or socially reared age mates. However, they displayed remarkable recoveries when regularly exposed to younger, socially experienced infants (Harlow & Suomi, 1971).

Clinical impressions suggest that positive effects also occur among humans. In many cultures, a woman's sense of adequacy and physical integrity—her feeling of personal worth—is intimately linked with her ability to bear and rear offspring successfully. In the United States, mothers of blind infants sometimes find a new sense of adequacy and competence when they learn to interpret the "meanings" of their babies' hand movements (Fraiberg, 1974). For the father, too, begetting young may enhance self-esteem and provide evidence of both his masculinity and his union with his mate (Howells, 1971).

In short, the presence or characteristics of the young may have a wide range of effects on the emotional state of the caregiver. In man, caregiving can either decrease or increase perceived well-being. These phenomena can be seen as complements of the effects of early experience on later emotionality of the young and of human adults' effects on the child's feelings of self-worth.

Feeding behavior.   Most developmentalists would agree that caregivers influence offspring diet; the converse is less often considered. Nevertheless, pregnancy and lactation do lead to altered feeding patterns in many species. Gestation places new energy demands on the mother; depending on the species or strain, either the fetus or the mother may suffer under conditions of mild starvation. In the latter case, the mother's body may be "robbed" even of essential elements to support the development of the young (Eichorn, 1970). Under favorable conditions, the mother simply eats more. The mother rat's food consumption varies with the number of pups she is nursing; it declines abruptly when the litter is weaned. Part of this effect can be attributed directly to stimulation by the young. Anesthetizing the mother's teats prevents increases in food consumption even when milk production is maintained by hormone injections (Ota & Yokoyama, 1967a; 1967b). Even the food items selected can be determined by metabolic needs. For example, Leshner (1972) provided pregnant and nonpregnant rats with diets that had equal caloric value and that were optimal for fat, minerals, and vitamins, but which varied in protein content. When allowed to select from several diets, the mothers consumed more protein than did controls when they were between the last third of pregnancy and the second week of lactation.

Apart from nausea, pregnant women often experience changes in appetite. Across cultures and ethnic groups, the frequency of cravings and aversions was estimated to range between 30 and 70%. In addition to individual peculiarities, which possibly reflect altered taste sensitivities (Trethowan & Dickens, 1972), cultures frequently prescribe changes in the diet of pregnant or postpartum mothers (Newton & Newton, 1972a). In addition to the traditional obstetric concern with the mother's gaining too much weight, folklore in "advanced" cultures also dictates that certain foods be emphasized or avoided (cf. Hubert, 1974). Thus, directly, in response to the metabolic alterations accompanying pregnancy, or indirectly, as a result of others' recognizing the pregnant state, the mother's diet is often altered.

Among such species as dogs and wolves, in which the mother's feeding is restricted by her tendency to remain with her offspring, other members of the pack assist in providing food (Estes & Goddard, 1967; Murie, 1944). In contrast, mothers in semisolitary forms such as squirrels, who gather and store food during periods of abundance, frequently get a late start on their winter supplies, because they have to consume what they gather in order to meet the demands of their litters (Smith, 1968). In man, there is currently widespread concern about the extreme hardships imposed upon impoverished families who attempt to provide enough food for their offspring. At the same time, as a result of advertising in the mass media, the young of the more affluent sometimes are persuaded to act as salesmen for processed foods (Harper, 1975).

Activity patterns.   Theories of socialization often stress the imposition of restrictions on the physical activity of the young. Not considered are the corresponding restrictions on parental behavior. From the later stages of pregnancy through the early dependence of the young, the mothers' and other caregivers' motor activities are often affected.

As term approaches, the mother's mobility may be reduced. Regardless of their personal predilections, many human cultures require expectant mothers to restrict or augment their activity (Newton & Newton, 1972a). In Western culture, it is common to curtail the activities of pregnant women. London working class women were treated by their mothers "as if they were marginally ill" during their first pregnancy; they were urged to rest, keep their feet up, and avoid strenuous activity (Hubert, 1974).

Likewise, maternal activity can also be affected after delivery. For example, Beach's (1939) pouchless opossum had to alter her posture when the young were clinging to her belly. Compared with her stance when unencumbered, the mother's hindquarters were more elevated when carrying her offspring. The young may cause alterations in caregiver locomotion even in precocial species. A "peculiar, springy gait" is adopted by the mother caribou, whose neonate calf is still too weak to flee from danger (Lent, 1966). Mothers of lame or severely injured ponies alter their movements to accommodate their offspring (Tyler,

1972), and zebra groups adjust their pace to that of the foals when chased by African wild dogs (van Lawick–Goodall & van Lawick–Goodall, 1971). Such adjustments in caregiver locomotion are common among primates whose young learn to walk only gradually. When crossing between trees, mother orangutans hang suspended between branches, providing a bridge for their offspring (Mackinnon, 1974), and most human caregivers will adjust their rate of movement to that of small children when they are not carrying them.

Many mammals show distinctive patterns of behavior only when interacting with the young. Le Boeuf et al. (1972) described vocalizations peculiar to mother elephant seals, and Lent (1966) listed a number of postures and gestures specific to adult–calf relationships in caribou. Several observers of human caregiver–young relationships have remarked how adults adopt exaggerated variability in intonation patterns and stereotyped facial expressions when interacting with small infants (Brazelton et al., 1974; Stern, 1974). In short, caregiving affects the amount and patterning of adult activity in man and other mammals.

Use of space. Caregivers of many species affect the offspring's exposure to their environments. As the foregoing descriptions of altered responsiveness to stimuli, feeding habits, and motor patterns suggest, the presence or prospect of offspring can also affect the caregiver's use of space.

In several mammals, pregnant females return to the site of their birth to bear their own young. Among others, expectant mothers seek the same locations in successive years. Even when the specific site varies, many pregnant females appear to seek certain kinds of settings prior to giving birth. Whether or not infantile experience determines the initial site preference, it seems likely that the pregnant state is one determinant of the timing of the female's return and the nature of the terrain chosen (Geist, 1971; Harper, 1970; Le Boeuf et al., 1972; Sandgren, Chu, & Vandevere. 1973).

Among species in which the offspring remain in hiding or in remote locations while the mother forages, the location of the young becomes a point of reference for the mother's activities. For example, when mother Steller sea lions return to nurse after foraging at sea, they swim closest to the location in the rookery at which they left their pups (Ono, 1972). Under normal conditions, female black-tailed deer do not return to previous bed sites. However, does whose fawns have died or wandered away repeatedly come back to the sites where they last interacted with their young (F. L. Miller, 1971).

When the caregiver remains with the young, movement may depend upon offspring locomotor capacities. Among such otherwise diverse burrowing forms as group-living African hunting dogs (van Lawick–Goodall & van Lawick–Goodall, 1971) and semi-solitary marmots (Barash, 1973), the group or the mother may have a restricted range of movement during the early postpartum period. When the young emerge from the burrow and begin to move about more freely, the foraging patterns of the caregiver(s) increase in extent and duration. An obvious example of offspring effects on caregiver movements in humans is the young parents who are reluctant to leave their firstborn with a capable sitter in order to go out for an evening.

On the other hand, the young may also directly contribute to changes or increases in the areas frequented by caregivers. Mother Steller sea lions will leave the main rookery to join their pups when the latter are swept to adjacent reefs in heavy weather (Orr & Poulter, 1967). And in hyenas, when they are capable of walking, cubs may move from one den to another on their own, causing the parent to move to the new site (van Lawick–Goodall & van Lawick–Goodall, 1971). In addition, maturing young of several species cause adult caregivers to seek new homesites. Similarly, human caregivers who have the means may change their place of residence to accommodate their offspring. Parents also take their children places to which they would not have gone otherwise (cf. Harper, 1970; 1975). In short, caregiver use of space may be localized, restricted, or expanded as a result of the presence of the young.

Exposure to danger.   Almost by definition, caregiving involves sheltering the young from danger. Field studies show that increased demands posed by feeding offspring may cause parents to venture into unsafe territory in search of food. Protecting the young from predators may also cause the caregiver to be less cautious in face of potential harm. For example, wild flying squirrel mothers will climb onto a human's clothing in order to retrieve their pups (Muul, 1970), and captive vervet monkeys defend their offspring when humans attempt to handle them. On the other hand, in the absence of the dominant male, young captive male vervets will also attack humans who attempt to capture their *mothers* (Bramblett, 1973). Here, then, we have an example of the young providing greater security for their caregivers. Among humans, one frequently encounters news articles recounting how caregivers risked—or lost—their lives in attempts to rescue their offspring from dangerous situations. Similarly, it is not uncommon for children to attack someone they feel is threatening their parents.

In summary, caring for the young may lead to either increased risk of or protection against danger.

Gregariousness.   A central concern of socialization theory is how the young "imprint upon" or form attachments to caregivers; the fact that bearing or caring for young leads to changes in interadult interactions has been neglected. In Chapter 7, we noted that the mother–young relationship may constitute solitary species' only prolonged social contacts. In other mammals, seasonal changes in gregariousness relate directly or indirectly to the prospect or presence of young. Gray squirrels who inhabit the suburban Washington, D.C., area share closely adjacent nest sites in holes in oak trees during the winter months. However, in the spring and summer, when the females are pregnant and nursing, each mother has her own nest, and sites too close to one another are uninhabited until after the young become independent (Harper, unpublished observations, 1967–1969).

Even in nearly continuously gregarious mammals, pregnant females may leave the group to give birth. Others may avoid species-mates while the young are very small, and some may remain remote from the larger group until the offspring can move about on their own (Kruuk, 1972; Rowell et al., 1968; Schenkel, 1966). In still other species, pregnant females may become actively hostile toward males and/or congregate in all-female subgroups (van Lawick–Goodall & van Lawick–Goodall, 1971; Du Mond, 1968).

The presence of young also may lead to increases in certain kinds of "friendly" contacts among adults. Female rhesus monkeys without offspring of their own sometimes begin to interact with a mother just after delivery. Similar "aunt" relationships have been observed in a number of other species. For example, Rowell et al., (1968) described a five- to ten-fold increase in mother baboons' contacts with new mothers. This phenomenon is not limited to primates; it occurs in several mammalian orders (Spencer–Booth, 1970). Among humans, mothers and fathers frequently develop friendships with the parents of their offsprings' playmates.

In summary, relationships with the young may represent the only enduring social interactions of the species; they may cause transient reductions or limitations in social interaction; or they may lead to increases in the frequency or range of contacts between adult caregivers and other members of the group.

Dominance relations.   Another facet of socialization is preparing the young to assume a position within the social group. Alterations in an individual's relationships with others as a result of parenthood also indicate that the presence of young sometimes changes the caregiver's status. In some species in which males are usually dominant, nursing females may drive males away from the nestsite. This suggests that the females' status has been altered as a result of their motherhood (Geist, 1971; Hall & Mayer, 1967). In at least four mammalian orders,[1] females with young are dominant over barren females and sometimes even over males. Like gray squirrels, mother marmots dominate at least the region of their burrows (Barash, 1974). In several primate species, a mother may attain higher status by virtue of the fact that the males protect infants and those associated with them. Young male monkeys may even associate with infants and juveniles as a means of self-protection or as a "passport" into areas that are otherwise exclusively occupied by the most dominant adult males (Itani, 1959; Kummer, 1968; Williams, 1968).

In many human societies, bearing children is a criterion for achieving adult status—for both husband and wife. In Western cultures, the nuclear family with children has been considered the "basic unit" about which society is organized (Busfeld, 1974). Many wives regard pregnancy and large families as "confirmation" that they are "proper women," and begetting offspring often has a com-

[1] Primates (Jay, 1963; Jolly, 1966; Schaller, 1963); ungulates (Espmark, 1964; Lent, 1966); carnivores (Sharp & Sharp, 1956); rodents (Horner & Taylor, 1968).

parable effect on the father's concept of himself (Hopkins & Clyne, 1972; Howells, 1971). Parenthood in the West may also affect a couple's social standing by affecting their standards of living. For many fathers, parenthood provides motivation for increased effort and a sense of legitimacy for competitive economic striving (Busfeld, 1974). Furthermore, practices associated with caregiving may serve as sources of status. Bottle-feeding is sometimes regarded as a symbol of affluence in developing nations (Newson & Newson, 1974). On the negative side, social disapproval and rejection may be directed toward families producing malformed or sickly offspring (Mead & Newton, 1967; Sontag, 1962), and legal action can be taken against child abusers.

Clearly, then, caregiving or parenthood can affect an individual's standing in his group. In the foregoing examples, the caregivers' bearing, possession of the young, or responses to the young were the critical factors in determining their status. However, among primates, the actions of the young also can affect caregiver status directly. We have seen that in the absence of the dominant male in a captive group, young male vervet monkeys will attempt to protect their mothers from human handlers. Presumably, they also might defend her during disputes within the group. In rhesus monkeys, offspring do rally to the aid of their parents. Males have been observed defending their mothers in a free-ranging colony (Wilson & Vessey, 1968), and, in a captive group, female offspring similarly came to the aid of their mother during disputes with other adults (Marsden, 1968). Not surprisingly, this also occurs among apes; wild chimpanzees sometimes defend their mothers during conflicts (van Lawick–Goodall, 1971). Among humans, in addition to direct physical support, the positive achievements or notoriety attained by offspring may lead to honor or disgrace.

In summary, among mammals it is quite common for individuals who have assumed a caregiving role to experience a change in social status within their group directly or indirectly as a result of their relationship to the young.

Sexual behavior.   Traditional theory stresses the effects of caregivers on the development of offspring sexual attitudes and practices. Less attention is given to the fact that offspring can affect parental sexual behavior. Although some mammalian mothers mate shortly after delivery, under "natural" conditions, many others remain unreceptive or inaccessible until after their offspring are of weaning age. Among the latter, especially those species in which there is a sharply defined period of "heat," stimulation from the suckling young may block hormonal changes underlying sexual receptivity (cf. Maneckjee, Srinath, & Moudgal, 1976). We already noted that nursing in rats could be extended well beyond the normal duration by repeatedly fostering "fresh" pups. One other consequence of this procedure is to extend the period of lactation diestrus for up to twice its normal duration (Bruce, 1961). Even without litter replacement, the effects of the young can be demonstrated in rats. Tucker and Thatcher (1968) observed that mothers not only produced more milk when nursing larger litters, but mothers nursing many pups also resumed estrus cycling later than mothers nursing smaller litters. Females whose offspring were removed at birth resumed cycling within 1 week after delivery; mothers who suckled two young came into heat on the average within 15 days; and none of those nursing six or twelve pups resumed cycling in less than 16 days. Even after estrus cycling has been resumed as a consequence of litter removal, litter replacement can reinduce lactation diestrus in rats (Ota & Yokoyama, 1965).

Inhibitory effects of suckling on sexual receptivity have been observed in a number of species. Fletcher (1971) found a positive relationship between the frequency of lambs' suckling during the first 2 weeks after birth and the time elapsed between delivery and the mother sheep's coming into heat. Lactation diestrus has been reported in representatives of four mammalian orders including monkeys and apes (Harper, 1970). Human mothers who breastfeed their young may also fail to conceive for as long as 1 year. Furthermore, the commonly encountered decrease in sexual desire experienced by pregnant women may, in some cases, persist and even be intensified in the postpartum period (Newton & Newton, 1962; Kaij & Nilsson, 1972). Thus, nursing and caregiving can often be related to temporary cessations of sexual activity in man and other mammals.

On the other hand, among humans, whose offspring are viewed as affirmations of one's personal adequacy, there may be considerable additional incentive for intercourse, at least until the woman is pregnant. Once the young are present, the decision to have additional offspring may be influenced by the size of the family and relationships with present young. For instance, families are less likely to have an additional child if the last one is a male (Busfeld, 1974; Sears, Maccoby, & Levin, 1957). Where considerations such as these affect the frequency of intercourse, the young may be said to indirectly affect parental sexual behavior. Other effects of the young may be seen in cultural restrictions on sexual activity during pregnancy and after delivery. Often the child must pass a developmental milestone before the parents are permitted to resume sexual relations (Mead & Newton, 1967).

Communicative behavior. The unidirectional view emphasizes how caregivers provide models for the young to emulate. However, the evidence indicates that adult communicative behavior is also affected by offspring. In representatives of at least three mammalian orders, parents and other adults employ distinctive vocal or postural signals only when interacting with the young. Given that these actions are indeed primarily directed toward offspring, it is fair to say that the young affect the communicative behavior of their adult caregivers (Le Boeuf et al., 1972; Lent, 1966; Nelson, 1965).

Among humans, there are numerous reports that parental verbal behavior depends upon offspring gender, age, presence, verbal competence, and cognitive ability (cf. Harper, 1975). A particularly obvious example of Western young influencing adult vocabulary—if not usage—is the widespread adoption by the mass media of many idioms originating with the "youth culture" of the 1960s and 1970s.

Thus, in both man and infrahuman mammals, the communicative patterns displayed by adult caregivers can be influenced by the young.

Effects of the Young on the Larger Group

Theories of socialization usually portray the young as the recipients of group influences; the offspring are seldom considered as contributors to the form or content of culture. Yet, we have seen that young have far reaching effects upon the social relationships of their caregivers. This fact implies that among gregarious species there will be repercussions throughout the larger social group.

Social cohesion.   It has been suggested that the parent–offspring relationship may be the basis for mammalian social organization (Eisenberg, 1966). Whether or not this hypothesis proves true, the parent–offspring bond appears to provide the basis for group formation in Soay sheep (Grubb & Jewell, 1966), patterns of associations among chimpanzees (van Lawick–Goodall, 1968), and troop division in Japanese monkeys (Sugiyama, 1960). In several species of old-world monkeys and among lions, the presence of young is associated with increased rates of "friendly" social exchanges within the group (cf. Harper, 1970).

It has been argued that human society is "organized around" the parent–child nuclear family (Busfeld, 1974). Certainly, conventions establishing kinship lineages are found in virtually all cultures, and having children is a central factor in legitimizing, defining, or maintaining male–female bonds in most human groups (Mead & Newton, 1967). Even among members of industrialized societies for whom birth control is accepted practice, there are strong pressures for married couples to produce or nurture children. From the Early Greeks until the present, childless couples either have been pitied for their inability to have young or considered selfish for failing to procreate (Busfeld, 1974).

In other mammals, the birth season may herald either an increase or a decrease in mothers' tendencies to congregate with their kind, and it may sometimes signal segregation of the sexes. In man, the bearing of children frequently strengthens the bond between the grandparents and parents. On the other hand, just as bearing or adopting young can increase family cohesion, it can also lead to disharmony and separation even when the young are healthy (Ryder, Kafka, & Olson, 1971). The assumption of a caregiving relationship exposes individuals to forces that often simultaneously strain and reinforce family ties. The outcome depends upon complex interactions between caregiver and offspring characteristics and cultural expectations (Howells, 1971). For example, in societies frowning upon illegitimacy, out-of-wedlock pregnancies can seriously upset family harmony.

Care of dependent young may also extend interadult contacts beyond the family. In the previously mentioned "aunt" relationships, females develop or strengthen social bonds with mothers, apparently as an offshoot of their interest in the young. In some species, such associations may lead to lasting alliances among adults. The near simultaneous birth of young under conditions of close proximity may lead to a sort of communal caregiving in species that do not have strongly exclusive mother–young bonds (Zimmerman, 1974). Even among sheep and ponies, where the mother–offspring bond is exclusive, "nursery bands" form during the birth season (Geist, 1971; Tyler, 1972). Similarly, in man, there are many examples of the ways in which the presence and (inter)actions of the young may cause a widening of parental social relationships (cf. Harper, 1975). Although these changes obviously reflect many different causes, they do indicate that the young can affect group cohesion.

Intragroup conflict.   Despite the fact that widened social contacts may be predominantly amicable, in many species hostile encounters also result from offspring presence or activity. Among laboratory mice, increased maternal aggressiveness represents an interaction between maternal state and the presence of young. Mother mice who are housed alone with their litters attack intruders; the severity of these attacks decreases as the pups grow older. However, if the litter is removed 5 hours prior to the introduction of an intruder mouse, the severity of the attack is reduced. Returning the litter after a 5-hour separation and introducing an intruder 5 or 10 minutes later restores the intensity of maternal attack. The mere presence of the pups behind a wire screen induces ferocious defense by the mother (Svare & Gandelman, 1973). Suckling stimuli appear to be a major factor in the development of this response to strangers. Mothers whose nipples have been removed before birth and "induced" virgin females fail to show such defensive behavior. If nipple growth is stimulated in virgin females by hormone injections so that their teats are large enough to permit pups to suck, they will attack alien males after 1 day or less with pups. If the pups are removed for a day or more, attacks upon intruders cease, but they resume within 24 hours of litter replacement. The crucial factor seems to be whether the pups can attach to the females' teats (Svare & Gandelman, 1976). Clearly then, pups are a central factor in the mother mouse' hostility toward unfamiliar species-mates.

In other mammals, the young may be the direct cause of intragroup confrontations. Among monkeys, infants whose rough play elicits distress signals from playmates are often threatened by their victims' mothers. The mothers of the offending young may also be threatened or attacked as a result; and mothers may attack adults who are simply in the vicinity of distressed young (Hall & Mayer, 1967; Harlow & Harlow, 1965). Analogous situations among humans are matters of common experience. Furthermore, in man, failure to conform to group expectations concerning proper caregiving practices may lead to conflicts. For example, mothers in Israeli *kibbutzim* occasionally have to accept sole responsibility for the care of their infants for a period of weeks after delivery. They usually form intense attachments to the babies even though their caregiving is not a matter of choice. Despite the fact that they have willingly committed previous offspring to communal care, many of the mothers resist surrendering these infants to the group. Such refusals to conform to commune expectations have caused serious dissention within kibbutzim and occasionally withdrawals from the group (Bettleheim, 1969; L. Miller, 1971). To the extent that early, extensive exposure to their infants induced these strong maternal attachments (cf. Chapter 8), the young can be considered to have contributed to group conflicts.

Social organization and role performance.   If dominance standings and patterns of hostilities within the group change when an individual adopts a caregiving role, social hierarchies are modified with the advent of young. In some human societies, a family's status is enhanced by the advent of (male) offspring, and such enhancement accrues to the extended lineage as well (Mead & Newton, 1967). Among cultures in which social positions involve relatively fixed patterns of behavior, such offspring-related redefinitions of a parent's or a family's standing can involve far-reaching readjustments within the group. For example, among the traditional Masai of Africa, a transition to the next higher social rank occurs for each of the older-age cohorts of males when a new generation "comes of age" (van den Berghe, 1973).

Even when age gradations of social position are not so sharply delineated, the birth of an infant can lead to the redefinition of an individual's position within the extended family. In Western, industrialized societies, women whose own offspring have achieved independence often eagerly accept the position of "granny," and a resumption of a socializing role, albeit sometimes a secondary one. Among poor Americans, grandparents may be the primary socializing agents. In such cases, as a consequence of the advent of another generation, grandparents return to a caregiving role (Money & Ehrhardt, 1972). This phenomenon may not be uniquely human. It is possible that grandparental care occurs among African elephants (Douglas–Hamilton & Douglas–Hamilton, 1975), and the strong and long-lasting mother–offspring ties among chimpanzees (van Lawick–Goodall, 1968) suggest that a similar pattern may be observable in that species as well.

This brings us to a consideration of the overall contribution to the group made by the parent. Even among mammals in which mother and offspring have little contact with species mates, parenthood may affect others insofar as the mother defends a specified range or intensifies her use of available food supplies. If some kind of cooperation of group coordination is involved in obtaining food, pregnancy and caregiving may directly affect the behavior of other members of the group. Among certain pack-hunting carnivores, the mother remains at the den and does not participate in the hunt for some weeks after littering. The other members of the pack provide food for the mother, and later, the weaning-age young. As the young mature, but before they are effective hunters themselves, adults allow them preferred access to the kill. Thus, the other members of the group have to assume additional burdens in the search for food: They must not only hunt without the contribution of the mother, but they must capture enough additional game to supply her and her offspring (Murie, 1944; van Lawick–Goodall & van Lawick–Goodall, 1971).

Among humans, parenthood involves increased economic burdens on the family for several years; in almost all societies, the young make little contribution to family subsistence until after the fourth year. Even in industrialized cultures in which childcare services constitute economic institutions in themselves, most working wives will spend several months on maternity leave, and many young women withdraw from the labor force permanently. Thus, parenthood can alter the makeup of the available work force. Among very small groups, or if the mother possesses unique skills or experience, her loss to the productive force may necessitate significant adjustments on the part of other members (cf. Bettleheim, 1969).

Furthermore, as suggested above, affluent societies frequently develop economic institutions devoted to providing for the young. Common examples are laundry services that specialize in cleaning infants' diapers or bedding, food processors who produce a wide assortment of baby formulae, and toy makers who tout their products as having educational value. As societies free themselves from day-to-day subsistence pursuits and become concerned with the welfare of subsequent generations, older, established service institutions also feel the impact of interest in the young (Busfeld, 1974). For example, academic institutions respond to the demand with expanded programs of instruction in child development.

In short, socialization involves preparing the young to contribute to the group's functioning, but the group's economic activities often change during the preparatory period—or permanently—in response to the need to care for offspring.

Parenthood also may affect an individual's contribution to intergroup relations. Among Ceylon gray langurs, many females make at least token threats and chases during encounters with other groups of langurs. Females with infants, however, usually do not engage in these intergroup aggressive displays (Ripley, 1967). Thus, among some mammals, parenthood may be a condition that absents certain individuals from an aggressive–defensive role in the group. An obvious human parallel can be seen in the rules governing conscription of young men for military service. During the Korean and Vietnam wars, young married North American males with dependent children were often excused from the draft. Here too, parenthood was a condition that exempted otherwise eligible individuals from participation in intergroup conflict.

Extending social contacts.   Even in such species as Hamadryas baboons, in which dominant males attempt to prevent their females from interacting with members of other groups, the young are relatively free to play with one another "across" family lines. In addition, females with very young infants sometimes cluster together during the birth season, "violating" the otherwise typical harem organization imposed by the males (Kummer, 1968). The van Lawick–Goodalls (1971) suggested that juvenile, but not adult hyenas also may be tolerated by adults from other "clans" and Koford (1957) reported that juvenile play groups of vicunas cross territorial boundaries.

The young are not only more socially mobile themselves, but they may also enhance the social mobility of caregivers. As an example of offspring influence on dominance, we have already considered how male Japanese macaques may adopt a caregiving relationship to infants in order to gain access to the "inner circle" of the troop. Similarly, relationships with young may provide a means by which outsiders can gain admittance to a foreign group. Poirier (1969a) reported that play relationships formed with juvenile members seemed to be a significant factor in facilitating an alien male's acceptance into a troop of langurs. On the other hand, the young may also provide occasions for intergroup hostilities. Yoshiba (1968) has observed conflict triggered by the "kidnapping" of infants in the natal coat among troops of Indian langurs. Thus, primate young may provide the links for the development of either positive or negative contacts between groups within a species. Furthermore, relationships can even develop across species as exemplified by play among young baboons and chimpanzees (van Lawick–Goodall, 1968; 1971).

In humans, commitments involving the young (especially females) historically have been one of the major cultural means for creating or cementing intergroup bonds (van den Berghe, 1973). Even in more recent times, interclass and interethnic play contacts or marital unions have provided the basis for expanded communication and interaction (negative, as well as positive) across cultural or subcultural lines.

In summary, then, the prospect or presence of young affect not only the caregivers' relationships with species-mates, but caregiving can influence the patterns of interaction and responsibilities within the wider group, and sometimes, across groups. Although such offspring–effects are clearly not mirror images of parent–effects, they nevertheless indicate that unidirectional models can not adequately capture the full complexity of the caregiving relationship.

EFFECTS OF THE YOUNG ON THE EVOLUTION OF THE SPECIES

It is obvious that the young of sexually reproducing forms represent new and "untested" combinations of a species' genetic potential. As such, they provide the raw material upon which the selective process operates, and, in a very real sense, they represent the future of the species (cf. Dobzhansky, 1970). When a group of animals adopts a strategy of caregiving, the environment in which the young develop tends to be more homogeneous. This reduces the need for genetic buffering of growth and allows for more developmental plasticity, which, in turn, can accelerate the rate of evolution of the species. It has been proposed that a prolonged period of development in the womb followed by postnatal nursing permitted a reduction in the genetic canalization of mammalian behavioral development and thereby gave rise to a greater range of offspring responses. This behavioral plasticity, particularly as expressed in such activities as play and exploratory behavior, has been considered a major contributor to mammalian evolution (Harper, 1970).[2] Furthermore, in view of the fact that components of the parent–offspring relationship appear in a variety of other social contexts, Wickler (1972) has suggested that the match between parental solicitousness and offspring characteristics provided the raw material for the evolution of complex social relationships. Thus, characteristics of the young, in and of themselves, as well as the adjustments involved in the development of caregiving, must be considered when attempting to understand mammalian evolution.

Although these considerations are important as background, they are remote from the dominant theme of this treatise: the more immediate effects of the young upon their caregivers and their group—effects that are apparent within a few generations. Now, while the evolution of a species or a subspecies cannot occur within such a brief time span, the rate of evolution of a group tends to increase when it adopts a new way of life, expanding its range to include unexploited aspects of the environment (Dobzhansky, 1970). As a result of modifying its relationship to its environment (where the environment is otherwise stable), a group exposes itself to new demands and thus to new selective pressures. New selective pressures in turn imply modifications in the gene–pool. If these modifications confer increased viability, and the environmental demands remain constant for appreciable periods of time, then speciation or subspeciation is likely to occur (cf. Mayr, 1970). The crucial question is thus whether the young are able to affect the behavior of a group so extensively as to alter the selective pressures to which it is subjected.

Several lines of evidence converge in support of the hypothesis that young mammals do play an important role in the colonization of new habitats and thereby expose their group to changed selection pressures.

Dispersal.   Most vigorous species are capable of producing more young than required to maintain a stable population. Although different species have adopted various strategies for keeping their numbers within the carrying capacities of their environments, a common means to this end involves driving away supernumerary young (cf. Jewell & Loizos, 1966; Wynne–Edwards,

---

[2] Although the constraints imposed upon caregivers by parturition and lactation may have acted to maintain a terrestrial phase in the life cycle of pinnipeds (Peterson, 1968), there is no reason to believe that caregiving sets absolute limits upon the adaptation of mammals, because mating, parturition, and caregiving in whales and dolphins is aquatic (for example, Tavolga & Essapian, 1957).

1962). In some cases, the young may regulate this process. For example, among Olympic marmots, two-year-olds are the ones who are forced to leave the colony; the degree of "pressure" exerted upon them by the adult generation is apparently determined by the number of yearlings who survive winter hibernation. However, the tendency to wander already resides in the two-year-olds; adult intolerance is manifest only when they return from exploratory sorties (Barash, 1973). Similarly, mother orangutans allow their offspring to sleep and travel with them until a new infant is born; then the juveniles are forced to travel, nest, and feed on their own (Mackinnon, 1974). When a species regulates its population in this way, it is, in effect, "deporting" colonists, forcing the offspring to attempt to inhabit as yet unexploited regions. Thus, the younger generation provides individuals who are most likely to expand the range of the group.

Given that juveniles of several species are frequently forced to leave the vicinity of the parental group and are thereby required to colonize new habitats, is there any evidence that they exploit previously unused sites? Although available data are scanty, there are observations consistent with this hypothesis. Le Boeuf, Ainley, and Lewis (1974) observed events leading to the re-establishment of a breeding colony of elephant seals on an island off the California coast, a site that had not been used for several decades. Because these investigators had been involved in a long-term study of the behavior of the region's elephant seal population, many of the members of the new breeding colony were identifiable by means of tags affixed to their flippers as pups. Both from the tags and from the overall estimates of the animals' ages based on size, etc., it was concluded that the colonists were predominantly subadults and young adults—individuals who usually compete unsuccessfully for space in established breeding colonies. Thus, there is some evidence that when young elephant seals are forced to the periphery by their elders, they respond by establishing new colonies wherever hospitable locations can be found in the vicinity.

Curiosity. In addition to enforced dispersal, we have noted that the young are more likely than their caregivers to wander afield. This juvenile wanderlust is perhaps part of younger animals' overall tendency to approach and investigate the unfamiliar (cf. Menzel, 1966). The possible adaptive value of such behavior is suggested by several studies of primate groups.

Suzuki (1965) observed the behavior of Japanese monkeys inhabiting an area at the extreme north of the species' range, a region having regular winter snowfall. In order to survive where their usual sources of food, leaves and green shoots, were unavailable for significant periods of time during winter, the members of this group had to strip and eat the bark of trees. The important observation for our purposes is that bark-eating was observed only among the juveniles of other groups living in adjacent, but more favorable, settings. The evidence thus suggests that young animals may have been the innovators of bark-eating and the colonists of this rather extreme habitat. Support for the foregoing conjecture comes from Poirier's (1969b) observations of south-Indian langurs inhabiting either "stable" environments or habitats that were being modified as a result of human activity. In changing settings, the troops' dietary habits were different from those of animals inhabiting more natural areas. Here too, in both environments, the young were the ones who sampled new and atypical food items. Thus, the curiosity or food-sampling behavior of the young appeared to be a likely factor in expanding the species' means of subsistence and thereby its geographical range.

Expansion of the species' habitat.   The foregoing observations imply that the curiosity and greater dietary flexibility of the young may lead them to exploit regions previously unused by the species. Although not involving food preferences directly, expansions of Japanese monkeys' habitats have been observed to occur as a result of the innovative activity of the young. In addition to his analysis of feeding behavior, Suzuki (1965) observed the onset of an apparently novel behavior in the cold-climate troop, bathing in the naturally heated springs typical of the area. The first individual observed indulging in this behavior was a juvenile female. Although the practice became more common over the next 2 years, it was the juveniles, almost without exception, who first acquired the behavior.

The second example derives from the now-classic reports of "sweet-potato-washing" by Itani (1958), Kawamura (1963), and Kawai (1965). These authors had been feeding an island-dwelling troop sweet potatoes. The food was strewn along open sections of the beach so that the observers could obtain an unobstructed view of the animals' behavior. The food was readily accepted by the monkeys; the adhering sand was not. The animals' usual response was to brush away the sand with one hand while holding the potato in the other. After a considerable period during which no animal had shown such behavior, a juvenile female picked up a sweet potato and immersed it in the water to wash off the sand. This behavior quickly spread to her playmates and occasionally to their adult caregivers. As more of the younger animals acquired this habit, their use of the sea increased. The sea had been avoided previously, but after they began to wash their food, the young animals ventured into the water to play. Eventually, through their playful explorations, the young began to gather and eat shellfish from the rocks along the coastline. In this case, then, we have direct evidence of an expansion of the troop's range into a new medium, one which not only increased the group's geographical range, but also afforded them a new source food.

In summary, we have direct evidence that young Japanese monkeys are responsible for an expansion of the species' range, and additional data suggest that the same may be true for other mammals. In view of the magnitude of the change in range resulting from the acquisition of sweet-potato-washing, it seems reasonable to conclude that the troop involved is now subject to different selection pressures. Thus, the conditions for an increased rate of evolution have been met as a result of offspring activity. If the younger generations survive and prosper in their expanded habitat, the conditions for a change in the gene pool are present (Howard, 1965).[3]

HUMAN CULTURAL EVOLUTION

As indicated in Chapter 3, there seems to be a lingering notion that man is somehow different—not just as all species are different from one another, but as set apart from all other forms. Whether or not cultural adaptations make man entirely unique among mammals, it appears that humans evolved within a cultural context (Dobzhansky, 1962). Thus we can evaluate evidence for the effects of the young on human evolution by considering the ways in which the young affect culture itself.

"Culture" has been variously defined, but at least one common theme is the transmission of certain behavioral attributes from one generation to the next by largely nonhereditary means. A basic premise in the social sciences has been that there is a relationship between culturally conditioned childhood experiences and adult behavior (cf. Buettner–Janusch, 1966; von Mering & Mulhare, 1970). Although it is obvious that offspring are shaped by the behavior and institutions of their elders, there is no empirical reason to believe that the direction of cultural transmission need always be from caregiver to young. The concept of a "match" implies interaction.

Although the possibility that endogenous predispositions of the young contribute to child-rearing practices and national character is open to debate,[4] there is evidence of considerable offspring influence on the culture at large. It is a common observation that the value systems of the young are based primarily upon parental exhortation and example (cf. Mussen, Conger, & Kagan, 1974). However, given the fact that adults do not always conform to their stated ideals, the young may affect cultural change by "internalizing" the preachments of their parents and by practicing them more fully. The civil rights movement in the United States during the 1960s provides an example of youthful idealists demanding that their society live up to its stated ideals (Horn & Knott, 1971).

[3]For additional discussions of the importance of mammalian young as innovators, see Frisch (1968); Harper (1970); Kummer (1971); Menzel (1966); and Reynolds (1972).

[4]Freedman (1974) has argued that the genetically determined behavioral predispositions of the young could have been responsible for caregiving practices as often as the opposite, and van den Berghe (1973) has noted a similar possibility with regard to the socialization of sex differences. However, Mead (1963) has presented an equally convincing case for the possibility that selection favors a biobehavioral "fit" between infants and already existing child-rearing practices. Thus, at this point, we must consider the question open until more extensive data are available from a variety of ethnic and cultural groups.

Without the activism of the younger generation, the far-reaching social legislation passed by the United States Congress during the 1960s probably would have
been achieved much later.

Not only do the young spur their elders toward greater adherence to their own
values, but they also are likely to be innovators in this realm. In his extensive
study of the relationship between age and culturally significant achievements,
Lehman (1953) noted that most new religions were introduced by the young.
The older generation usually became entrusted with leadership only after these
systems had become established. Other institutions for the transmission of culture also are influenced by the young. The history of Western European education is filled with episodes in which the students demanded—and sometimes
won—far-reaching changes in personnel, governance, and curriculum of universities (Eisenberg, 1970; Feuer, 1969). Clearly then, the young may influence
changes in cultural institutions.

However, with the possible exception of religious innovation, it is not immediately apparent how the above mentioned phenomena might alter the selective pressures affecting mankind. The most commonly acknowledged means of
affecting the rate of evolution of a group is to alter the kinds of environments
with which its members have to cope. Here too, we have reason to believe that
human young contributed directly to colonizing new habitats and creating environmental changes. These changes would seem to have far-reaching consequences for the evolution—and perhaps the maintenance—of the species *homo
sapiens*.

One of the most remarkable aspects of human evolution, as it is currently
understood, is man's expansion from a primarily open, savannah habitat to almost
every corner of the globe—from equatorial deserts to arctic tundra. Although we
cannot prove that the young constituted the bulk of the pioneering hominids who
ventured into new regions, a reasonably good case can be made for this contention. We noted that the young of many other mammalian species—including
primates—are more geographically mobile than their elders. Thus, it would
seem likely that man descended from stock possessing a similar tendency. Furthermore, the recorded history of Western Europe shows that the pioneering
exploratory ventures were accomplished by young men, usually under the age of
35 when the excursion was *completed* (Lehman, 1953).[5] In short, the available
evidence is consistent with the view that the younger generation must be credited
with at least a good portion of man's extensive colonization of this planet.

But, after all, in order for a "naked ape" to successfully colonize polar
regions, more than a mere wanderlust was required. Indeed, that aspect of

---

[5] Before taking this age as too old to represent "the younger generation," one should consider the
fact that many societies do not permit males to marry or participate in governing councils until they
are in their thirties (van den Berghe, 1973). Even in the United States, the Constitution specifies a
minimum age of 30 for members of Congress and 35 for the President. As the counterculture slogan
of the 1960s proclaimed, people were suspect when *over* 30.

culture which probably was most important in human adaptive radiation was the ability to harness the forces of nature, or at least, to modify the environment. In so doing, man opened up new habitats and with them exposed himself to new environmental demands. The tensions characteristic of industrialization and the harnessing of fossil fuel and atomic energy provide abundant evidence for the ways in which man's ingenuity has altered his environment and, very probably, the kinds of selection pressures to which his species is subject.

On the basis of recorded Western European history, we must conclude that the young were largely responsible for technological innovation. Lehman's (1953) study documents how the major scientific and technological advances were the products of young people. They usually were under the age of 25 when they published their first important creative works and under the age of 35 when their major contributions were completed. Analysis of major contributors to the social sciences (Deutsch, Platt, & Senghass, 1971) and a study of late 19th- and early 20th-century physicists (Feuer, 1974) have led to essentially the same conclusions. Most innovators undoubtedly were several years younger than 25 when they first formulated their ideas. It must have taken them at least a year or two to refine their concepts, test them against the evidence, and get them published. Thus, at the outset, we are probably talking about individuals in their late teens who were not yet accepted as members of the "establishment," youths who were just beginning to strike out on their own before they started families. (It may be significant that their major contributions were *completed* at an age when their own families would have been underway.)

SUMMARY

Here, then, is documented evidence for the contribution of the young to increased exploitation of human habitats during the last 1,000 years. The data indicate that the younger generations showed a greater wanderlust and a tendency to produce the technological innovations that made such migrations and settlement possible. Furthermore, "protocultural innovation" among the young of other primates indicates the possibility that similar age differences characterized early man and played a major role in prehistoric human evolution. From this we may conclude that, for man and other mammals, the effects of offspring behavior can have far-reaching consequences that may extend beyond the lifetimes of the young and their groups of origin—to the very evolution of their species.

12
Summary and Conclusions

Richard Q. Bell and Lawrence V. Harper

Our survey began with an historical overview from which it became apparent that parents and other adults have been highly responsive to the distinctive characteristics of infants and young children—from the ancient Mediterranean civilizations through the present. The power or importance of the young can be seen in the writings of philosophers and religious leaders. Then, just as now, there were those who saw potential threat to the morality and political structure of adult society in the spontaneity and capability for innovation shown by the young. There were also the optimists—educators who saw ''good'' seeds that should be left to flower and develop in their own beautiful way. Scientists, too, have variously seen in the child's development the history of man's evolution, the emergence of biological forces in the form of instincts, the battle of instincts against suppressive societal structures, and a photographic process in which parents and educators registered their imprint at will by using the principles of learning. All in all, if we didn't know better, we might be inclined to say that down through time the child has been merely an excellent inkblot in which anyone can see whatever they want.

Since the end of the 19th century, animal behaviorists have been aware of complementarity in social behavior, and they documented the effects of young mammals as early as 1933. Yet students of human socialization have only recently begun to appreciate the extent to which the young determine caregiver behavior. Experts who have reviewed specific areas of the vast literature on human socialization have in the last few years come to recognize that a unidirectional approach involving exclusive attention to the effects of parents is no longer defensible. Nonetheless, just as we are still discovering soldiers on remote islands who are under the impression that they are fighting World War II, some investigators still assume that the most plausible and parsimonious explanations of relationships between parent and child characteristics are those that primarily

212

depict the parent as an agent of socialization. Part of the problem is that these investigators have not looked beyond the product to the process by which it is achieved. If they were to do so, they would see that the process could not be inferred from the final outcome (in terms of how parent and child function at a given moment) and that the child plays a substantial role in shaping the process by which any particular end state is reached. In a nutshell, the love-oriented, permissive parent and the sweet little child who is obediently doing chores may have done some real shouting and hair-pulling before you appeared on the scene to observe their currently peaceful truce.

To maintain the momentum of the newer bidirectional approach and to offset nearly 40 years of exclusive attention to the unidirectional approach, we have attempted to show that the few consistent findings emerging from these many decades of research could easily be reinterpreted as due to the effects of children on parents. An adequate explanatory model now exists for such effects, and there are good reasons to believe that child–effects are more than a logical possibility. We have then gone on to review the advantages and disadvantages of research strategies that offer ways of isolating child– and parent–effects. We have done this in order to counter overreliance on field or correlational studies which, when done at a single time period, yield directionally ambiguous statistical associations between parent and child characteristics.

Given that many investigators are no longer content with the traditional uni-directional approach and that new strategies are available which could isolate determinants, there is a pressing need for hypotheses about child–effects that would provide the impetus for a new wave of empirical research. To this end, we have presented a control systems model of how parents and children regulate each other's behavior and a theory of how human young contribute to the very beginning of the socialization system in the first year of life. In addition, in order to broaden what has been a rather narrow perspective in the field of human socialization, we have attempted to indicate where parallels might exist between caregiver–offspring relationships in man and experimentally demonstrated offspring–effects in other mammals. A summary of some of the major features of the caregiving cycle, and a review of the long- and short-term effects of the young in nonhuman mammals, were presented in order to suggest new ways of viewing interactions in man.

At the risk of overkill, we have provided a myriad of examples in mammalian behavior to illustrate each class of effect, then cross-classified the effects, and bombarded you with choice factual tidbits all over again. We didn't leave anything to chance. An evolutionary perspective was stressed in most of the book, because it reminds us that behaviors which appear to be distinctively human probably originated in ways similar to those characterizing other species. Also, in analyzing the behavior of other forms, the data has led to a recognition of the necessity for a mutual matching of parent and filial behavior systems.

Our survey of mammalian caregiver–offspring relationships has shown that the young affect their caregivers from conception to—and often past—the point at which they no longer require care. This has led us beyond the question of the specific effects of offspring on caregiver behavior to a consideration of the ways in which mammalian young may influence other adult responses. We have found that the presence and activities of the young have repercussions throughout the group. Indeed, the evidence seems very strong that the behavioral peculiarities of the young may have been among the more important factors leading to the proliferation of mammalian species and the adaptive radiation of hominids. This is a very elegant way of saying that the Little People are more curious than cautious, and it is they who blunder into a Garden of Eden and take a bite of the apple.

References

Ainsworth, M. D. S., & Bell, S. M.   Attachment, exploration, and separation: Illustrated by the behavior of one-year-olds in a strange situation. *Child Development,* 1970, *41,* 49–67.

Aldred, C.   *Akhenaten.* New York: McGraw-Hill, 1968

Anderson, A. B. M., & Turnbull, A. C.   Comparative aspects of factors involved in the onset of labor in ovine and human pregnancy. In A. Klopper & J. Gardner (Eds.), *Endocrine factors in labour. Memoirs of the Society for Endocrinology,* No. 20. Cambridge: Cambridge University Press, 1973.

Anderson, J. W.   Attachment behaviour out of doors. In N. G. Blurton–Jones (Ed.), *Ethological studies of child behavior.* New York: Academic Press, 1972.

Anokhin, P. K.   Systemogenesis as a general regulator of neural development. In W. A. Himiwich & H. E. Himiwich (Eds.), *Progress in brain research* (Vol. 9). Amsterdam: Elsevier, 1964.

Aries, P.   *Centuries of childhood: A social history of family life.* (Robert Baldick, trans.). New York: Knopf, 1962. Originally published 1960.

Baer, D. J., & Ragosta, T. A.   Relationship between perceived child-rearing practices and verbal and mathematical ability. *Journal of Genetic Psychology,* 1966, *108,* 105–108.

Baldwin, A. L.   The study of child behavior and development. In P. H. Mussen (Ed.), *Handbook of research methods in child development.* New York: Wiley, 1960.

Baldwin. A. L.   *Theories of child development.* New York: Wiley, 1967.

Baldwin, B. A., & Shillito, E. E.   The effects of ablation of the olfactory bulbs on parturition and maternal behaviour in Soay sheep. *Animal Behaviour,* 1974, *22,* 220–223.

Balsdon, J. P. V. D.   *Life and leisure in ancient Rome.* New York: McGraw-Hill, 1969.

Baltes, P. B.   Longitudinal and cross-sectional sequences in the study of age and generation effects. *Human Development,* 1968, *11,* 145–171.

Bandura, A., Ross, D., & Ross, S. A.   A comparative test of the status envy, social power, and secondary reinforcement theories of identificatory learning. *Journal of Abnormal and Social Psychology,* 1963, *67,* 527–534.

Barash, D. P.   The social biology of the Olympic marmot. *Animal Behaviour Monographs,* 1973, *6,* 171–245.

Barash, D. P.   The social behavior of the hoary marmot *(Marmota caligata). Animal Behaviour,* 1974, *22,* 256–261.

Barnett, C. R., Leiderman, P. H., Grobstein, R., & Klaus, M.   Neonatal separations: the maternal side of interactional deprivation. *Pediatrics,* 1970, *45,* 197–205.

Barnett, S. A., & Burn, J.   Early stimulation and maternal behaviour. *Nature*, 1967, *213*, 150–152.

Bartholomew, G. A.   Mother–young relations and maturation of pup behaviour in the Alaskan fur seal. *Animal Behaviour*, 1959, *7*, 163–172.

Bates, J. E.   Effects of a child's imitation versus nonimitation on adults' verbal and nonverbal positivity. *Journal of Personality and Social Psychology*, 1975, *31*, 840–851.

Baumrind, D.   Effects of authoritative parental control on child behavior. *Child Development*, 1966, *37*, 887–907.

Baumrind, D., & Black, A. E.   Socialization practices association with dimensions of competence in preschool boys and girls. *Child Development*, 1967, *38*, 291–327.

Bayley, N., & Schaefer, E. S.   Correlations of maternal and child behaviours with the development of mental abilities: Data from the Berkeley Growth Study. *Monographs of the Society for Research in Child Development*, 1964, *29* (6, Whole No. 97).

Beach, F. A.   Maternal behavior of the pouchless marsupial *(Marmosa cinerea)*. *Journal of Mammalogy*, 1939, *20*, 315–321.

Beach F. A. Instinctive behavior: Reproductive activities. In S. S. Stevens (Ed.), *Handbook of experimental psychology*. New York: Wiley, 1951.

Beach, F. A.   The de-scent of instinct. *Psychological Review*, 1955, *62*, 401–410.

Beach, F. A., & Jaynes, J.   Studies of maternal retrieving in rats I: Recognition of young. *Journal of Mammalogy*, 1956, *37*, 177–180. (a)

Beach, F. A., & Jaynes, J.   Studies of maternal retrieving in rats II: Sensory cues involved in the lactating female's reponse to her young. *Behaviour*, 1956, *10*, 104–125. (b)

Beck, A. G.   *Greek education 450–350 B.C.* London: Metheun, 1964.

Becker, W. C., & Krug, R. S.   The parent attitude research instrument—A research review. *Child Development*, 1965, *36*, 329–365.

Beckwith, L.   Relationships between attributes of mothers and their infants' I.Q. scores. *Child Development*, 1971, *42*, 1083–1097.

Beckwith, L.   Relationship between infants' social behavior and their mothers' behavior. *Child Development*, 1972, *43*, 397–411.

Beckwith, L., Cohen, S. E., & Parmelee, A. H.   *Risk, sex, and situational influences in social interactions with premature infants.* Paper presented at the meeting of the American Psychological Association, Montreal, September 1973.

Bell, R. W.   Ultrasounds in small rodents: Arousal-produced and arousal-producing. *Developmental Psychobiology*, 1974, *7*, 39–42.

Bell, R. W., Nitschke, W., Bell, N., & Zachman, T. A.   Early experience, ultrasonic vocalizations, and maternal responsiveness in rats. *Developmental Psychobiology*, 1974, *7*, 235–242.

Bell, R. W., Nitschke, W., Gorry, T. N., & Zachman, T. A.   Infantile stimulation and ultrasonic signaling: A possible mediator of early handling phenomena. *Developmental Psychobiology*, 1971, *4*, 181–191.

Bell, R. Q.   The effect on the family of a limitation in coping ability in the child: A research approach and a finding. *Merrill–Palmer Quarterly*, 1964, *10*, 129–142. (a)

Bell, R. Q.   Structuring parent–child interaction situations for direct observation. *Child Development*, 1964, *35*, 1009–1020. (b)

Bell, R. Q.   A reinterpretation of the direction of effects in studies of socialization. *Psychological Review*, 1968, *75*, 81–95.

Bell, R. Q.   Stimulus control of parent or caretaker behavior by offspring. *Developmental Psychology*, 1971, *4*, 63–72.

Bell, R. Q.   Contributions of human infants to caregiving and social interaction. In M. Lewis & L. A. Rosenblum (Eds.), *The effect of the infant on its caregiver*. New York: Wiley, 1974.

Bell, R. Q.   A congenital contribution to emotional response in early infancy and the preschool period. In R. Porter & M. O'Connor (Eds.), *Parent–infant interaction* (CIBA Foundation Symposium 33). New York: Associated Scientific Publishers, 1975.

Bell, R. Q., Weller, G. M., & Waldrop, M. F.   Newborn and preschooler: Organization of behavior and relations between periods. *Monographs of the Society for Research in Child Development*, 1971, *36* (1, 2, Serial No. 142).

Bell, S. M., & Ainsworth, M. D.   The development of the concept of object as related to infant–mother attachment. *Child Development*, 1970, *41*, 291–311.

Bell, S. M., & Ainsworth, M. D.   Infant crying and maternal responsiveness. *Child Development*, 1972, *43*, 1171–1190.

Benedict, R.   Child rearing in certain European countries. *American Journal of Orthopsychiatry*, 1949, *19*, 342–350.

Berberich, J. P.   Do the child's responses shape the teaching behavior of an adult? *Journal of Experimental Research in Personality*, 1971, *5*, 92–97.

Berkowitz, L.   Control of aggression. In B. M. Caldwell & H. N. Ricciuti (Eds.), *Review of child development research*. Chicago: University of Chicago Press, 1973.

Bernal, J. F.   Crying during the first ten days of life, and maternal responses. *Developmental Medicine and Child Neurology*, 1972, *14*, 362–372.

Bernal, J. F.   Night waking in infants during the first 14 months. *Developmental Medicine and Child Neurology*, 1973, *15*, 760–769.

Bernstein, N.   *The coordination and regulation of movements*. London: Pergamon Press, 1967.

Bettleheim, B.   *The children of the dream*. Toronto: Collier–Macmillan, 1969.

Bing, E.   Effect of childrearing practices on development of differential cognitive abilities. *Child Development*, 1963, *34*, 631–648.

Birch, H. E., & Lefford, A.   Visual differentiation, intersensory integration, and voluntary motor control. *Monographs of the Society for Research in Child Development*, 1967, *32* (2, Serial No. 110).

Blalock, H. M., Jr.   *Causal inferences in nonexperimental research*. Chapel Hill, North Carolina: The University of North Carolina Press, 1961.

Booth, C.   Some observations on behavior of *Cercopithecus* monkeys. *Annals of the New York Academy of Sciences*, 1962, *102*, 477–487.

Boring, E.   *History of experimental psychology*. New York: Appleton–Century–Crofts, 1957.

Bowlby, J.   Separation anxiety. *International Journal of Psychoanalysis*, 1960, *41*, 89–113.

Bowlby, J.   *Attachment and loss* (Vol. 1). New York: Basic Books, 1969.

Bramblett, C. A.   Social organization as an expression of role behavior among old world monkeys. *Primates*, 1973, *14*, 101–112.

Brazelton, T. B., Koslowski, B., & Main, M.   The origins of reciprocity: The early mother–infant interaction. In M. Lewis & L. A. Rosenblum (Eds.), *The effect of the infant on its caregiver*. New York: Wiley, 1974.

Bridges, R., Zarrow, M. X., Gandelman, R., & Denenberg, V. H.   Differences in maternal responsiveness between lactating and sensitized rats. *Developmental Psychobiology*, 1972, *5*, 123–127.

Brody, S. *Patterns of mothering*. New York: International Universities Press, 1956.

Bronfenbrenner, U.   *A theoretical perspective for research on human development*. Unpublished paper, Cornell University, 1971.

Bronfenbrenner, U.   Developmental research, public policy, and the ecology of childhood. *Child Development*, 1974, *45*, 1–5.

Brooks, R. J., & Banks, E. M.   Behavioral biology of the collared lemming *(Dicrostonyx groenlanclicus* (Trail)): An analysis of acoustic communication. *Animal Behaviour Monographs*, 1973, *6*, 1–83.

Brooks, V., & Hochberg, J.   A psychophysical study of "cuteness." *Perceptual and Motor Skills*, 1960, *11*, 205.

Brown, L. E.   Home range and movement of small mammals. In P. A. Jewell & C. Loizos (Eds.), *Play, exploration and territory in mammals. Symposia of the Zoological Society of London*, Vol. 18. London: Academic Press, 1966.

Bruce, H. M.   Observations on the suckling stimulus and lactation in the rat. *Journal of Reproduction and Fertility*, 1961, *2*, 17–34.

Bruner, J. S.   Nature and uses of immaturity. *American Psychologist*, 1972, *27*, 687–708.

Buettner–Janusch, J.   *Origins of man*. New York: Wiley, 1966.

Bulmer, M. G.   *The biology of twinning in man*. London: Oxford University Press, 1970.

Busfeld, J.   Ideologies and reproduction. In M. P. M. Richards (Eds.), *The integration of a child into a social world*. London: Cambridge University Press, 1974.

Caldeyro–Barcia, R.   Factors controlling the actions of the pregnant human uterus. In M. Knowlessar (Ed.), *The physiology of prematurity*. New York: Josiah Macy Foundation, 1961.

Caldwell, B. M.   The effects of infant care. In M. L. Hoffman & L. W. Hoffman (Eds.), *Review of child development research* (Vol. 1). New York: Russell Sage Foundation, 1964.

Carlier, C., & Noirot, E.   Effects of previous experience on maternal retrieving by rats. *Animal Behaviour*, 1965, *13*, 423–426.

Carlsmith, L.   Effect of early father absence on scholastic aptitude. *Harvard Educational Review*, 1964, *34*, 3–21.

Carpenter, C. R.   A field study in Siam of the behavior and social relations of the gibbon. *Comparative Psychology Monographs*, 1940, *16* (Whole No. 5).

Chappell, P. F., & Meier, G. W.   Behavior modification in a mother–infant dyad. *Developmental Psychobiology*, 1974, *7*, 296.

Chard, T.   The posterior pituitary and the induction of labour. In A. Klopper & J. Gardner (Eds.), *Endocrine factors in labour. Memoirs of the Society for Endocrinology*, No. 20. Cambridge: Cambridge University Press, 1973.

Charles–Picard, G., & Charles–Picard, C.   *Daily life in Carthage*. New York: Macmillan, 1958.

Chess, S.   Genesis of behaviour disorders. In J. G. Howells (Eds), *Modern perspectives in international child psychiatry*. New York: Brunner/Mazel, 1971.

Clark, K.   *Civilization*. New York: Harper, 1969.

Clarke–Stewart, K. A.   Interactions between mothers and their children: Characteristics and consequences. *Monographs of the Society for Research in Child Development*, 1973, *38*(6–7, Serial No. 153).

Clausen, J. A.   The organism and socialization. *Journal of Health and Social Behavior*, 1967, *8*, 243–252.

Coates, B., Anderson, E. R., & Hartup, W. W.   Interrelations in the attachment behavior of human infants. *Developmental Psychology*, 1972, *6*, 218–230.

Cohen, S. E.   Developmental differences in infants' attentional responses to face–voice incongruity of mother and stranger. *Child Development*, 1974, *45*, 1155–1158.

Collias, N. E.   The analysis of socialization in sheep and goats. *Ecology*, 1956, *37*, 228–239.

Collis, G. M., & Schaffer, H. R.   Synchronization of visual attention in mother–infant pairs. *Journal of Child Psychology and Psychiatry*, 1975, *16*, 315–320.

Colvin, M. A.   Analysis of acoustic structure and function in ultrasounds of neonatal *Microtus*. *Behaviour*, 1973, *44*, 234–263.

Condon, W. S., & Sander, L. W.   Synchrony demonstrated between movements of the neonate and adult speech. *Child Development*, 1974, *45*, 456–462.

Contenau, G.   *Everyday life in Babylon and Assyria*. London: Edwin Arnold, 1954.

Cross, B. A.   Neural control of oxytocin secretion. In L. Martini & W. F. Ganong (Eds.), *Neuroendocrinology* (Vol I). New York: Academic Press, 1966.

Darwin, C.   *The origin of species*. London: Murray, 1859.

Darwin, C.   *The expression of emotions in man and animal*. London: Appleton, 1872. Reprinted by University of Chicago Press, 1972.

David, M., & Appell, G.   A study of nursing care and nurse–infant interaction. In B. M. Foss (Ed.), *Determinants of infant behaviour* (Vol. 1). New York: Wiley, 1961.

David, M., & Appell, G.   Mother–child relationship. In J. G. Howells (Ed.), *Modern perspectives in international child psychiatry*. New York: Brunner/Mazel, 1971.

Deets, A. C., & Harlow, H. F. Adoption of single and multiple infants by rhesus monkey mothers. *Primates,* 1974, *15,* 193–203.

Deis, R. P. The effects of an exteroceptive stimulus on milk ejection in lactating rats. *Journal of Physiology,* 1968, *197,* 37–46.

Deis, R. P., & Orias, R. The effect of an exteroceptive stimulus on the concentration of melanocyte-stimulating hormone in the pituitary of lactating rats. *Journal of Physiology,* 1968, *197,* 47–51.

DeMause, L. The evolution of childhood. *History of Childhood Quarterly: The Journal of Psychohistory,* 1974, *1,* 503–575.

Demos, J. *A little commonwealth: Family life in Plymouth colony.* New York: Oxford University Press, 1970.

Dennis, W. Historical beginnings of child psychology. *Psychological Bulletin,* 1949, *46,* 224–235.

Deutsch, K. W., Platt, J., & Senghaas, D. Conditions favoring major advances in social science. *Science,* 1971, *171,* 450–459.

DeVore, I. Mother–infant relationships in free-ranging baboons. In H. L. Rheingold (Ed.), *Maternal behavior in mammals.* New York: Wiley, 1963.

DeVore, I. (Ed.) *Primate behavior. Field studies of monkeys and apes.* New York: Holt, Rinehart and Winston, 1965.

De Vos, A., Brokx, P., & Geist V. A review of social behavior of the North American cervids during the reproductive period. *American Midland Naturalist,* 1967, *77,* 390–417.

De Vries, P. *The tunnel of love.* Boston: Little, Brown & Co., 1954.

Dobzhansky. T. *Mankind evolving.* New Haven: Yale University Press, 1962.

Dobzhansky. T. *Genetics of the evolutionary process.* New York: Columbia University Press, 1970.

Douglas–Hamilton, I., & Douglas–Hamilton, O. *Among the elephants.* New York: Viking, 1975.

Doyle, G. A., Anderson, A., & Bearder, S. K. Maternal behavior in the lesser bushbaby *(Galago senegalensis moholi)* under semi-natural conditions. *Folia Primatologica,* 1969, *11,* 215–238.

Du Mond, F. V. The squirrel monkey in a semi-natural environment. In L. A. Rosenblum & R. W. Cooper (Eds.), *The squirrel monkey.* New York: Academic Press, 1968.

Eibl–Eibesfeldt, I. *Ethology: The biology of behavior.* New York: Holt, Rinehart and Winston, 1970.

Eichorn, D. Physiological development. In P. H. Mussen (Ed.), *Carmichael's manual of child psychology* (3rd ed.). New York: Wiley, 1970.

Eisenberg, J. F. The behavior of heteromyid rodents. *University of California Publications in Zoology,* 1963, *69,* 1–78.

Eisenberg, J. F. The social organization of mammals. *Handbuch der Zoologie,* 1966, *8,* 1–92.

Eisenberg, L. Student unrest: Sources and consequences. *Science,* 1970, *167,* 1688–1692.

Eisenberg, R. B. Auditory sensory processes: Some gleanings from the developmental lode. In J. W. Prescott, M. S. Read, & D. Coursin (Eds.), *Brain function and malnutrition: Neuropsychological methods of assessment.* New York: Wiley, 1975.

Ellingson, R. J. Cerebral electrical responses to auditory and visual stimuli in the infant (human and subhuman studies). In P. Kellaway & I. Petersen (Eds.), *Neurological and electroencephalographic correlative studies in infancy.* New York: Grune and Stratton, 1964.

Emde, R. N., Gaensbauer, T. J., & Harmon, R. J. Emotional expression in infancy: A biobehavioral study. *Psychological Issues,* 1976, *10*(1, Monograph 37).

Emmerich, W. Continuity and stability in early social development. *Child Development,* 1964, *35,* 311–332.

Epple, G. Comparative studies on vocalization in marmoset monkeys *Hapalidae. Folia Primatologica,* 1968, *8,* 1–40.

Epstein, W. Experimental investigations of the genesis of visual space perception. *Psychological Bulletin*, 1964, *61*, 115–128.

Erikson, E. H. *Childhood and society*. New York: Norton, 1950.

Erlanger, H. S. Social class and corporal punishment in childrearing: A reassessment. *American Sociological Review*, 1974, *39*, 65–85.

Erman, A. *The ancient Egyptians*. New York: Harper, 1966.

Eron, L. D., Lefkowitz, M. M., Huesmann, L. R., & Walder, L. O. Does television violence cause aggression? *American Psychologist*, 1972, *27*, 253–263.

Escalona, S. *The roots of individuality*. Chicago: Aldine, 1968.

Espmark, Y. Studies in dominance–subordination relationships in a group of semi-domestic reindeer (*Rangifer tarandus*, L.). *Animal Behaviour*, 1964, *12*, 420–426.

Espmark, Y. Individual recognition by voice in reindeer mother–young relationship. Field observations and play-back experiments. *Behaviour*, 1971, *40*, 295–301.

Estes, R. D., & Goddard, J. Prey selection and hunting behavior of the African wild dog. *Journal of Wildlife Management*, 1967, *31*, 52–70.

Etzel, B. C., & Gewirtz, J. L. Experimental modification of caretaker-maintained high-rate operant crying in a 6- and a 20-week-old infant (Infans tyrannotearus): Extinction of crying with reinforcement of eye contact and smiling. *Journal of Experimental Child Psychology*, 1967, *5*, 303–317.

Feshbach, S. Aggression. In P. H. Mussen (Ed.), *Carmichael's manual of child psychology* (3rd ed.). New York: Wiley, 1970.

Feuer, L. *The conflict of generations*. New York: Basic Books, 1969.

Feuer, L. *Einstein and the generations of science*. New York: Basic Books, 1974.

Findlay, A. L. R. Nursing behaviour and the condition of the mammary gland in the rabbit. *Journal of Comparative and Physiological Psychology*, 1969, *69*, 115–118.

Flacelière, R. *Daily life in Greece at the time of Pericles*. (Peter Green, trans.). New York: Macmillan, 1965. Originally published 1959.

Fleming, A. S., & Rosenblatt, J. S. Olfactory regulation of maternal behavior in rats: I. Effects of olfactory bulb removal in experienced and inexperienced lactating and cycling females. *Journal of Comparative and Physiological Psychology*, 1974, *36*, 221–232. (a)

Fleming, A. S., & Rosenblatt, J. S. Olfactory regulation of maternal behavior in rats: II. Effect of peripherally induced anosmia and lesions of the lateral olfactory tract in pup-induced virgins. *Journal of Comparative and Physiological Psychology*, 1974, *86*, 233–246. (b)

Fleming, A. S., & Rosenblatt, J. S. Maternal behavior in the virgin and lactating rat. *Journal of Comparative and Physiological Psychology*, 1974, *86*, 957–972. (c)

Fletcher, I. C. Relationship between frequency of sucking, lamb growth, and post-partum oestrus behaviour in ewes. *Animal Behaviour*, 1971, *19*, 108–111.

Fontana, A. F. Familial etiology of schizophrenia: Is a scientific methodology possible? *Psychological Bulletin*, 1966, *66*, 214–227.

Formby, D. Maternal recognition of infant's cry. *Developmental Medicine and Child Neurology*, 1967, *9*, 293–298.

Fraiberg, S. Blind infants and their mothers: An examination of the effects of the sign system. In M. Lewis & L. A. Rosenblum (Eds.), *The effect of the infant on its caregiver*. New York: Wiley, 1974.

Frank, G. H. The role of the family in the development of psychopathology. *Psychological Bulletin*, 1965, *65*, 191–205.

Frankfort, H., Frankfort, H. A. G., Jacobsen, T., & Wilson, J. *Before philosophy*. Baltimore: Penguin, 1946.

Freedman, D. G. Hereditary control of early social behavior. In B. M. Foss (Ed.), *Determinants of infant behavior* (Vol. III). New York: Wiley, 1965.

Freedman, D. G. *Human infancy: An evolutionary perspective*. Hillsdale, New Jersey: Lawrence Erlbaum Associates, 1974.

Freud, S.   Civilization and its discontents. In *The standard edition of the complete works of Sigmund Freud* (Vol. 21). London: Hogarth Press, 1953.

Frisch, J. E.   Individual behavior and intertroop variability in Japanese macaques. In P. Jay (Ed.), *Primates: Studies in adaptation and variability*. New York: Holt, Rinehart and Winston, 1968.

Fullard, W., & Reiling, A. M.   An investigation of Lorenz's "babyness." *Child Development*, 1976, *47*, 1191–1193.

Gandelman, R., Zarrow, M. X., & Denenberg, V. H.   Stimulus control of cannibalism and maternal behavior in anosmic mice. *Physiology and Behavior*, 1971, *7*, 583–586.

Gardner, B. T., & Wallach, L.   Shapes of figures identified as a baby's head. *Perceptual and Motor Skills*, 1965, *20*, 135–142.

Gardner, D. B., & Pease, D.   The use of situational tests with preschool children. *Journal of Nursery Education*, 1958, *14*, 18–20.

Geist, V.   *Mountain sheep*. Chicago: University of Chicago Press, 1971.

Gesell, A., & Ames, L. B.   Early evidence of individuality in the human infant. *Scientific Monthly*, 1937, *45*, 217–225.

Gesell, A., Halverson, M., Thompson, H., Ilg, F. L., Castner, B. M., Ames, L. B., & Amatruda, C. S.   *The first five years of life: A guide to the study of the preschool child*. New York: Harper, 1940.

Gewirtz, J. L.   A learning analysis of the effects of normal stimulation, privation, and deprivation on the acquisition of social motivation and attachment. In B. M. Foss (Ed.), *Determinants of infant behaviour*. (Vol. I) New York: Wiley, 1961.

Gewirtz, J. L., & Boyd, E. F.   Does maternal responding really reduce infant crying?: A critique of the 1972 Bell and Ainsworth Report. *Child Development*, 1977.

Gewirtz, J. L., & Boyd, E. F.   Experiments in mother–infant interaction, mutual attachment, acquisition: The infant conditions his mother. In T. Alloway, L. Krames, & P. Pliner (Eds.), *Advances in the study of communication and affect* (Vol. 3). New York: Plenum, 1976.

Gewirtz, J. L., & Gewirtz, H. B.   Stimulus conditions, infant behaviors, and social learning in four Israeli child-rearing environments: A preliminary report illustrating differences in environment and behavior between the "only" and the "youngest" child. In B. M. Foss (Ed.), *Determinants of infant behaviour*, III. New York: Wiley, 1965.

Gewirtz, H. B., & Gewirtz, J. L.   Visiting and caretaking patterns for Kibbutz infants: Age and sex trends. *American Journal of Orthopsychiatry*, 1968, *38*, 427–443.

Gewirtz, H. B., & Gewirtz, J. L.   Caretaker settings, background events and behavior differences in four Israeli child-rearing environments: Some preliminary trends. In B. M. Foss (Ed.), *Determinants of infant behaviour* (Vol. IV). London: Methuen, 1969.

Gill, D. G.   *Violence against children*. Cambridge, Mass.: Harvard University Press, 1970.

Gill, J. C., & Thompson, W.   Observations on the behaviour of suckling pigs. *British Journal of Animal Behaviour*, 1956, *4*, 46–52.

Gordon, C.   *Hammurabi's code*. New York: Holt, Rinehart & Winston, 1957.

Gould, E.   Studies of maternal–infant communication and development of vocalizations in the bats *Myotis* and *Eptesicus*. *Communications in Behavioral Biology*, 1971, *5*, 263–313.

Gould, E., & Eisenberg, J. F.   Notes on the biology of the *Tenrecidae*. *Journal of Mammalogy*, 1966, *47*, 660–686.

Grimm, R. J.   Catalogue of sounds of the pigtailed macaque *(Macaca nemestrina)*. *Journal of Zoology*, 1967, *152*, 361–373.

Grosvenor, C. E., & Mena, F.   Evidence that suckling pups through an exteroceptive mechanism inhibit the milk stimulatory effects of prolactin in the rat during late lactation. *Hormones and Behavior*, 1973, *4*, 209–222.

Grota, L. J.   Factors influencing the acceptance of caesarean-delivered offspring by foster mothers. *Physiology and Behavior*, 1968, *3*, 265–269.

Grota, L. J.   Effects of litter size, age of young and parity on foster mother behaviour in *Rattus norvegicus*. *Animal Behaviour*, 1973, *21*, 78–82.

Grubb, P., & Jewell, P. A.   Social grouping and home range in feral Soay sheep. In P. A. Jewell & C. Loizos (Eds.), *Play, exploration and territory in mammals. Symposia of the Zoological Society of London,* No. 18. London: Academic Press, 1966.

Gruenberg, E. M.   On the psychosomatics of the not-so-perfect fetal parasite. In S. A. Richardson & A. F. Guttmacher (Eds.), *Childbearing: Its social and psychological aspects.* Baltimore: Williams & Wilkins, 1967.

Gunther, E. M.   Infant behaviour at the breast. In B. M. Foss (Ed.), *Determinants of Infant Behaviour* (Vol. I). New York: Wiley, 1961.

Gurney, O. R.   *The Hittites.* Baltimore: Penguin, 1954.

Guskin, S.   Social psychologies of mental deficiencies. In N. R. Ellis (Ed.), *Handbook of mental deficiencies.* New York: McGraw-Hill, 1963.

Haaf, R. A., & Brown, C. J.   *Developmental changes in infants' response to complex facelike patterns.* Paper presented at the biennial meeting of the Society for Research in Child Development, Denver, April 1975.

Hafez, E. S. E., & Lineweaver, J. A.   Sucking behavior in natural and artificially fed neonate calves. *Zeitschrift für Tierpsychologie,* 1968, *25,* 187–198.

Haley, J.   Testing parental instructions to schizophrenic and normal children. *Journal of Abnormal Psychology,* 1968, *73,* 559–565.

Hall, K. R. L., & De Vore, I.   Baboon social behavior. In I. De Vore (Ed.), *Primate behavior.* New York: Holt, Rinehart and Winston, 1965.

Hall, K. R. L., & Mayer, B.   Social interactions in a group of captive patas monkeys *Erythrocebus patas. Folia Primatologica,* 1967, *5,* 213–236.

Halverson, C. F., & Victor, J. B.   Minor physical anomalies and problem behavior in elementary school children. *Child Development,* 1976, *47,* 281–285.

Halverson, C. F., & Waldrop, M. F.   Maternal behavior toward own and other preschool children: The problem of "ownness." *Child Development,* 1970, *41,* 839–845.

Haour, F., & Saxena, B. B.   Detection of a gonadotropin in rabbit blastocyst before implantation. *Science,* 1974, *185,* 444–445.

Hannan, T. E.   *Possible role of mother–infant separation in the development of the post-partum blues syndrome in man.* Unpublished manuscript, Department of Applied Behavioral Sciences, University of California at Davis, 1975.

Harlow, H. F., & Harlow, M. K.   The affectional system. In A. M. Schrier, H. F. Harlow, & F. Stollnitz (Eds.), *Behavior of nonhuman primates* (Vol. II). New York: Academic Press, 1965.

Harlow, H. F., Harlow, M. K., Dodsworth, R. O., & Arling, G. L.   Maternal behavior of rhesus monkeys deprived of mothering and peer associations in infancy. *Proceedings of the American Philosophical Society,* 1966, *110,* 58–66.

Harlow, H. F., Harlow, M. K., & Hansen, E. W.   The maternal affectional system in rhesus monkeys. In H. L. Rheingold (Ed.), *Maternal behavior in mammals.* New York: Wiley, 1963.

Harlow, H. F., & Suomi, S. S.   Social recovery by isolation-reared monkeys. *Proceedings of the National Academy of Science,* 1971, *68,* 1534–1538.

Harper, L. V.   Ontogenetic and phylogenetic functions of the parent–offspring relationship in mammals. In D. S. Lehrman, R. A. Hinde, & E. Shaw (Eds.), *Advances in the study of behavior,* Vol. 3. New York: Academic Press, 1970.

Harper, L. V.   The young as a source of stimuli controlling caretaker behavior. *Developmental Psychology,* 1971, *4,* 73–88.

Harper, L. V.   The scope of offspring effects: From caregiver to culture. *Psychological Bulletin,* 1975, *82,* 784–801.

Harper, L. V.   Behavior. In J. E. Wagner & P. J. Manning (Eds.), *Biology of the Guinea Pig.* New York: Academic Press, 1976.

Hart, F. M., & King, J. A.   Distress vocalizations in the young in two subspecies of *Peromyscus maniculatus. Journal of Mammalogy,* 1966, *47,* 287–293.

Hayes, C. *The ape in our house.* New York: Harper, 1951.

Herrenkohl, L. R., & Lisk, R. D. The effects of sensitization and social isolation on maternal behavior in the virgin rat. *Physiology and Behavior,* 1973, *11,* 619–624.

Herrenkohl, L. R., & Rosenberg, P. A. Hypothalamic deafferentiation during early and late pregnancy suppresses milk ejection but not nursing behavior in the primiparous rat. *American Zoologist,* 1972, *12,* 651. (a)

Herrenkohl, L. R., & Rosenberg, P. A. Exteroceptive stimulation of maternal behavior in the naive rat. *Physiology and Behaviour,* 1972, *8,* 595–598. (b)

Herrenkohl, L. R., & Sachs, B. D. Sensory regulation of maternal behavior in mammals. *Physiology and Behaviour,* 1972, *9,* 689–692.

Hersher, L., Richmond, J. B., & Moore, A. U. Maternal behavior in sheep and goats. In H. L. Rheingold (Eds.), *Maternal behavior in mammals.* New York: Wiley, 1963.

Hess, J. P. Some observations on the sexual behaviour of captive lowland gorillas *Gorilla g. gorilla* (Savage and Wyman). In R. P. Michael & J. H. Crook (Eds.), *Comparative ecology and behaviour of primates.* London: Academic Press, 1973.

Hillenbrand, E. D. *The relationship of psychological, medical, and feeding variables to breast feeding.* Unpublished master's thesis, George Washington University, 1965.

Hilton, I. Differences in the behavior of mothers toward first- and later-born children. *Journal of Personality and Social Psychology,* 1967, *7,* 282–290.

Hinde, R. A. *Biological bases of human social behaviour.* New York: McGraw-Hill, 1974.

Hinde, R. A., Rowell, T. E., & Spencer–Booth, Y. Behaviour of socially living rhesus monkeys in their first six months of life. *Proceedings of the Zoological Society of London,* 1964, *143,* 609–649.

Hinde, R. A., & Spencer–Booth, Y. The behaviour of socially-living rhesus monkeys in their first two and a half years. *Animal Behaviour,* 1967, *15,* 169–196.

Hinde, R. A., & Spencer–Booth, Y. Towards understanding individual differences in rhesus mother–infant interaction. *Animal Behaviour,* 1971, *19,* 165–173.

Hoffman, M. L. Moral development. In P. H. Mussen (Ed.), *Carmichael's manual of child psychology* (3rd ed.). New York: Wiley, 1970.

Hoffman, M. L. Moral internalization, parental power, and the nature of the parent–child interaction. *Developmental Psychology,* 1975, 228–239.

Holm, L. W. Prolonged pregnancy. In C. A. Brandy & C. Cornelius (Eds.), *Advances in veterinary science,* Vol. 11. New York: Academic Press, 1967.

Honzik, M. P. Environmental correlates of mental growth: Prediction from the family setting at 21 months. *Child Development,* 1967, *38,* 337–364.

Hopkins, P., & Clyne, M. B. Management of the home confinement. In J. G. Howells (Ed.), *Modern perspectives in psycho-obstetrics.* New York: Brunner/Mazel, 1972.

Horn, J. L., & Knott, P. D. Activist youth of the 1960's: Summary and prognosis. *Science,* 1971, *171,* 977–985.

Horner, B. E., & Taylor, J. M. Growth and reproductive behavior in the southern grasshopper mouse. *Journal of Mammalogy,* 1968, *49,* 644–660.

Howard, W. E. Interaction of behavior, ecology and genetics of introduced mammals. In H. G. Baker & G. L. Stebbins (Eds.), *The genetics of colonizing species.* New York: Academic Press, 1965.

Howells, J. G. Fathering. In J. G. Howells (Ed.), *Modern perspectives in international child psychiatry.* New York: Brunner/Mazel, 1971.

Hubert, J. Belief and reality: Social factors in pregnancy and childbirth. In M. P. M. Richards (Ed.), *The integration of a child into a social world.* Cambridge: Cambridge University Press, 1974.

Hudgens, G. A., Chilgren, J. D., & Palardy, D. D. Mother–infant interactions: Effects of early handling of offspring on rat mothers' open-field behavior, *Developmental Psychobiology,* 1972, *5,* 61–70.

Huesmann, L. R., Eron, L. D., Lefkowitz, M. M., & Walder, L. O. Television violence and aggression: The causal effect remains. *American Psychologist*, 1973, *28*, 617–620.

Hutt, S. J., Hutt, C., Lenard, H. G., Bernuth, H. V., & Muntjewerff, W. J. Auditory responsivity in the human neonate. *Nature*, 1968, *218*, 888–890.

Itani, J. On the acquisition and propagation of a new food habit in the natural group of the Japanese monkey at Takasaki–Yama. *Primates*, 1958, *1*, 84–86.

Itani, J. Paternal care in the wild Japanese monkey *Macaca fuscata*. *Primates*, 1959, *2*, 61–93.

James, W. *The principles of psychology* (Vol. II). New York: Henry Holt, 1890.

Jay, P. Mother–infant relations in langurs. In H. L. Rheingold (Ed.), *Maternal behavior in mammals*. New York: Wiley, 1963.

Jenkins, J. R., & Deno, S. L. Influence of student behavior on teacher's self evaluation. *Journal of Educational Psychology*, 1969, *60*, 439–442.

Jensen, G. D., & Bobbitt, R. A. Sex differences in the development of independence of infant monkeys. *Behaviour*, 1968, *30*, 1–14.

Jensen, G. D., Bobbitt, R. A., & Gordon, B. N. Mothers' and infants' roles in the development of independence of *Macaca nemestrina*. *Primates*, 1973, *14*, 79–88.

Jewell, P. A., & Loizos, C. (Eds.). *Play, exploration and territory in mammals. Symposia of the Zoological Society of London*, No. 18. London: Academic Press, 1966.

Joffe, J. M. Genotype and prenatal and premating stress interact to affect adult behavior in rats. *Science*, 1965, *150*, 1844–1845.

Jolly, A. *Lemur behavior*. Chicago: University of Chicago Press, 1966.

Jones, M. C. Psychological correlates of somatic development. *Child Development*, 1965, *36*, 899–911.

Jones, S. J., & Moss, H. A. Age, state, and maternal behavior associated with infant vocalizations. *Child Development*, 1971, *42*, 1039–1051.

Kagan, J. Discrepancy, temperament, and infant distress. In M. Lewis & L. A. Rosenblum (Eds.), *Origins of fear*. New York: Wiley, 1974.

Kaij, L., & Nilsson, A. Emotional and psychotic illness following childbirth. In J. G. Howells (Ed.), *Modern perspectives in psycho-obstetrics*. New York: Brunner/Mazel, 1972.

Kaplan, J. Responses of mother squirrel monkeys to dead infants. *Primates*, 1973, *14*, 89–91.

Kawamura, S. The process of sub-culture propagation among Japanese monkeys. In C. H. Southwick (Ed.), *Primate social behavior*. New York: Van Nostrand, 1963.

Kawai, M. Newly-acquired pre-cultural behavior of the natural troop of Japanese monkeys on Koshima Islet. *Primates*, 1965, *6*, 1–30.

Kaye, K., & Brazelton, T. B. *Mother–infant interaction in the organization of sucking*. Paper presented at the biennial meeting of the Society for Research in Child Development at Minneapolis, Minnesota, April 1971.

Kennell, J. H., Jerauld, R., Wolfe, H., Chesler, D., Kreger, N. C., McAlpine, W., Steffa, M., & Klaus, M. H. Maternal behavior one year after early and extended post-partum contact. *Developmental Medicine and Child Neurology*, 1974, *16*, 172–179.

Kessen, W. Research design in the study of developmental problems. In P. H. Mussen (Ed.), *Handbook of research methods in child development*. New York: Wiley, 1960.

Kessen, W. *The child*. New York: Wiley, 1965.

Kessen, W., Haith, M. M., & Salapatek, P. H. Human infancy: A bibliography and guide. In P. H. Mussen (Ed.), *Carmichael's manual of child psychology* (3rd ed.). New York: Wiley, 1970.

Klaus, M. H., Jerauld, R., Kreger, N. C., McAlpine, W., Steffa, M., & Kennell, J. H. Maternal attachment, importance of the first post-partum days. *New England Journal of Medicine*, 1972, *286*, 460–463.

Klaus, M. H., & Kennell, J. H. Mothers separated from their newborn infants. *Pediatric Clinics of North America*, 1970, *17*, 1015–1037.

Klaus, M. H., Kennell, J. H., Plumb, N., & Zuehlke, S. Human maternal behavior at the first contact with her young. *Pediatrics*, 1970, *46*, 187–192.

Klein, M., & Stern, L.   Low birth weight and the battered child syndrome. *American Journal of Diseases of Childhood,* 1971, *122,* 15–18.

Klopfer, P. H., & Gamble, J.   Maternal "imprinting" in goats: The role of chemical senses. *Zeitschrift für Tierpsychologie,* 1966, *23,* 588–592.

Klopfer, P. H., & Hailman, J. P.   *An introduction to animal behavior.* Englewood Cliffs, N.J.: Prentice-Hall, 1967.

Klopfer, P. H., & Klopfer, M. S.   Maternal "imprinting" in goats: Fostering of alien young. *Zeitschrift für Tierpsychologie,* 1968, *25,* 862–866.

Klopper, A.   The role of oestrogens in the onset of labour. In A. Klopper & J. Gardner (Eds.), *Endocrine factors in labour. Memoirs of the Society for Endocrinology,* No. 20. Cambridge: Cambridge University Press, 1973.

Klopper, A., & Gardner, J.(Eds.).   *Endocrine factors in labour. Memoirs of the Society for Endocrinology,* No. 20. Cambridge: Cambridge University Press, 1973.

Koford, C. B.   The vicuna and the puña. *Ecological Monographs,* 1957, *27,* 153–219.

Kohlberg, L.   Stage and sequence: The cognitive–developmental approach to socialization. In D. A. Goslin (Ed.), *Handbook of socialization theory and research.* Chicago: Rand McNally, 1969.

Konner, M. J.   Aspects of the developmental ethology of a foraging people. In N. G. Blurton–Jones (Ed.), *Ethological studies of child behaviour.* Cambridge: Cambridge University Press, 1972.

Korner, A. F.   The effect of thestate, level of arousal, sex, and ontogenetic stage on the caregiver. In M. Lewis & L. A. Rosenblum (Eds.), *The effect of the infant on its caregiver.* New York: Wiley, 1974.

Korner, A. F., & Thoman, E. B.   The relative efficacy of contact and vestibular–proprioceptive stimulation in soothing neonates. *Child Development,* 1972, *43,* 443–453.

Kramer, S. N.   *The Sumerians.* Chicago: University of Chicago Press, 1963.

Kruuk, H.   *The spotted hyena. A study of predation and social behavior.* Chicago: University of Chicago Press, 1972.

Kummer, H.   *Social organization of hamadryas baboons.* Chicago: University of Chicago Press, 1968.

Kummer, H.   *Primate societies.* Chicago: Aldine, 1971.

Lakin, M.   Personality factors in mothers of excessively crying (colicky) infants. *Monographs of the Society for Research in Child Development,* 1957, *22,*(1 Serial No. 64).

Landauer, T. K., Carlsmith, J. M., & Lepper, M.   Experimental analysis of the factors determining obedience of four-year-old children to adult females. *Child Development,* 1970, *41,* 601–612.

Langer, W.   Infanticide: A historical survey. *History of Childhood Quarterly: The Journal of Psychohistory,* 1973, *1,* 353–367.

Leach, P. J., & Costello, A. J.   A twin study of infant–mother interaction. In F. J. Monks, W. W. Hartup, & J. Dewwit (Eds.). *Determinants of behavioral development.* New York: Academic Press, 1972.

Le Boeuf, B. J., Ainley, D. G., & Lewis, T. J.   Elephant seals on the Farralones: Population structure of an incipient breeding colony. *Journal of Mammalogy,* 1974, *55,* 370–385.

Le Boeuf, B., Whiting, R. J., & Gantt, R. F.   Perinatal behavior of northern elephant seal females and their young. *Behaviour,* 1972, *43,* 121–156.

Lefkowitz, M. M., Walder, L. O., & Eron, L. D.   Punishment, identification and aggression. *Merrill–Palmer Quarterly,* 1963, *9,* 159–174.

Lehman, H. C.   *Age and achievement.* Princeton, N.J.: Princeton University Press, 1953.

Lehrman, D. S.   On the organization of maternal behavior and the problem of instinct. In P. P. Grasse (Ed.), *L'Instinct dans le comportement des animaux et de l'homme.* Paris: Masson, 1956.

Lehrman, D. S.   Ethology and psychology. In J. Wortis (Ed.), *Recent advances in biological psychology* (Vol. IV). New York: Plenum Press, 1962.

Leifer, A. D., Leiderman, P. H., Barnett, C. R., & Williams, J. A.   Effects of mother–infant separation on maternal attachment behavior. *Child Development,* 1972, *43,* 1203–1218.

Leik, R. K.   Instrumentality and emotionality in family interaction. *Sociometry*, 1963, *26*, 131–145.

Lenneberg, E. H., Rebelsky, F. G., & Nichols, I. A.   The vocalizations of infants born to deaf and hearing parents. *Human Development*, 1965, *8*, 23–37.

Lent, P. C.   Calving and related social behavior in the barren-ground caribou. *Zeitschrift für Tierpsychologie*, 1966, *23*, 701–756.

Leon, M., & Moltz, H.   The development of the pheromonal bond in the albino rat. *Physiology and Behaviour*, 1972, *8*, 683–686.

Leshner, I. A.   Dietary self-selection by pregnant and lactating rats. *Physiology and Behavior*, 1972, *8*, 151–154.

Levy, D. M.   *Behavioral analysis: Analysis of clinical observations of behavior as applied to mother–newborn relationship.* Springfield, Ill.: Charles C. Thomas, 1958.

Lewis, M., & Ban, P.   *Stability of attachment behavior: A transformational analysis.* Paper presented at the biennial meeting of the Society for Research in Child Development, Minneapolis, April 1971.

Lewis, M., Goldberg, S., & Rausch, M.   Attention distribution as a function of novelty and familiarity. *Psychonomic Science*, 1967, *7*, 227–228.

Lewis, M., & Freedle, R.   Mother–infant dyad: The cradle of meaning. In P. Pliner, L. Kranes, & T. Alloway (Eds.), *Communication and affect: Language and thought.* New York: Academic Press, 1973.

Lewis, M., & Lee–Painter, S.   An interactional approach to the mother–infant dyad. In M. Lewis & L. A. Rosenblum (Eds.), *The effect of the infant on its caregiver.* New York: Wiley, 1974.

Linsdale, J. M., & Tomich, P. Q.   *A herd of mule deer.* Berkeley and Los Angeles: University of California Press, 1953.

Lipton, E. L., Steinschneider, A., & Richmond, J. B.   Autonomic function in the neonate. *Psychosomatic Medicine*, 1960, *22*, 57–65.

Livingston, R. B.   Brain circuitry relating to complex behavior. In G. C. Quarton, T. Melnechuk, & F. O. Schmitt ((Eds.), *The Neurosciences.* New York: Rockefeller University Press, 1967.

Lorence, B. W.   Parents and children in eighteenth-century Europe. *History of Childhood Quarterly: The Journal of Psychohistory*, 1974, *2*, 1–30.

Lorenz, K. Z.   Companionship in bird life. In C. Schiller (Ed.), *Instinctive behavior.* New York: International Universities Press, 1957, 83–128. (Abridged from "Der Kumpan in der Umwelt des Vogels," *Journal of Ornithology*, 1935, *83*, 137–213.)

Lusk, D., & Lewis, M.   Mother–infant interaction and infant development among the Wolof of Senegal. *Human Development*, 1972, *15*, 58–69.

Lynn, D. B.   *The father: His role in child development.* Belmont, California: Brooks/Cole, 1974.

Lytton, H., & Zwirner, W.   Compliance and its controlling stimuli observed in a natural setting. *Developmental Psychology*, 1975, *11*, 769–779.

Maccoby, E. E., & Feldman, S. S.   Mother-attachment and stranger reactions in the third year of life. *Monographs of the Society for Research in Child Development*, 1972, *37*(1, Series No. 146).

Maccoby, E. E., & Masters, J. C.   Attachment and dependency. In P. H. Mussen (Ed.), *Carmichael's manual of child psychology* (3rd ed.). New York: Wiley, 1970.

Mackinnon, J.   The behaviour and ecology of wild orang-utans *(Pongo pygmaeus). Animal Behaviour*, 1974, *22*, 3–74.

Maneckjee, R., Srinath, B. R., & Moudgal, N. R.   Prolactin suppresses release of luteinising hormone during lactation in the monkey. *Nature*, 1976, *262*, 507–508.

Marsden, H. M.   Agonistic behaviour of young rhesus monkeys after changes induced in social rank of their mothers. *Animal Behaviour*, 1968, *16*, 38–44.

Mayr, E.   *Populations, species and evolution.* Cambridge, Mass.: Harvard University Press, 1970.

McBride, A. F., & Kritzler, N.   Observations on pregnancy, parturition and postnatal behavior in the bottlenose dolphin. *Journal of Mammalogy*, 1951, *32*, 251–266.

McCoy, N., & Zigler, E.   Social reinforcer effectiveness as a function of the relationship between child and adult. *Journal of Personality and Social Psychology,* 1965, *1,* 604–612.

McCullers, J. C. G.   Stanley Hall's conception of mental development and some indications of its influence on developmental psychology. *American Psychologist,* 1969, *24,* 1109–1114.

McLaughlin, M. M.   Survivors and surrogates: Children and parents from the ninth to the thirteenth century. In Lloyd DeMause (Ed.), *The history of childhood.* New York: Psychohistory Press, 1974.

Mead, M.   Some general considerations. In P. H. Knapp (Ed.), *Expression of the emotions in man.* New York: International Universities Press, 1963.

Mead, M., & Newton, N.   Cultural patterning of perinatal behavior. In S. A. Richardson & A. F. Guttmacher (Eds.), *Childbearing: Its social and psychological aspects.* Baltimore: Williams and Wilkins, 1967.

Meites, J.   Control of mammary growth and lactation. In L. Martini & W. F. Ganong (Eds.), *Neuroendocrinology* (Vol. 1). New York: Academic Press, 1966.

Mena, F., & Grosvenor, C. E.   Effect of number of pups upon suckling-induced fall of pituitary prolactin concentration and milk ejection in the rat. *Endocrinology,* 1968, *82,* 623–626.

Menzel, E. W., Jr.   Responsiveness to objects in free-ranging Japanese monkeys. *Behaviour,* 1966, *26,* 130–150.

Merrill, B.   A measurement of mother–child interaction. *Journal of Abnormal and Social Psychology,* 1946, *41,* 37–49.

Michener, G. R.   Maternal behaviour in Richardson's ground squirrel, *Spermophilus richardsonii richardsonii:* Retrieving of young by lactating females. *Animal Behaviour,* 1971, *19,* 653–656.

Miller, F. L.   Behaviour of maternal black-tailed deer *(Odocoileus hemionus columbianus)* associated with the death of fawns. *Zeitschrift für Tierpsychologie,* 1971, *28,* 527–538.

Miller, L.   Childrearing in the kibbutz. In J. G. Howells (Ed.), *Modern perspectives in international child psychiatry.* New York: Brunner/Mazel, 1971.

Minton, C., Kagan, J., & Levine, J. A.   Maternal control and obedience in the two-year-old. *Child Development,* 1971, *42,* 1873–1894.

Mischel, W.   Sex-typing and socialization. In P. H. Mussen (Ed.), *Carmichael's manual of child psychology* (3rd ed.). New York: Wiley, 1970.

Mishler, E. G., & Waxler, N. E.   *Interaction in families: An experimental study of family processes and schizophrenia.* New York: Wiley, 1968.

Mitchell, G. D.   Attachment differences in male and female monkeys. *Child Development,* 1968, *39,* 611–620.

Mitchell, G., & Schroers, L.   Birth order and parental experience in monkeys and man. In H. W. Reese (Ed.), *Advances in child development and behavior* (Vol. 8). New York: Academic Press, 1973.

Moltz, H., Geller, D., & Levin, R.   Maternal behavior in the totally mammectomized rat. *Journal of Comparative and Physiological Psychology,* 1967, *64,* 225–229.

Moltz, H., & Leon, M.   Stimulus control of the maternal pheromone in the lactating rat. *Physiology and Behavior,* 1973, *10,* 69–71.

Money, J., & Ehrhardt, A.   *Man and woman, boy and girl.* Baltimore: Johns Hopkins University Press, 1972.

Montet, P.   *Everyday life in Egypt in the days of Ramesses the Great.* London: Edwin Arnold, 1958.

Moore, T., & Ucko, L. E.   Night waking in early infancy. Part I. *Archives of Diseases of Childhood,* 1957, *32,* 333–342.

Morris, D.   The psychological management of handicapped children in the first year of life. In J. G. Howells (Ed.), *Modern perspectives in psycho-obstetrics.* New York: Brunner/Mazel, 1972.

Morse, C., Sahler, L., & Friedman, S.   A three-year follow-up study of abused and neglected children. *American Journal of Diseases of Children,* 1970, *120,* 439–446.

Moss, H. A. Sex, age, and state as determinants of moth3r–infant interaction. *Merrill–Palmer Quarterly*, 1967, *13*, 19–36.

Moss H. A. Communication in mother–infant interaction. In Krames, L., Pliner, P., & Alloway, T. (Eds.), *Nonverbal communication: Comparative aspects*. New York: Plenum Press, 1974.

Moss, H. A., & Kagan, J. Maternal influences on early IQ scores. *Psychological Reports*, 1958, *4*, 655–661.

Moss, H. A., & Robson, K. S. The role of protest behavior in the development of the mother–infant attachment. In J. L. Gewirtz (Chm), *Attachment behaviors in humans and animals*. Symposium presented at the meeting of the American Psychological Association, San Francisco, September 1968.

Moynihan, M. Communication in the titi monkey, *Callicebus*. *Journal of Zoology*, 1966, *150*, 77–127.

Müller–Schwartze, D. Pheromones in black-tailed deer *(Odocoileus hemionus columbianus)*. *Animal Behaviour*, 1971, *19*, 141–152.

Murie, A. *The wolves of Mount McKinley. U.S. National Park Service Fauna Series*, No. 5. Washington, D.C.: U.S. Government Printing Office, 1944.

Mussen, P. H. (Ed.). *Carmichael's manual of child psychology* (3rd ed.). New York: Wiley, 1970.

Mussen, P. H., Conger, J. S., & Kagan, J. *Child development and personality* (4th ed.). New York: Harper and Row, 1974.

Muul, I. Intra and interfamilial behaviour of *glaucomys volans* (Rodentia) following parturition. *Animal Behaviour*, 1970, *18*, 20–25.

Naaktgeboren, C. The birth of the dog. (Translated from the Dutch by the Translating Unit, N.I.M.H.). *Hondenweld*, 1964, Christmas issue, 1–20.

Nadler, R. D. Preparuritional behavior of a primiparous lowland gorilla. *Primates*, 1974, *15*, 55–73.

Nelson, J. E. Vocal communication in Australian flying foxes. *Zeitschrift für Tierpsychologie*, 1964, *21*, 857–870.

Nelson, J. E. Behaviour of Australian *Pteropodidae (Megachiroptera)*. *Animal Behaviour*, 1965, *13*, 544–557.

Newson, J., & Newson, E. Cultural aspects of childrearing in the English-speaking world. In M. P. M. Richards (Ed.), *The integration of a child into a social world*. Cambridge: Cambridge University Press, 1974.

Newton, M., & Newton, N. The normal course and management of lactation. *Obstetrics and Gynecology*, 1962, 44–63.

Newton, N., & Newton, M. Childbirth in crosscultural perspective. In J. C. Howells (Ed.), *Modern perspectives in psycho-obstetrics*. New York: Brunner/Mazel, 1972. (a)

Newton, N., & Newton, M. Lactation—Its psychologic components. In J. G. Howells (Ed.), *Modern perspectives in psycho-obstetrics*. New York: Brunner/Mazel, 1972. (b)

Newtson, D. Foundations of attribution: The perception of ongoing behavior. In J. Harvey, W. Ickes, & R. Kidd (Eds.), *New directions in attribution research*. Hillsdale, New Jersey: Lawrence Erlbaum Associates, 1976.

Noirot, E. Changes in responsiveness to young in the adult mouse: I. The problematic effect of hormones. *Animal Behaviour*, 1964, *12*, 52–58. (a)

Noirot, E. Changes in responsiveness in the adult mouse: The effect of external stimuli. *Journal of Comparative and Physiological Psychology*, 1964, *57*, 97–99. (b)

Noirot, E. Changes to young in the adult mouse: IV. The effect of an initial contact with a strong stimulus. *Animal behaviour*, 1964, *12*, 442–448. (c)

Noirot, E. Changes in responsiveness to young in the adult mouse: III. The effects of immediately preceding performances. *Behaviour*, 1965, *24*, 318–325.

Noirot, E. Ultrasounds in young rodents: I. Changes with age in albino mice. *Animal Behaviour*, 1966, *14*, 459–462.

Noirot, E.   Ultrasounds in young rodents: II. Changes with age in albino rats. *Animal Behaviour,* 1968, *16,* 129–134.

Noirot, E.   Changes in responsiveness to young in the adult mouse: V. Priming. *Animal Behaviour,* 1969, *17,* 542–546. (a)

Noirot, E.   Serial order of maternal responses in mice. *Animal Behaviour,* 1969, *17,* 547–550. (b)

Noirot, E.   The onset of maternal behavior in rats, hamsters and mice. A selective review. In D. S. Lehrman, R. A. Hinde, & E. Shaw (Eds.), *Advances in the study of behavior,* Vol. 4. New York: Academic Press, 1972. (a)

Noirot, E.   Ultrasounds and maternal behavior in small rodents. *Developmental Psychobiology,* 1972, *5,* 371–387. (b)

Noirot, E.   Nest-building by the virgin female mouse exposed to ultrasound from inaccessible pups. *Animal Behaviour,* 1974, *22,* 410–420.

Noirot, E., & Goyens, J.   Changes in maternal behavior during gestation in the mouse. *Hormones and Behavior,* 1971, *2,* 207–215.

Noirot, E., & Richards, M. P. M.   Maternal behavior in virgin female golden hamsters: Changes consequent upon initial contact with pups. *Animal Behaviour,* 1966, *14,* 7–10.

Novakowski, N. S.   The influence of vocalization on the behavior of beaver, *Castor canadensis* Kuhl. *American Midland Naturalist,* 1969, *81,* 198–204.

Nowlis, V.   The search for significant concepts in a study of parent–child relationships. *American Journal of Orthopsychiatry,* 1952, *22,* 286–299.

Olley, G.   *Mother–infant interaction during feeding.* Paper presented at the biennial meeting of the Society for Research in Child Development, Philadelphia, Pa., March 1973.

Ono, K. A.   *Mother–pup interaction in the Steller sea lion (Eumetopias jubatus).* Paper presented at the 9th annual conference on Biological Sonar and Diving Mammals, Menlo Park, California, October 1972.

Orlansky, H.   Infant care and personality. *Psychological Bulletin,* 1949, *46,* 1–48.

Orr, R. T., & Poulter, T. C.   Some observa5ions on reproduction, growth, and social behavior in the Steller sea lion. *Proceedings of the California Academy of Sciences,* 1967, *35,* 193–226.

Osofsky, J. D.   Children's influences upon parental behavior: An attempt to define the relationship utilizing laboratory tasks. *Genetic Psychology Monographs,* 1971, *83,* 147–169.

Osofsky, J. D., & Danzger, B.   *Relationships between neonatal characteristics and mother–infant interaction.* Paper presented at the biennial meeting of the Society for Research in Child Development, Philadelphia, Pa., March 1973.

Osofsky, J. D., & O'Connell, E. J.   Parent–child interaction: Daughters' effects upon mothers' and fathers' behaviors. *Developmental Psychology,* 1972, *7,* 157–168.

Ostwald, P. F.   *Soundmaking.* Springfield, Ill.: C. C. Thomas, 1963.

Ota, K., & Yokoyama, A.   Resumption of lactation by suckling in lactating rats after removal of litters. *Journal of Endocrinology,* 1965, *33,* 185–194.

Ota, K., & Yokoyama, A.   Body weight and food consumption of lactating rats: Effects of ovariectomy and of arrest and resumption of suckling. *Journal of Endocrinology,* 1967, *38,* 251–261. (a)

Ota, K., & Yokoyama, A.   Body weight and food consumption of lactating rats nursing various sizes of litters. *Journal of Endocrinology,* 1967, *38,* 263–268. (b)

Owen, F. W., Adams, P. A., Forrest, T., Stolz, L. M., & Fisher, S.   Learning disorders in children: Sibling studies. *Monographs of the Society for Research in Child Development,* 1971, *36*(4, Series No. 144).

Palmer R. R.   *The age of the democratic revolution: Vol II. The struggle.* Princeton: Princeton University Press, 1964.

Papousek, H.   Conditioning during early postnatal development. In Y. Brackbill & G. G. Thompson (Eds.), *Behavior in infancy and early childhood.* New York: Free Press, 1967.

Paradise, J. L.   Maternal and other factors in the etiology of infantile colic. *Journal of the American Medical Association,* 1966, *197,* 191–199.

Parmelee, A. H., Jr.   Development of states in infants. In C. Clemente, D. Purpura, & F. Mayer (Eds.), *Maturation of brain mechanisms related to sleep behavior*. New York: Academic Press, 1972.

Patterson, G. R.   A basis for identifying stimuli which control behaviors in natural settings. *Child Development*, 1974, *45*, 900–911.

Patterson, G. R., & Cobb, J. A.   Stimulus control for classes of noxious behaviors. In J. F. Knutson (Ed.), *The control of aggression: Implications from basic research*. Chicago: Aldine, 1973.

Patterson, G. R., Cobb, J. A., & Ray, R. S.   A social engineering technology for retraining the families of aggressive boys. In H. E. Adams & I. P. Unikel (Eds.), *Issues and trends in behavior therapy*. Springfield, Ill.: Charles C. Thomas, 1973.

Paxton, P. S.   *Effects of drug-induced behavior change in hyperactive children on maternal attitudes and personality*. Ph.D. dissertation, Department of Psychology, University of Minnesota, 1971.

Payne, G. H.   *The child in human progress*. New York: Putman, 1916.

Peiper, A.   *Cerebral function in infancy and childhood*. New York: Consultant's Bureau, 1963.

Peterson, R. S.   Social behavior in pinnipeds with particular reference to the northern fur seal. In R. J. Harrison, R. C. Hubbard, R. S. Peterson, C. E. Rice, & R. J. Schusterman (Eds.), *The behavior and physiology of Pinnipeds*. New York: Appleton–Century–Crofts, 1968.

Peterson, R. S., & Bartholomew, G. D.   Airborne vocal communication in the California sea lion. *Animal Behaviour*, 1969, *17*, 17–24.

Petrinovich, L.   Individual recognition of pup vocalizations by northern elephant seal mothers. *Zeitschrift für Tierpsychologie*, 1974, *34*, 308–312.

Pfeffer, P.   Le mouflon de Corse (*Ovis ammon musimon*. Schreber, 1872). Position systematique, écologic et éthologie comparées. *Mammalia*, 1967, *31* (Supp. pp. 262).

Plume, S., Fogarty, C., Grota, L. J., & Ader, R.   Is retrieving a measure of maternal behavior in the rat? *Psychological Reports*, 1968, *23*, 627–630.

Poirier, F. E.   The Nilgiri langur (*Presbytis Johnii*) troop: Its composition, structure, function and change. *Folia Primatologica*, 1969, *10*, 20–47. (a)

Poirier, F. E.   Behavioral flexibility and intertroop variation among Nilgiri langurs (*Presbytis Johnii*) of south India. *Folia Primatologica*, 1969, *11*, 119–125. (b)

Pollitt, E.   Behavior of infant in causation of nutritional marasmus. *American Journal of Clinical Nutrition*, 1973, *26*, 264–270.

Pratt, K. C.   The neonate. In L. Carmichael (Ed.), *Manual of child psychology* (2nd ed.). New York: Wiley, 1954.

Prechtl, H. F. R.   The mother–child interaction in babies with minimal brain damage. In B. M. Foss (Ed.), *Determinants of infant behaviour: II*. New York: Wiley, 1963.

Preistnall, R.   Effects of handling on maternal behaviour in the mouse (*Mus musculus*): An observational study. *Animal Behaviour*, 1973, *21*, 383–386.

Preyer, W. *Die Seele des Kindes. Beobachtungen uber die geislige Entwicklung des Menschen in den ersten Lebensjahren*. Leipzig: T. Grieben, 1882.

Rappaport, M. M., & Rappaport, H.   The other half of the expectancy equation: Pygmalion. *Journal of Educational Psychology*, 1975, *67*, 531–536.

Rathbone, C.   Teachers' information handling behavior when grouped with students by conceptual level. *Dissertation Abstracts*, 1971, *32*, 798A.

Rebelsky, F. G., Seavey, C., & Blotner, R.   *Maternal control techniques and resistance to temptation in young children*. Paper presented at the biennial meeting of the Society for Research in Child Development, Minneapolis, Minnesota, April 1971.

Ressler, R. H.   Parental handling in two strains of mice reared by foster parents. *Science*, 1962, *137*, 129–130.

Reynolds, H. C.   Studies on reproduction in the opossum *(Didelphis virginiana virginiana)*. *University of California Publications in Zoology*, 1952, *52*(Whole No. 3).

Reynolds, P. C.   *Play and human evolution*. Paper presented at the annual meeting of the American Association for the Advancement of Science, Washington, D.C., December 1972.

Rheingold, H. L.   The effects of environmental stimulation upon social and exploratory behaviour in the human infant. In B. M. Foss (Ed.), *Determinants of infant behavior* (Vol. I). New York: Wiley, 1961.

Rheingold, H. L. (Ed.).   *Maternal behavior in mammals*. New York: Wiley, 1963.

Rheingold, H. L.   The development of social behavior in the human infant. In H. W. Stevenson (Ed.), Concept of development: A report of a conference commemorating the 40th anniversary of the Institute of Child Development, University of Minnesota. *Monographs of the Society for Research in Child Development*, 1966, *31*(5, Whole No. 107).

Rheingold, H. L., Gewirtz, J. L., & Ross, H. W.   Social conditioning of vocalizations in the infant. *Journal of Comparative and Physiological Psychology*, 1959, *52*, 68–73.

Richards, M. P.   Social interaction in the first weeks of human life. *Psychiatria, Neurologia, Nuerochirurgia*, 1971, *74*, 35–42.

Richards, M. P.   First steps in becoming social. In M. P. Richards (Ed.), *The integration of a child into a social world*. Cambridge: Cambridge University Press, 1974.

Ripley, S.   Intertroop encounters among Ceylon gray langurs *(Presbytis entellus)*. In S. A. Altmann (Ed.), *Social communication among primates*. Chicago: University of Chicago Press, 1967.

Robson, K. S.   The role of eye-to-eye contact in maternal–infant attachment. *Journal of Child Psychology and Psychiatry*, 1967, *8*, 13–25.

Robson, K. S., & Moss, H. A.   Patterns and determinants of maternal attachment. *Journal of Pediatrics*, 1970, *77*, 976–985.

Rosen, B. C., & D'Andrade, R.   The psychosocial origins of achievement motivation. *Sociometry*, 1959, *22*, 185–218.

Rosenberg, B. G., & Sutton–Smith, B.   Family interaction effects on masculinity–femininity. *Journal of Personality and Social Psychology*, 1968, *8*, 117–120.

Rosenblatt, J. S.   The development of maternal responsiveness in the rat. *American Journal of Orthopsychiatry*, 1969, *39*, 36–56.

Rosenblatt, J. S.   Nonhormonal basis of maternal behavior in the rat. *Science*, 1967, *156*, 1512–1513.

Rosenblatt, J. S., & Lehrman, D. S.   Maternal behavior of the laboratory rat. In H. L. Rheingold (Ed.), *Maternal behavior in mammals*. New York: Wiley, 1963.

Rosenblith, J. F., & Anderson, R. B.   Prognostic significance of discrepancies in muscle tension between upper and lower limbs. *Developmental Medicine and Child Neurology*, 1968, *10*, 322–330.

Rosenblum, L. A., & Youngstein, K. P.   Developmental changes in compensatory dyadic response in mother and infant monkeys. In M. Lewis & L. A. Rosenblum (Eds.), *The effect of the infant on its caregiver*. New York: Wiley, 1974.

Rosenson, L. M.   Observations of the maternal behavior of two captive greater bushbabies *(Galago crassicaudatus argentatus)*. *Animal Behaviour*, 1972, *20*, 677–688.

Rosenthal, D.   A program of research on heredity in schizophrenia. *Behavioral Science*, 1971, *16*, 191–201.

Rosenthal, M. K.   The generalization of dependency behaviors from mother to stranger. *Dissertation Abstracts*, 1966, *26*, 6841–6842.

Rosenthal, R., Baratz, S. S., & Hall, C. M.   Teacher behavior, teacher expectation, and gains in pupils' rated creativity. *Journal of Genetic Psychology*, 1974, *124*, 115–121.

Ross, S., Sawin, P. B., Zarrow, M. X., & Denenberg, V. H.   Maternal behavior in the rabbit. In H. L. Rheingold (Ed.), *Maternal behavior in mammals*. New York: Wiley, 1963.

Rowell, T. E. On retrieving of young and other behaviour in lactating golden hamsters. *Proceedings of the Zoological Society of London*, 1960, *135*, 265–282.

Rowell, T. E., Din, N. A., & Omar, A. The social development of baboons in their first three months. *Journal of Zoology*, 1968, *155*, 461–483.

Rowell, T. E., & Hinde, R. A. Vocal communication by the rhesus monkey *(Macaca mulatta)*. *Proceedings of the Zoological Society of London*, 1962, *138*, 279–294.

Rubenstein, J. A concordance of visual and manipulative responsiveness to novel and familiar stimuli in six-month-old infants. *Child Development*, 1974, *45*, 194–195.

Rubin, J. Z., Provenzano, F. J., & Luria, Z. The eye of the beholder: Parents' views on sex of newborns. *American Journal of Orthopsychiatry*, 1974, *44*, 512–519.

Ryder, R. G. Longitudinal data relating marriage satisfaction and having a child. *Journal of Marriage and the Family*, 1973, *35*, 604–606.

Ryder, R. G., Kafka, J. S., & Olson, D. H. Separating and joining influences in courtship and early marriage. *American Journal of Orthopsychiatry*, 1971, *41*, 450–467.

Ryszkowski, L. The space organization of nutria *(Myocastor coypus)*. In P. A. Jewell & C. Loizos (Eds.), *Play, exploration and territory in mammals. Symposia of the Zoological Society of London*, No. 18. New York: Academic Press, 1966.

Sackett, G. P. *A nonparametric lag sequential analysis for studying dependency among responses in observational scoring systems.* Unpublished preliminary research report, Regional Primate Research Center, University of Washington, 1975.

Sackett, G., Griffin, G. A., Pratt, C., Joslyn, G. D., & Ruppenthal, G. Mother–infant and adult female choice behavior in rhesus monkeys after various rearing experiences. *Journal of Comparative and Physiological Psychology*, 1967, *63*, 376–381.

Sackett, G. P., & Ruppenthal, G. C. Some factors influencing the attraction of adult female macaque monkeys to neonates. In M. Lewis & L. A. Rosenblum (Eds.), *The effect of the infant on its caregiver.* New York: Wiley, 1974.

Saggs, H. W. F. *Everyday life in Babylonia and Assyria.* New York: Putnam, 1965.

Sander, L. W. Infant and caretaking environment: Investigation and conceptualization of adaptive behavior in a system of increasing complexity. In E. Anthony (Ed.), *The child psychiatrist as investigator.* New York: Plenum Press, 1974.

Sandgren, F. E., Chu, E. W., & Vandevere, J. E. Maternal behavior of the California sea otter. *Journal of Mammalogy*, 1973, *54*, 668–679.

Sauer, E. G. T. Mother–infant relationship in Galagos and the oral child-transport among primates. *Folia Primatologica*, 1967, *7*, 127–149.

Scarr, S. The inheritance of sociability. *American Psychologist*, 1965, *20*, 524 (Abstract).

Scarr, S. Environmental bias in twin studies. *Eugenics Quarterly*, 1968, *15*, 34–40.

Schaefer, E. S. Parent–child interactional patterns and parental attitudes. In D. Rosenthal (Ed.), *The Genain Quadruplets.* New York: Basic Books, 1963.

Schaefer, E. S. Development of hierarchical, configurational models for parent behavior and child behavior. In J. P. Hill (Ed.), *Minnesota Symposia on child psychology* (Vol. 5). Minneapolis: University of Minnesota Press, 1971.

Schaffer, H. R., Greenwood, A., & Parry, M. H. The onset of wariness. *Child Development*, 1972, *43*, 165–175.

Schaller, G. B. *The mountain gorilla.* Chicago: University of Chicago Press, 1963.

Schaller, G. B. *The deer and the tiger.* Chicago: University of Chicago Press, 1967.

Schalock, H. D. Observation of mother–child interactions in the laboratory and in the home. *Dissertation Abstracts*, 1956, *16*, 707.

Schenkel, R. Play, exploration and territoriality in the wild lion. In P. A. Jewell & C. Loizos (Eds.), *Play, exploration and territoriality in mammals. Symposia of the Zoological Society of London*, No. 18. London: Academic Press, 1966.

Schneider, D. G., Mech, L. D., & Tester, J. R. Movements of female raccoons and their young as determined by radio-tracking. *Animal Behaviour Monographs*, 1971, *4*, 1–43.

Schneirla, T. C., & Rosenblatt, J. S.   Critical periods in the development of behavior. *Science,* 1963, *139,* 1110–1115.

Schneirla, T. C., Rosenblatt, J. S., & Tobach, E.   Maternal behavior in the cat. In H. L. Rheingold (Ed.), *Maternal behavior in mammals.* New York: Wiley, 1963.

Schoggen, P.   Environmental forces in the everyday lives of children. In R. G. Barker (Ed.), *The stream of behavior: Explorations of its structure and content.* New York: Appleton–Century–Crofts, 1963.

Scudder, H.   *Childhood in literature and art.* New York: Houghton-Mifflin, 1894.

Sears, R. R.   A theoretical framework for personality and social behavior. *American Psychologist,* 1951, *6,* 476–482.

Sears, R. R., Maccoby, E. E., & Levin, H.   *Patterns of child rearing.* Evanston, Ill.: Row, Peterson, 1957.

Seitz, P. F. D.   The maternal instinct in animal subjects. I. *Psychosomatic Medicine,* 1958, *20,* 215–226.

Selye, H., & McKeown, T.   Further studies on the influence of suckling. *Anatomical Record,* 1934, *60,* 323–332.

Serbin, L. A., O'Leary, K. D., Kent, R. N., & Tonick, I. J.   A comparison of teacher response to the preacademic and problem behavior of boys and girls. *Child Development,* 1973, *44,* 796–804.

Sewell, G. D.   Ultrasonic communication in rodents. *Nature,* 1970, *227,* 410.

Sewell, W. H.   Some recent developments in socialization theory and research. *Annals of the American Academy of Political and Social Science,* 1963, *349,* 163–181.

Sharman, G. B.   The red kangaroo. *Science Journal,* 1967, March, 53–60.

Sharp, W. M., & Sharp, L. H.   Nocturnal movement and behavior of wild raccoons at a winter feeding station. *Journal of Mammalogy,* 1956, *37,* 170–177.

Shaver, B. A.   Maternal personality and early adaption as related to infantile colic. In P. M. Shereshefsky & L. J. Yarrow (Eds.), *Psychological aspects of a first pregnancy and early postnatal adaptation.* New York: Raven Press, 1973.

Sherrod, K. B., Connor, W. H., & Meier, G. W.   Transient and enduring effects of handling on infant and maternal behavior in mice. *Developmental Psychobiology,* 1974, *7,* 31–37.

Siegel, G. M.   Adult verbal behavior with retarded children labeled as "high" or "low" in verbal ability. *American Journal of Mental Deficiency,* 1963, *68,* 417–424.

Silman, R. E., Chard, T., Lowry, P. J., Smith, I., & Young, I. M.   Human foetal pituitary peptides and parturition. *Nature,* 1976, *260,* 716–718.

Simpson, W. K.   *The literature of ancient Egypt.* New Haven: Yale University Press, 1972.

Skinner, B. F.   Behaviorism at fifty. In T. W. Wann (Ed.), *Behaviorism and phenomenology.* Chicago: University of Chicago Press, 1964.

Skinner, B. F.   *Beyond freedom and dignity.* New York: Knopf, 1971

Slotnick, B. M.   Intercorrelations of maternal activities in the rat. *Animal Behaviour,* 1967, *15,* 267–269.

Smith, C. C.   The adaptive nature of social organization in the genus of tree squirrels *Tamiasciurus. Ecological Monographs,* 1968, *38,* 31–63.

Smith, F. V., Van–Toller, C., & Boyes, T.   The 'critical period' in the attachment of lambs and ewes. *Animal Behaviour,* 1966, *14,* 120–125.

Snow, C. J.   Some observations on the behavioral and morphological development of coyote pups. *American Zoologist,* 1967, *7,* 353–355.

Sommerville, C.   Toward a history of childhood and youth. *Journal of Interdisciplinary History,* 1972, *3,* 438–447.

Sontag, L. W.   Psychosomatics and somatopsychics from birth to three years. In A. Merminod (Ed.), *The growth of the normal child during the first three years of life. Modern problems in pediatrics* (Vol. VII). New York: Karger, 1962.

Southwick, C. H., Pal, B. C., & Siddiqi, M. F.   Experimental studies on social intolerance in wild rhesus monkeys. *American Zoologist,* 1972, *12,* 651–652.

234 REFERENCES

Spencer–Booth, Y. The relationships between mammalian young and conspecifics other than their mothers and peers: A review. In D. S. Lehrman, R. A. Hinde, & E. Shaw (Eds.), *Advances in the study of behavior* (Vol. 3). New York: Academic Press, 1970.

Stern, D. N. Mother and infant at play: The dyadic interaction involving facial, vocal, and gaze behaviors. In M. Lewis & L. A. Rosenblum (Eds.), *The effect of the infant on its caregiver*. New York: Wiley, 1974.

Stern, D. N. A micro-analysis of mother–infant interaction: Behavior regulating social contact between a mother and her 3½-month-old twins. *Journal of the American Academy of Child Psychiatry,* 1971, *10,* 501–517.

Stevens, A. G. Attachment behaviour, separation anxiety and stranger anxiety. In H. R. Schaffer (Ed.), *The origins of human social relations*. London: Academic Press, 1971, 146.

Stevenson, H. W., Keen, R., & Knights, R. M. Parents and strangers as reinforcing agents for children's performance. *Journal of Abnormal and Social Psychology,* 1963, *67,* 183–186.

Struhsaker, T. T. Behavior of elk *(Cervus canadensis)* during the rut. *Zeitschrift für Tierpsychologie,* 1967, *24,* 80–114. (a)

Struhsaker, T. T. Auditory communication among vervet monkeys *(Cercopithecus aethiops)*. In S. A. Altmann (Ed.), *Social communication among primates*. Chicago: University of Chicago Press, 1967. (b)

Sugiyama, Y. On the division of a natural troop of Japanese monkeys at Takasakiyama. *Primates,* 1960, *2,* 109–148.

Sundaram, K., Connell, K. G., & Passantino, T. Implication of absence of HCG-like gonadotrophin in the blastocyst for control of corpus luteum function in pregnant rabbit. *Nature,* 1975, *256,* 739–740.

Sunley, R. Early nineteenth-century American literature on child rearing. In M. Mead and M. Wolfenstein (Eds.), *Childhood in contemporary culture*. Chicago: University of Chicago Press, 1955.

Suzuki, A. An ecological study of wild Japanese monkeys in snowy areas—Focused on their food habits. *Primates,* 1965, *6,* 31–72.

Svare, B., & Gandelman, R. Postpartum aggression in mice: Experiential and environmental factors. *Hormones and Behavior,* 1973, *4,* 323–334.

Svare, B., & Gandelman, R. Suckling stimulation induces aggression in virgin female mice. *Nature,* 1976, *260,* 606–608.

Tavolga, M. C., & Essapian, F. S. The behavior of the bottle-nosed dolphin *(Tursiops truncatus)*: Mating, pregnancy, parturition and mother–infant behavior. *Zoologica,* 1957, *42,* 11–31.

Terkel, J., & Rosenblatt, J. S. Aspects of nonhormonal maternal behavior in the rat. *Hormones and Behavior,* 1971, *2,* 161–171.

Terkel, J., & Rosenblatt, J. S. Humoral factors underlying maternal behavior at parturition: Cross transfusions between freely moving rats. *Journal of Comparative and Physiological Psychology,* 1972, *80,* 365–371.

Thoman, E. B., Leiderman, P. H., & Olson, J. P. Neonate–mother interaction during breast-feeding. *Developmental Psychology,* 1972, *6,* 110–118.

Tinbergen, N. *The study of instinct*. Oxford: Oxford University Press, 1951.

Trethowan, W. H. The couvade syndrome. In J. C. Howells (Ed.), *Modern perspectives in psycho-obstetrics*. New York: Brunner/Mazel, 1972.

Trethowan, W. H., & Dickens, G. Cravings, aversions and pica of pregnancy. In J. C. Howells (Ed.), *Modern perspectives in psycho-obstetrics*. New York: Brunner/Mazel, 1972.

Trivers, R. L. Parent–offspring conflict. *American Zoologist,* 1974, *14,* 249–264.

Tucker, H. A., Paape, M. J., Sinha, A., Pritchard, D. E., & Thatcher, W. W. Relationship among nursing frequency, lactation, pituitary prolactin and adrenocorticotropic hormone content in rats. *Proceedings of the Society for Experimental Biology and Medicine,* 1967, *126,* 100–103.

Tucker, H. A., & Thatcher, W. W. Pituitary growth hormone and luteinizing hormone content after various nursing intensities. *Proceedings of the Society for Experimental Biology and Medicine*, 1968, *129*, 578–580.

Tyler, S. J. The behaviour and social organization of the New Forest ponies. *Animal Behaviour Monographs*, 1972, *5*, 85–196.

Valanne, E. H., Vuorenkoski, V., Partanen, T. J., Lind, J., & Wasz–Hockert, O. The ability of human mothers to identify hunger cry signals of their own new-born infants during the lying-in period. *Experientia*, 1967, *23*, 1–4.

van den Berghe, P. *Age and sex in human societie   : A biosocial perspective.* Belmont, California: Wadsworth, 1973.

Vandevere, J. E. *Behavior of southern sea otter pups.* Paper presented at the 8th annual Conference on Biological Sonar and Diving Mammals, Menlo Park, California, October 1972.

van Gennep, A. *The rites of passage.* Chicago: University of Chicago Press, 1960.

van Lawick–Goodall, H., & van Lawick–Goodall, J. *Innocent killers.* Boston: Houghton-Mifflin, 1971.

van Lawick–Goodall, J. The behaviour of free-living chimpanzees in the Gombe Stream preserve. *Animal Behaviour Monographs*, 1968, *1*, 165–311.

van Lawick–Goodall, J. *In the shadow of man.* Boston: Houghton-Mifflin, 1971.

Voci, V. E., & Carlson, N. E. Enhancement of maternal behavior and nest-building following systemic and diencephalic administration of prolactin and progesterone in the mouse. *Journal of Comparative and Physiological Psychology*, 1973, *33*, 388–393.

von Mering, O., & Mulhare, M. T. Anthropological perspectives on socialization. In E. J. Anthony and T. Benedek (Eds.), *Parenthood.* Boston: Little, Brown & Co., 1970.

Vuorenkoski, V., Wasz–Hockert, O., Koivisto, E., & Lind, J. The effect of cry stimulus on the temperature of the lactating breast of primipara: A thermographic study. *Experientia*, 1969, *25*, 1286–1287.

Waldrop, M. F., Bell, R. Q., & Goering, J. D. Minor physical anomalies and inhibited behavior in elementary school girls. *Journal of Child Psychology and Psychiatry*, 1976, *17*, 113–122.

Waldrop, M. F., & Halverson, C. F. Minor physical anomalies and hyperactive behavior in young children. In J. Hellmuth (Ed.), *The exceptional infant* (Vol. 2). Seattle: Special Child Publications, 1971.

Waldrop, M. F., Pederson, F. A., & Bell, R. Q. Minor physical anomalies and behavior in preschool children. *Child Development*, 1968, *39*, 391–400.

Walters, R. H. On the high-magnitude theory of aggression. *Child Development*, 1964, *35*, 303–304.

Walters, R. H., & Parke, R. D. The role of the distance receptors in the development of social responsiveness. In L. P. Lipsitt & C. C. Spiker (Eds.), *Advances in child development and behavior* (Vol. 2). New York: Academic Press, 1965.

Wasz–Hockert, O., Partanen, T. J., Vuorenkoski, V., Valanne, E. H., & Michelsson, K. Effect of training on ability to identify preverbal vocalizations. *Developmental Medicine and Child Neurology*, 1964, *6*, 393–396.

Watson, J. S. The development and generalization of "contingency awareness" in early infancy: Some hypotheses. *Merrill–Palmer Quarterly*, 1966, *12*, 123–135.

White, B. L., & Held, R. Plasticity of sensorimotor development in the human infant. In J. R. Rosenblith and W. Allinsmith (Eds.), *The causes of behavior: Readings in child development and educational psychology.* Boston: Allyn & Bacon, 1966.

White, J. *Everyday life in ancient Egypt.* New York: Putnam, 1963.

Wickler, W. *The sexual code.* Garden City, N.J.: Doubleday, 1972.

Wiesner, B. P., & Sheard, N. M. *Maternal behaviour in the rat.* Edinburgh: Oliver and Boyd, 1933.

Williams, L. *Man and monkey.* Philadelphia, Pa.: J. P. Lippincott, 1968.

Wilson, A. P., & Vessey, S. H. Behavior of free-ranging castrated rhesus monkeys. *Folia Primatologica*, 1968, *9*, 1–14.

Wolff, P. H.   The developmental psychologies of Jean Piaget and psychoanalysis. *Psychological Issues,* 1960, *2*(No. 1).

Wolff, P. H.   The causes, controls and organization of behavior in the neonate. *Psychological Issues,* 1966, *5*(No. 1).

Wolff, P. H.   Mother–infant relationships at birth. In J. G. Howells (Ed.), *Modern perspectives in international child psychiatry.* New York: Brunner/Mazel, 1971.

Wright, H. F.   *Recording and analyzing child behavior.* New York: Harper & Row, 1967.

Wynne–Edwards, V. C.   *Animal dispersion in relation to social behaviour.* New York: Hafner, 1962.

Yarrow, L. J.   Research in dimensions of early maternal care. *Merrill–Palmer Quarterly,* 1963, *9,* 101–114.

Yarrow, M. R., Campbell, J. D., & Burton, R. V.   *Child rearing: An inquiry into research and methods.* San Francisco: Josey–Bass, 1968.

Yarrow, M. R., Waxler, C. Z., & Scott, P. M.   Child effects on adult behavior, *Developmental Psychology,* 1971, *5,* 300–311.

Yee, A. H., & Gage, N. L.   Techniques for estimating the source and direction of causal influence in panel data. *Psychological Bulletin,* 1968, *70,* 115–126.

Yoshiba, L.   Local and intertroop variability in ecology and social behavior of common Indian Langurs. In P. Jay (Ed.), *Primates: Studies in adaptation and variability.* New York: Holt, Rinehart and Winston, 1968.

Zarrow, M. X., Denenberg, V. H., & Anderson, C. O.   Rabbit: Frequency of suckling in the pup. *Science,* 1965, *150,* 1835.

Zimmerman, G. D.   Cooperative nursing behavior observed in *Spermophilus tridecemlineatus* (Mitchell). *Journal of Mammalogy,* 1974, *55,* 680–681.

Author Index

Numbers in *italics* refer to the pages on which the complete references are listed.

Subject Index

V

Verbal ability
  labeling and, 113
  parent-child relationships and, 82–83
Vision, caregiving and, 154, 155
Vocalization
  development of, 97
  as response, 140, 141–142, 146

W

Wakefulness, infant development and, 128

Warmth, parent-offspring bond and, 184
Watson, John B.
  views of, 37, 38, 41
Weaning, patterns of, 166
Women, childcare and, 4–5

Y

Young, *see* Children, Infant, Juvenile,
  Offspring